LAND OF THE MILLRATS

# Land of the Millrats

RICHARD M. DORSON

HARVARD UNIVERSITY PRESS          1981

Cambridge, Massachusetts, and London, England

Printed in the United States of America
Library of Congress Cataloging in Publication Data
Dorson, Richard Mercer, 1916-
    Land of the millrats.
    Bibliography: p.
    Includes index.
    1. Folk-lore—Indiana—Calumet region.   2. Calumet region (Ind.)—Social
life and customs.   3. Cities and towns (in religion, Folklore, etc.)—Indiana—
Calumet region.   I. Title.
GR110.I6D67        398'.097772'99        81-2944
ISBN 0-674-50855-6                        AACR2

For Inta

# ACKNOWLEDGMENTS

The National Endowment for the Humanities provided the grant that enabled me to spend six months during 1975 and 1976 in the Calumet Region. The grant also permitted graduate students to work with me there for periods totaling six weeks, and I greatly benefited from their presence. A fellowship from the National Humanities Center made possible writing up my material during the academic year 1978–79 in their marvelous facility in Research Triangle Park, North Carolina.

Many persons in the Region assisted me in my quest, although I have sometimes changed their names to protect their privacy. I wish especially to thank students at Indiana University Northwest who became close friends: Diane Banks, Rick Broadstone, Angela Maniak, Gil Razo, and Vicki Voller; the Regans, Larry, Sandy, and Jennie, who made Jennie's restaurant a second home for us; and Harold Malone, Dick Van Orman, and Fred and Naomi Stern, who did me special favors. Many others befriended me and have left warm memories of the Region in my heart.

To my team—the "Gary Gang" of Thomas Adler, Elena Bradunas, Gilbert E. Cooley, Philip B. George, John Hasse, Richard March, and

# Acknowledgments

Adrienne L. Seward—you were my comrades and supporters and fellow-explorers.

For valuable suggestions on the manuscript I am deeply indebted to Roger D. Abrahams and Alan Dundes. Zora Zimmerman kindly assisted on the Serbian sections. Jeff Dorson prepared the index. My editor at Harvard University Press, Ann Louise McLaughlin, gave unstintingly of her time and talents. The responsibility for the data and interpretations is mine.

My debt to Inta Carpenter, coordinator of the project, editorial critic of the manuscript, and my partner in the Folklore Institute, I express on another page.

Bloomington, Indiana                                              R.M.D.

# CONTENTS

ix

# ILLUSTRATIONS

# Illustrations

LAND OF THE MILLRATS

# INTRODUCTION: FORAY INTO "DE REGION"

For thirty years I followed the customary trails of the folklorist leading away from the centers of population to the hinterland. A goodly company had preceded me in such pursuits of the folk, trekking to backcountry towns, mountain hollows, and the fringes of civilization to trap the elusive lore. In the United States, Cecil Sharp journeyed to the southern Appalachians to collect traditional ballads, John Lomax obtained folksongs from cowboys and black convicts, Vance Randolph scoured the Ozarks for tales, songs, and beliefs, the Reverend Harry Hyatt amassed Afro-American hoodoo and witchcraft from southern blacks. In my own fieldwork I followed the same thinking and explored country regions in Michigan's Upper Peninsula, Maine's down-East coast, and the Mississippi Delta. Then, in 1975, I reversed a lifetime's practice and headed for the industrial metropolis in pursuit of folklore.

In recent years a turnabout in folkloric concepts has redirected field inquiries from the country to the city, and from the marginal to the mainstream culture. Folklore, instead of being considered a matter of survivals and antiquities, as William John Thoms conceived the subject when he baptized it in 1846, is now regarded as the direct reflection of the central anxieties, aspirations, and concerns of the contemporary era. In *America in Legend* (1973) I divided American history into four periods, each characterized by a distinctive folklore mirroring the dominant energies of the times. The old and the new models of folklore research can be contrasted in this way. The old long-accepted model directed fieldwork to the marginal culture of village peasants and interpreted the resulting data as a mirror on the remote past. The recent revised model directs fieldwork to the mainstream culture of urban centers and interprets the data as a mirror on the present.

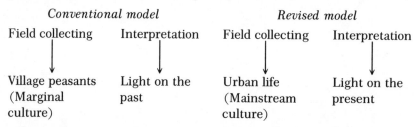

| *Conventional model* | | *Revised model* | |
|---|---|---|---|
| Field collecting | Interpretation | Field collecting | Interpretation |
| Village peasants (Marginal culture) | Light on the past | Urban life (Mainstream culture) | Light on the present |

The inference emerges that we have done very little to collect our own folklore, or even to recognize its forms.

To test the new model, and determine for myself its validity, I undertook a foray into the Calumet Region of northwest Indiana, self-styled as the most heavily industrialized sector of the United States, with its steel mills and oil refineries and diversified manufactures. In some respects this enterprise paralleled my first field expedition, to the Upper Peninsula in 1946, that led, six years later, to the publication of *Bloodstoppers and Bearwalkers*. In both cases I was departing from a university base downstate to a well-defined, semi-legendary region upstate, seemingly blocked off from ordinary channels of commerce with the outside world. Both regions possessed highly visible ethnic populations. But there the parallels ended, for the one was a region of villages and small towns, farmers and fishermen, lumberjacks and miners, and the other was a conurbation of grimy cities peopled with blue-collar laborers.

My plan was not simply to collect city folklore, for I had little idea what shapes such folklore would take, if indeed it existed at all, but to take a folklorist's walk in the city, to live for a while in the urban environment as a folklorist in the field observing the urban folk. I marked five targets in the Calumet Region. The first was the mystique of the Region itself. The Region was composed of a cluster of small urban centers linked by historical, economic, and ecological ties. Its residents, and downstaters even more, recognized its special personality and invidiously referred to the general area as "de Region." As a folklorist interested in regional theory and the common traditions shaping a region, I was intrigued by the notion of an urbanized region, seemingly a contradiction in terms, and one so self-aware that it pinned the label on itself. Had the Region generated a distinctive folklore within its boundaries and become a subject of talk and legends?

This was an urban region of heavy industry, notably steelmaking and oil refining, and posed the additional challenge of discovering folklore among blue-collar workers. Collectors had heaped up songs of the cowboys, lumberjacks, and miners and unearthed a cycle of tales from and about Gib Morgan in the oilfields. Steel was the number one industry in the United States, yet no one had plumbed its operations for possible folkloric spinoff. Did steelworkers possess a body of traditions comparable to that shared by men who herded cattle, cut timber, mined ore, and drilled for oil?

This was a heavily ethnic urban region, with various nationalities pouring into the mills from eastern Europe and Latin America and mingling with the southern whites and blacks who had migrated north to work in the mills. Ethnicity fascinates historians, sociologists, political scientists, and above all folklorists, who have attempted to extract the essence of ethnic tradition from the hyphenated groups that constitute so large a part of the American population. The Region included strong and highly visible ethnic enclaves, notably of Serbs, Greeks, Mexicans, and Puerto Ricans. How did their folkways and cultural systems fit into and influence the rhythms of city life?

The transformation of Gary, a city built by steel in 1906, into a community governed and dominated by blacks, with the election of Richard Gordon Hatcher as mayor in 1967, intrigued me. We knew a good deal about the tales, songs, and beliefs of lower-class southern blacks from impressive collections by white and black fieldworkers, and we had learned about the strident folklore of Philadelphia's black ghetto youths from Roger Abrahams' *Deep Down in the Jungle* (1964). But what folklore, if any, could one derive from the middle-class blacks of a northern city they now dominated?

Finally, I wished to inquire into crimelore, as a case example of how a pressure point in modern life might generate a body of folklore. Crime on the streets had become an incessant cause for apprehension and topic of conversation among city dwellers. Gary and East Chicago headed the list of incidence of violent crime in Indiana cities and offered an appropriate laboratory for the purpose. Did talk about muggings fall into narrative patterns that might be classed as modern folktales?

These five lines of inquiry became the prongs of my search into the nature of urban traditions. With the topics of steel and crime, I discovered that the lore took precedence over the folk, because of the wide-

spread knowledge of similar themes and incidents. In those topics dealing with the Region, ethnics, and blacks, the folk loomed larger than the
lore, which was filtered through personal histories and experiences. Accordingly, I have presented five reports in two different ways, one em-
phasizing the narratives, the other the conversational interviews.

To recount my meandering field strategies would require a separate
report. Suffice to say that for six months during 1975 and 1976 I lived in
the Region, interviewed and tape-recorded its citizens, attended civic
events, toured steel mills, visited black and ethnic churches, and entered
as much as I could into the life of the Region. To establish a base I twice
taught a course on "Folklore and Oral History of the Calumet Region" at
Indiana University Northwest in Gary, with the idea of enlisting students
in the project; some proved to be excellent informants and collectors and
good friends. From time to time each of seven doctoral candidates in the
Folklore Department in Bloomington participating in the project, under
our grant from the National Endowment for the Humanities, drove up
for limited stays to conduct special inquiries according to their expertise,
and to aid me in the endeavor to fathom the folklore mysteries of "de Region." Adrienne Seward and Gil Cooley (now Elon Kulii) concentrated
on the blacks, Richard March on the Serbs and Croatians, Elena Bradunas on the Lithuanians, Phil George on the Latinos, Tom Adler on the
southern whites, John Hasse on black gospel music. Richard Vidutis, a
graduate student who was a native of Gary, assisted with the video
equipment. All proved invaluable field collaborators.

Some fruits of these efforts appear in the chapters that follow.

"I'd say the Region is probably the most corrupt of any place I have lived all my life."—a millworker

# 1

# MYSTIQUE OF THE REGION

In considering the Region as a historical and spiritual phenomenon, we confront several questions. What distinguishing characteristics and markers have led observers to call the area a region? What images are attached to the Region by residents, downstaters, and out-of-staters? What are the physical dimensions and component parts of the Region as conceived by Regionites of varying backgrounds? And what are the perspectives and orbits of Region individuals in their daily rounds? These questions overlap, but they involve separate bodies of theory: about the definition and character of urban regions, about the nature of urban imagery, and about the shape of cognitive or mental maps in the minds of city dwellers that guide them through the urban jungle. The folklorist is intrigued by these questions, which lead him into what might be called the mystique or mythology of the Region.

## IDENTITY OF THE REGION

Historians, sociologists, geographers, economists, political scientists, and folklorists have all demonstrated interest in regional theory. Howard W. Odum and Harry Estill Moore have speculated on the concepts of regions employed by marketing managers, athletic conferences, the Federal Reserve Board, presidential campaigners, and other agencies and units which needed to divide up the country. In *American Regionalism* (1938) they pointed to regions of earlier historical significance, of newer administrative functions, of convenience and necessity, government and commerce, literary achievement and agricultural adjustment, of land and water, forests and minerals, flora and crops, of educational institutions and football arrangements, of wholesale trade and of Rotary and Kiwanis. These they divided into five groups most commonly recognized in the United States: the *natural* region, characterized by mountain range, river valley, or great plains; the *metropolitan* region, such as Greater New York or Chicagoland, with the city at the hub; the region for *convenience,* to provide administrative subdivisions for an industrial corporation or government agency; the *group of states* region, such as New England or the Gulf states; and the *section or provincial locality* to which loyalties, patriotism, and folkways adhere.

This last category defines very well the folklorist's concept of the region, which may involve historical, economic, geographical, and political factors, insofar as they contribute to a sense of one's home ground. Common points of reference, common attitudes and expressions and behavior patterns, define this folk region. Its residents share perceptions of socio-cultural forces and economic problems entwined in the fabric of their lives. A young man born in Colorado and teaching in North Dakota told me that he felt an immediate kinship on meeting individuals from any of the western prairie states and Canadian provinces, with whom he could talk about cattle, blizzards, water needs, the open range, and such aspects of the plains lifestyle. So in each folk region a set of traditional themes and values links the inhabitants, and the folklorist in his field inquiries should set his sights on those cementing ideas. The folk region, unlike the other regions defined by Odum and Moore, lies in the mind and spirit as much as in physical boundaries; consequently, those boundaries may shift as the social networks that maintain the region's folkways and symbols stretch or contract in spatial areas.

The concept of symbolic landscapes as formulated by cultural or human geographers, particularly Donald W. Meinig, bears on regional theory and imagery. Meinig and his colleagues emulate the interpretation of ordinary landscapes pioneered in by William G. Hoskins, who in

# Mystique of the Region

1955 opened new vistas with *The Making of the English Landscape*. In a brilliant essay on "Symbolic Landscapes: Some Idealizations of American Communities," Meinig singled out the New England Town with its steepled church and village green, the Main Street of Middle America dominated by the bank and places of business, and the single-story sprawling houses and green lawns of Southern California Suburbia, as key regional models for the United States. We might in turn "read" the Region's landscape in terms of the "aesthetics of ugliness," Jean Shepherd's phrase, and picture a grimy, dilapidated downtown, overshadowed by smokestacks of steel mills belching into the sky, dinosaur diesel trucks racing across freeways, glittering ashdumps and junkyards. The folklorist probes one step beyond the cultural geographer and peoples this landscape, then elicits cognitive maps from local residents.

Historians, too, have conceptualized the notion of region and on occasion written regional history. The several histories of northwest Indiana all confirm a general awareness of its separate identity and refer to it as a region. In 1915 *A Standard History of Lake County, Indiana, and the Calumet Region* stated: "In the Calumet Region, or northern Lake County, has occurred, within comparatively recent years, one of the greatest industrial expansions of modern times." The editor of the work, W. F. Howat, remarked on the difference in the kind of population between the Calumet Region and other parts of Lake County. Nearby Crown Point and Valparaiso, for instance, contained mostly old-stock German and Dutch families, while the more enterprising settlers had drifted into the lakefront cities.

In 1939 the Writers' Program of the Work Projects Administration in Indiana deviated from the pattern of state guidebooks to compose *The Calumet Region Historical Guide*. The project supervisor, Gordon F. Briggs, acknowledged that the volume was "unusual among the Writers' Program series for two reasons: first, because the book is a guide to a region that is wholly new and wholly industrial, and second, because it is a guide to four industrial cities, Gary, Hammond, East Chicago and Whiting, an unusual metropolitan area." Within three decades the Calumet Region has attained a population of 260,000 and has become one of the world's great industrial centers. Dominated by the heavy industries of steel, oil refining, chemicals, and railroad equipment, some 221 companies in the Region manufactured 1,217 products.

In 1959 Powell A. Moore wrote the only full-dress history of the area, *The Calumet Region: Indiana's Last Frontier*. He divided its history into three periods: 1675–1833, when the French, English, and Americans successively entered the land drained by the Great and Little Calumet rivers on the southern shore of Lake Michigan and occupied by the Potawatomi Indians; 1833–1869, marked by the arrival of the first settlers, the organization of Lake County in 1837, and the incorporation of the

7

first two towns, Valparaiso and Crown Point; and from 1869, when George H. Hammond established a meat-packing plant on the site of the city named for him, to 1933, end of the formative period of industrial development. In 1889 Standard Oil founded Whiting, in 1901 Inland Steel Company began operations in East Chicago, and in 1906 the United States Steel Corporation built Gary on the sand dunes of Lake Michigan. Moore devoted a chapter apiece to Hammond, Whiting, and East Chicago, and two chapters to Gary, as well as general chapters on such matters as population, education, labor and politics pertaining to all four cities. At the outset he, too, stated that the region "is today one of the most heavily industrialized centers of the United States."

The concentration of heavy industry in contiguous cities has given the Calumet Region its unifying characteristic and has created a uniform population throughout the Region of ethnics, blacks, and hillbillies who provide its labor force. The working class, blue-collar culture has dominated the lakefront cities and reinforced the sense of regional identity. Or, as a young steelworker, whose father also works in the mills, phrased it: "The Calumet Region was built by the steel mills. Where most regions overcame their dependence on a specific industry, the Calumet Region has not. Sure there are other businesses, but these are parasites of the mills. As the Region developed, the steel industry has become the power behind the Region, and the Region has responded by training the people to become steel educated and dependent. By the saying of steel dependent it is meant that, unless your dad is a big wheel in an independent business or unless you have a paper B.A., you are only good enough to work in the mills as a production-maintenance worker."

A young woman enrolled at Purdue-Calumet University in Hammond conducted a series of interviews in my behalf among middle-class whites, blacks, and Latinos who had lived in the Region at least fifteen years. Her informants all agreed that the economy of the mills tied together the Region and determined the lifestyle of its inhabitants. Families must adjust their rhythms to the shift work in the mills and accept the fact that the steelworking breadwinner often could not participate in family functions because of his changing work schedule. People described the mills as almost part of their families. Everyone knew when the main boulevards would be crowded with bumper-to-bumper traffic as the millworkers drove to or returned from work.

The Region stands in sharp contrast to the adjacent zones of Chicagoland to the east and the southern portions of Lake and Porter counties to the south. Chicago represents the high culture and lavish entertainment so conspicuously lacking in the Region, whose residents feel little pull toward that alien metropolis. Similarly, below the steel belt the rural, agricultural, white farmers in central Indiana constitute a separate world.

## IMAGES OF THE REGION

In his eye-opening *Images of the American City* (1961) Anselm L. Strauss broached the subject of urban personalities. We may evoke imaginative conceptions of metropolises by conjuring up distinctive landmarks, whether buildings or monuments or parks. We may seek to perceive the totality of a city by looking upon it from the air or from a nearby promontory. We may associate the city with particular activities—Mardi Gras in New Orleans, stockyards and slaughterhouses in Chicago.

The Region does create mental pictures in the minds of those who have lived within its borders or heard stories about its infamy. From the usual designation thirty years ago of "the Calumet Region" the name has been shortened to "de Region," denoting the rough speech and manners associated with its working-class society. One also hears less polite sobriquets, such as "the Armpit of America" and "the Hellhole (or Asshole) of the Universe." "Are you taking a gas mask?" "Will you carry a gun?" were among the wisecracks leveled at us when we announced we were going to de Region. Students coming to Indiana University in downstate Bloomington from Gary, East Chicago, and Hammond often said they learned of this derogatory image for the first time when they revealed their birthplaces to fellow-students. To avoid such harsh reactions some have disguised their origins, saying they come from thirty miles south of Chicago, or from northwest Indiana. When found out, they are often referred to as "Region rats."

Why is the Region so maligned? Crime, corruption, and pollution are customary explanations. In popular lore the Region is rough and tough, a dangerous place in which to live or even to visit or travel through. It is also a sink of pollution from the wastes of the steel mills and oil refineries. An Indiana University professor born in Hammond, whose father had held the post of school superintendent and who himself once taught junior high school there, states that "the whole Calumet Region is a sad story. It represents, with some exceptions, the worst that America has to offer. It's certainly a monument to lost opportunities." As a political scientist and an environmentalist, he sees the pilfering of local revenues by corrupt politicians and the bulldozing of the Dunes by the steel companies as the signs of the Region's decay.

A legacy of political graft further tarnishes the Region. In the words of a veteran millworker, who has resided in various parts of the country: "I'd say the Region is probably the most corrupt of any place I have lived all my life. And I think basically you can blame it on politics. It's not the rich people, it's the little bitty people trying to shove somebody out of the way so they move up a step." The aforementioned student at the Purdue-Calumet campus who interviewed forty-seven Hammond residents between the ages of thirty-seven and fifty-three, two-thirds male, with family incomes ranging from $17,000 to $35,000, thus summarized their attitudes toward the Region: "All agreed that the Calumet Region was so corrupt and voters so stupid that nothing short of a cataclysm could effect noticeable change. One man quipped that if political corruption could be cured with an enema, the Calumet Region would be the logical place to insert the syringe." Each of the forty-seven sought relief from living and working in the Region through a yearly vacation on which they spent considerable money; but other than for business purposes, they visited nearby Chicago only about once every two years. Not one planned to live in the Region after retirement.

Another student interviewer, who sampled a broader spectrum of age groups and ethnic groups, found comparable distaste for and boredom with the Region. Respondents commented on the stagnation and deterio-

The Region in 1975

ration of the Region, seen in the dying downtowns, the lack of entertainment and cultural satisfactions, the rising crime and pollution, the sheer ugliness. Youths looked upon college degrees as stepping-stones to escape; older folk looked forward to retirement in the Sun Belt. All tolerated the Region because of well-paying job opportunities in the mills, refineries, and railroads. The majority of millworkers could not transfer their skills to another occupation or to another part of the country. The most they could hope for was a move from the four core cities to the dormitory communities where they would be removed from the traffic, congestion, and crime. In concluding her report, the interviewer noted that only one of her informants admitted to enjoying this area.

Each of the core cities possesses its own subimage. Gary is the black city where nobody goes any more because of crime, particularly drug crime, but also because of the decay of the downtown shopping area and the air pollution from the "Big Mill," U.S. Steel. East Chicago evokes ethnic groups, particularly close-knit Latin families in the older part of the city, Indiana Harbor, which, too, is characterized by slow rot. One resident observed: "When I go downtown I see all the empty businesses and the trash all over. I see the steel mills illuminated in the distance and men falling out of taverns at every corner." Hammond conjures up endless railroad crossings downtown, a large Polish population, and a general drabness. Whiting, the smallest and least known of the four cities, is marked by its exclusion of blacks and predominance of Slovaks and by the dominance of Standard Oil's refineries. One commentator likened it to a small southern town.

As yet the fringe towns—the "white flight" or "bedroom" or "dormitory" communities—have not developed images comparable to those of the core cities, with the possible exception of Munster, known as "Snob City" and "Mortgage Row" because of the airs put on by its residents. One story claims that many Munster homes lack furniture because the new owners, in their anxiety to escape from the core cities and purchase houses in that desirable township, left themselves without funds to furnish the interiors. A Region-wise acquaintance performed a little skit to suggest the self-images of Munsterites and Garyites: "People in Munster do this," he said, sticking his chin up in the air, "and people in Gary do this," hanging his head down.

The image Regionites held in an earlier day, and which a few still maintain, reverses the picture. In his youth, recalls the distinguished Indiana University professor mentioned previously, he would never have dreamed of living downstate or of going to the university in Bloomington where he presently teaches. Forty years ago William Wirt, school superintendent in Gary, was developing a model school system that attracted the attention of the nation's educators. Intellectuals and professionals living in the Calumet Region looked to Chicago as their natural resource for concerts, museums, art galleries, theaters, and restaurants. Access then was easy by public transportation of streetcar, bus, and the South Shore railroad. An Indiana state senator from the Region, who has spent most of his working years in the mills, swore he would never send his children to the Bloomington campus, a center of drug traffic and abuse; the daughter of a close associate had died there from an overdose of drugs. (And indeed the senator's daughter enrolled in my Gary class.) A young Gary Serb expressed his delight in the Region with the metaphor of a salad bowl, rather than a melting pot, to suggest the variety of ethnic diversions available in brief compass.

Not all observers write off boarded-up downtown Gary. A shrewd legislator from Hammond comments:

✦ Downtown Gary, I think, will come back. I think the wisest thing that anyone could do if you wanted to make money would be buy the property on Broadway. Sit there and hold it or give it to your children. The next generation could be rich. Downtown Gary will come back. It will be a different service, but it will come back. It's going to take proper planning. The city of Hammond is going to have to tear down their buildings on Hohman and State Street, just like downtown Gary is. You have to start over again. I could take you into Hammond where there are no blacks and show you a downtown that's as dead as Gary is. It's not meeting the needs of the people; the people themselves are demanding different types of public places to shop. If you don't provide a more modern facility, they are going to go to shopping centers.

## BOUNDARIES OF THE REGION

Where exactly is this Region that aroused such strong emotions in many people? As I explored the question, I learned that this was the most folkloric aspect of all the Region's mystique, for people's conceptions shifted like the variants of a folktale. Although earlier historians considered the core cities of Gary, East Chicago, Hammond, and Whiting as the Region, white flight to the suburbs has dramatically expanded its perimeters. Within the past decade the Hammond *Times* and the Gary *Post Tribune* have dropped the city names from their mastheads, in recognition of the larger communities they now serve. The *Times* calls itself the "newspaper of the Calumet Region," but it excludes Gary and includes Lansing and Calumet City across the Illinois line.

An eloquent supporter of the *Times*'s perspective is Jean Shepherd, the writer, humorist, and radio, television, and platform personality who grew up in Hammond, worked in Inland Steel in East Chicago, and used this background in popular stories gathered in *Wanda Hickey's Night of*

## Mystique of the Region

*Golden Memories* and *In God We Trust, All Others Pay Cash*. Although he no longer resides there, Mr. Shepherd retains strong impressions and convictions about the Region. On September 1, 1977, at a conference in Bloomington he expressed this positive view: "The Region is only the cities and towns along the Greater Calumet River: Hammond, Whiting, East Chicago, Munster, Highland. *It definitely excludes Gary.* The original name was the Calumet Region. It is characterized by the Slavic, particularly the Polish element. Gary is younger, a company-built city, with a black population. The people in the Region look to Chicago, never to Gary. Dutch families settled in the Region and grew onions—they are a bulbous people. Hammond was, and is, all railroads. Gary is the Dunes."

In further conversation Mr. Shepherd told us about an executive with Borden's Milk Company in Hammond, who accompanied the driver of a milk delivery truck to Gary, where blacks robbed and, although they offered no resistance, shot them. None of the blacks standing around helped, and the driver had to crawl off to a telephone. The victim spent four months in the hospital. To many Hammond residents, Gary was enemy territory outside the Region.

Another conference participant, James B. Lane, professor of history at Indiana University Northwest, author of *"City of the Century": A History of Gary, Indiana,* and a resident of the Miller section of Gary, took issue with Shepherd. He pointed out the common climate of northwest Indiana, the steel mills shared by Gary and East Chicago, and the continuous presence of ethnic groups in Gary as well as in East Chicago and Hammond. In his view, steel and related industries define the Region, which thus extends from the Wisconsin Steel Company across the Illinois line to the two new steel mills of Bethlehem and Midwest in Porter County.

Different residents reveal different cognitive maps of the Region. Some see it as lying in the Harbor and Gary, which have the densest population and the closest proximity to the steel mills, as well as the most crime and violence and the highest number of blacks and Mexicans. Others see the Region extending a considerable direction west, east, and south. Some share the view of the Hammond *Times* that the outlying reaches of south Chicago join the Region in a continuous urban-ethnic-industrial band. Others, including a student who commuted nightly from Michigan City, visualized the Region as stretching eastward from Gary across the Dunes and enveloping the stretch from East Gary and Portage to Michigan City. (In 1978 East Gary changed its name to Lake Station.) But the southward push of the white ethnic population down Lake County has created the greatest reorientation in the mental map of Regionites. The first thrust, in the fifties and sixties, developed a tier of towns flanking Hammond, the trio of Munster, Highland, Griffith, plus Hobart, southeast of Gary. Then, in the seventies, the rush to the suburbs leapfrogged these communities to populate a second tier of bedroom communities, Merrillville (pronounced Merraville), Schererville (pronounced Scheraville), and Dyer. The growth of Merrillville, which successfully achieved incorporation after a bitter struggle with Glen Park, the ethnic residential neighborhood still willy-nilly part of Gary, illustrates the pattern. With Glen Park now the buffer zone into which the downtown blacks are moving, Merrillville has attracted ethnic churches, shopping centers, motels, restaurants, and new homes and schools. Along Route 30, a main east-west artery forming the southern edge of Merrillville which a number of Region residents now consider their new boundary line, sit conspicuous structures: the palatial Southlake Mall, a year old in 1975; just west of I-65, on the much-traveled freeway linking Gary and Indianapolis, a Holiday Inn and Convention Center throbbing with activity; and the newly completed Hellenic Center and St. Constantine's Greek Orthodox Church (a block from Route 30), its golden dome rising in a field, the site of an annual crowd-pulling Grecian Festival. In December 1975 the Gary National Bank announced that it would open an equal facility in Merrillville, and Sears, by then well-established in the Southlake Mall, made known that it was closing its Gary outlet. The Gary Country Club is located in Merrillville.

The tentacles of the Region are reaching farther out still, toward Crown Point, Valpo (Valparaiso), and St. John, a dozen miles or so beyond the present dormitory communities. Crown Point was originally a German settlement, whose rose-colored gingerbread courthouse has become the object of a historic preservation drive. It was in the courthouse jail that, according to legend, John Dillinger whittled away at a gun that he later used in escaping; letters thereafter poured in to "Wooden Gun, Indiana" (see Chapter 5). Valpo in Porter County has its own identity, home of Valparaiso University and Law School. St. John is an outpost south of Schererville, near the Illinois line. These are the places where retirees and young couples are moving, to put distance between themselves and the central city dangers of blacks and crime and pollution. And so the Region proliferates, as millworkers drive in to the plants from their suburban homes, and residents of the inner area drive out to the suburbs to visit retired parents and grandparents.

## ORBITS OF THE REGION

Whatever boundaries a resident might assign to the Region, he or she does not traverse the entire area. In terms of living space and routes of travel, a Region dweller moves in a particular orbit, determined by economic and social needs, personal preferences and fears. According to these orbits, Regionites construct mental maps, as does any city dweller, of familiar zones, danger spots, oases, blazed trails, and terra incognita. Urban legends and anecdotes illuminate these landmarks and pathways.

The interview-conversations that follow present the outlooks of a resident in each of the Region's core cities: Gary, East Chicago, Hammond, and Whiting. One was a housewife taking night classes to complete her college degree; another a retired accountant and former steelworker trapped in the inner city; a third a real-estate agent interested in local history; and a fourth a young college instructor, writing a dissertation on his immigrant parents' ethnic group. All four had thought deeply about the city and neighborhood in which they lived. Three felt positively, if with some degree of apprehension, about their situation; the other spoke bitterly about the Region's decline. They offer four windows onto the landscape of this blue-collar country.

### Dorothy Gale, Gary

A young woman with liberal convictions, who moved to a racially mixed neighborhood in Gary's Miller section, gives a vivid account of her reactions, and those of her friends. Dorothy and her husband, Tim, found themselves back in the Region in 1971, after her husband was discharged from the Navy, with a two-week-old baby and a thousand dollars. Dorothy had grown up in Hammond, where her family still lived, so they moved in with her parents and started looking for a home. But the banks wanted 20 percent down, a figure that would have restricted them to a five-thousand-dollar home. Finally, a bank that had repossessed a house in Miller informed her that it was available for immediate occupancy at $12,000, sight unseen, except from the road. (The bank was renting the property and did not wish the tenants to know it was for sale, lest they move, leaving the bank with a vacant house if the sale fell through.) All Dorothy and her husband knew about the house was that it had three bedrooms and a basement, and was between two homes of black families. So desperate were they for a place to live that they bought it without setting foot inside.

I visited several times in their pleasant, spacious home in a quiet residential area among the dunes near Miller Beach. Poised and sincere, Dorothy admitted she had paid a price for her boldness—a price she was perfectly willing to pay—the loss of bigoted friends. "People, our friends, started ridiculing us saying 'You are fools, why would you buy into a changing neighborhood? Why would you buy a house in between two black families?' " These fair-weather friends would not risk the trip through Gary to visit Dorothy, who found herself cut off from a former network of close peers. The erstwhile friends were high school graduates, who had gone into the mills or taken other moderate-income jobs. Most came from tight ethnic groups and believed what their parents told them about blacks. They married young, started families, and were constantly running from the black immigration. Dorothy deviated from this pattern and took night classes (as did her husband, who managed a shoe store in Hammond) at Indiana University Northwest, to accumulate credits toward a college degree. She understood and explained her friends' fears: panic at the thought of blacks moving in, causing the values of homes to depreciate. "I heard stories about people who owned $80,000 and $90,-000 homes that they sold for $20,000. The realtors with their 'For Sale' signs had added to the panic, warning 'Hurry up and sell your house now, before anyone else gets a sign up on the street, because if there's two on the street you won't sell your house.' That's how they spread the idea that blacks were going to move in, and the whites should get as much money for their houses as they could now. Then the realtors would turn around and sell the homes at a profit to black families." Hence the Miller's Citizen Corporation pressured the city to pass an ordinance banning "For Sale" signs. Now, in order to ascertain what houses are for sale, the prospective buyer must look up listings in the paper.

Dorothy did not conceal her motive in buying the house. "We didn't buy it to be provocative or to spread brotherhood throughout the world, you know. We bought it because it was cheap [laughs] and we needed a place to live. We knew that the black family to the east was a doctor with two children, and that the black family to the west were a retired couple, with five grown boys, but only two of the boys were home. Later I found out that one of their sons was in prison for rape, and I didn't tell a soul [laughs] 'cause I knew I would get even more flak about living in Gary."

Dorothy believed she had made a good investment, that if her husband received a promotion and they sold the house and moved away in the next few years they could double the purchase price. She quoted an article in the *Post Tribune* as saying that the Miller section of Gary offered the best buys for one's money anywhere in the Calumet Region. Only two partly white areas remained in Gary: the Glen Park section south of the university, adjacent to the midtown and downtown sections, which were now 95 percent black; and the Miller section to the east, separated from central Gary by scrub and wooded land. Actually Miller had once been a separate township, with a predominantly Jewish community. Attracted by the dunes and the beach and the relative proximity to their work, and excluded from the southern suburbs of Merrillville and Schererville, wealthier blacks commenced moving to Miller, along with lower-class whites, and the Jewish families departed, many to Munster. Miller would never become a slum, Dorothy confidently predicted.

Yet her former classmates prophesied that dire consequences would result from the move to Miller—and the folklore began to flow. When Dorothy pointed out she was within walking distance of the same Miller

Beach to which her parents had driven her twenty miles for the past twenty years, they scoffed.

+ And I heard several of the same stories repeated over and over again that there were youths, black gangs, that would go up and down the beach. They would hide in the brush and they would see a couple on the beach and they would come up and hold a gun to the man's head and rape the woman, and then they would beat them both. I've heard stories about how rape was so predominant in interchanging areas, you couldn't go out of your house.

And another story was there was a female impersonator, who would gain access to your home, posing as an Avon lady or something like that. And he would come into your home and ask to use the washroom. And he would go into the washroom, and he would stay in the washroom for a long time, and he would undress. And then of course, he was [revealed as] a man. And he would call for help. The woman would come in and he would attack her in the washroom. Which never made sense to me, because if he got in the home, why would he do it in the washroom?

Another story that I had heard was that a man had gained access to a woman's home through the basement and turned on the washing machine. The woman came downstairs to see why her washing machine was running, and the man was standing nude next to the washing machine. He attacked her and then ran out through the basement. And so that was another thing I couldn't understand: if he was in the house why did he make her come downstairs? But I guess you are not supposed to reason these things out.

The narrators of these stories did not specify whether the would-be rapists were black or white, but Dorothy knew of other reports identified with the black areas of Gary.

+ If you pull up to a stoplight and stop at night, you can be dragged from your car and beaten or raped. And if your doors were locked, they would take a pipe and bust the window and pull the lock up and drag you from the car. I believe that. That is one of the few stories that I've heard that I believe, and I believe it because I know it's happened. I know a person that it had happened to. He was a state representative, from Hammond in Lake County. And I do take precautions. I don't travel at night with my doors unlocked.

As a liberal sympathetic to and living among blacks, Dorothy felt guilty about having fears, but saw no way to dispel them. "I don't think whites are very well received [in midtown and downtown Gary] because those people really have a stinking life, and I empathize with them. I wish there were more that I could do about it, but I can't go around wearing a banner saying 'Hey, I live in an integrated area, I'm for you!' They can't recognize when I'm in my car at night that I'm on their side. But I *am* afraid to go through those areas, and my husband is too. It's not so much that I feel we might be pulled from the car at a stop sign; it's more the fact that if the car breaks down and we need help we are at their mercy. I think that we might get shot or raped or beaten just for the hell of it."

Blacks as well as whites feared to drive through midtown Gary. Dorothy told of a young black couple who had just moved from midtown to take up residence across the street from her and who refused to return to midtown even to visit their families: "John told me once, he said, 'I won't go back, 'cause I'm afraid one of my kids will get shot.' This was when The Family drug war was on, and there were bullets flying everywhere. I read in the paper once that sixty people had been killed. John knew what was going on and it scared him and he moved to Miller."

Although technically part of Gary, Miller conjured up quite distinct images—the Dunes, the beach, Marquette Park, its Jewish community—and blacks dissociated the neighborhood from Gary. Meeting a Gary black in her husband's store, Dorothy said, "I'm from Gary too," and he looked shocked. "And I told him that I was tired of getting that reception when I said that I was from Gary, because people acted as if you were a leper. I have never heard anything good said about Gary, even on TV." Here Dorothy identified Miller with Gary, contrary to the usual image of black Garyites. Her new acquaintance declared that the real Gary was midtown, where he lived, and that Miller was on the outskirts. Dorothy defined midtown as a big square, running north-south from the expressway and east-west from 15th and Grant to Broadway and Burr. "That is the ghetto. The red-light district is around Washington and Adams. I remember them talking about Washington and Adams when I was in second grade. I knew that's where the prostitutes in Gary were, where the predominance of crime is, and that's the section I am afraid to shop downtown." Because most of the big stores had departed—Sears, Gordon's, one after another had given up the ghost—Dorothy found it much simpler to shop at Southlake Mall in Merrillville or return to her old haunts in Hammond.

Living in integrated Miller entailed racial problems, but they did not stem from the blacks, who were well-to-do professionals. "The children that my son plays with are all black, and their parents have more middle-class values than I do. They are very, very conscious of professionalism. Their children have to have piano lessons and dancing lessons and they have to be refined and they are always immaculately clean, well-groomed. And my kid goes out and he has peanut butter and jelly on his sweatshirt

Rows of homes in the Region.

2. Jennie's Cafe, a popular meeting place in midtown Gary.

and he is barefoot half the time. I told my neighbor the other day—we were laughing about it—I said, 'There is definite advantage to having a black child. Their hair is never messed up and if their face is dirty you can't tell it [laughs]. And my son, he always looks terrible; he is just one of those grimy kids.' She just laughed it off. My next-door neighbor and I can talk about anything. We talk about race quite a bit, but basically, like I said, she is more white than I am. She frowns more than I do upon the black kids with the big wide-brimmed hats, the cool dudes who walk around and think they own the city. And I think that she's happy here. They moved here from midtown."

The presence of lower-class whites who could not afford to move from midtown to suburbs like Merrillville and had to settle for Miller led to tensions.

✦ For the most part the children are so foul-mouthed that they are the epitome of white trash, and this has infuriated the black people here more than anything else, because they have worked very hard to be where they are at and to move into Miller. My neighbor went down to complain to one of these people, about five doors down, who had four children. And the man of the house came to the door and he called her a dirty motherfucking nigger and said that she was married to a dirty motherfucking man and she had no business coming down there. Now this lady is a classy broad—I mean she has jewels like you can't believe, and furs, and she is terribly refined, and she is a beautiful woman and very literate.

And she told me they were looking for another home. She looked in Ogden Dunes, which is still an all-white section, and the most exclusive one in this part of the Region. So Cordelia went down there looking for a home, and she found a beautiful home that they could afford, right on the beach. She could pass; she is very fair. And then she asked the realtor: "How would you feel about a black family moving in?" "A black family! I thought you were white?" He said: "Lady, I couldn't sell you a home. I'd lose my job, your kids would have trouble in school; you would be the first black family here." Well, they were the second black family in Miller and they had a horrible time; they were terribly persecuted. Anyway she decided not to try to move out to Ogden Dunes, that the prices were terribly inflated for what you were getting, simply because it was an all-white area. They want to stay in Miller because they don't want to battle this racial thing, but they want to get in an area of Miller where the homes are all nice. See, here in this part of Miller you have one $20,000 home and a $60,000 home and a $10,000 home all next to each other, because everybody constructed what they could construct. And she wants to get in an area where they are all $60,000 homes, because then she doesn't feel that the white trash can permeate the area, that anyone who can spend $60,000 on a home must have her standard of living. I wish her luck. I don't think she will find it, but she is going to try.

Dorothy has ceased trying to justify her move to Miller and stopped defending herself against her peers. Her pastor at the Marquette Park Methodist Church told her: "As long as you are happy, you don't really have to defend yourself." Dorothy realizes that the ones who denigrate Gary are those who have run away—to Hobart and Merrillville, Shererville and St. John and Dyer to the south, and Portage to the east. They are bitter because in their flight to the suburbs they suffered exorbitant losses on their homes. She accepted the idea of living among blacks and raising her children with black playmates, and now she pays $112 a month on her mortgage instead of $350 a month, on a secluded street free from traveling salesmen and ice cream vendors, where so far no thefts or break-ins have marred her peace.

"I feel as secure here as I think I would anywhere, right now. And I'm happy. I love this area now. I love taking my son to the beach. I never encountered any problems at all on the beach, although I don't go there after dark. My husband and son and I went down there last Tuesday night and we were the only persons on the beach. This was four in the afternoon and it was a hot day. This beach directly in front of our house is almost always desolate, and if I ever have a problem I find it very tranquilizing just to go down and walk on the beach. It's very beautiful, and although you look to the east and see a steel mill, and look to the west and see a steel mill, when you look straight out you see water. It's very beautiful and it's very refreshing, just to be able to have such an easy access to tranquility."

This statement by a concerned young woman, who has lived in both Hammond and Gary, reveals in microcosm the troubles, and the folklore arising from those troubles, that beset the Region and other urban centers. Fear of black encroachment in white neighborhoods, panic over possible depreciation in housing values, stories of black violence, incidents of racial friction, intraracial resentments based on class differences—all come to a boil in this testament. Both the deteriorating image of Gary—a portent, Dorothy says, of what will happen to the rest of the Region—and the invigorating image of the Dunes that contribute to the mystique of the Region are apparent in her reflections.

*Philip Spalding, East Chicago*

A strident spokesman for the voices of doom in the Region, a self-proclaimed fascist and bigot, admirer of George Wallace and Lester Maddox, seventy-one-year-old Philip Spalding lived in the Harbor side of East Chicago in a state of siege. When I telephoned him, at the suggestion of a mutual acquaintance, Spalding said I could come right over. I found him in a rundown neighborhood populated by Mexicans and other ethnics and blacks, in a house so cluttered with books and furnishings we could scarcely find a place to sit. A bachelor, Spalding was the last of his family, an Anglo-Saxon Protestant whose ancestors had fought in the Revolution, the Civil War, and the Spanish-American War, had trekked through Cumberland Gap on a bull team, and were related to George Washington and General Custer. He despised the blacks and the browns who now engulfed him, but he was stuck. After arsonists set fire to a suburban home he had purchased, he had to bring all his household goods back to his Harbor residence, hence the disarray. Because of the depreciation of housing values in the area he could not sell his house for enough money to buy one elsewhere. "In 1952 this property was considered to be worth $24,000. And now, twenty-three years later, with the decline of the dollar about 60 percent, it's worth about $18,500. I was waiting, hoping for a rise in values, because if I go to Florida, to have an eight-room house like I have here, I have to find about $60,000. In addition to that, for me to move to Florida, the moving bill is $5,500. I estimate my losses in twenty years to be $300,000. In my area here we used to have an average of two to three persons per home. Now we have as many as fifty persons in one building."

White-haired and jowly, with a safari shirt, green shorts, and long yellow socks clothing his large frame, Spalding talked nonstop in an authoritative voice. A graduate of the University of Chicago, he claimed to have an IQ of over 145, putting him in the upper 1 percent of the population and making it difficult, he said, to find persons of equal intellectual level with whom to associate. As a youth he had worked for Inland Steel, where his father had been a surgeon. Now retired, he had made his living as a systems accountant, auditing books for business firms.

He viewed the Region with profound pessimism.

✦ Our area here, I've been watching it go down every single day for twenty-five years. Every year it declines more and more. Every year I have more broken glass in the alley to clean up. I had all my windows shot out in the back of my house. All my garage windows have been broken. And last year I had a Mexican fellow who used to bring his dog into my yard to defecate. And so I went out and remonstrated with him, and he didn't get out. And I went out and got my rifle and almost killed him in my back yard last year. Because of the fact that he had a perfect right to occupy my back yard for the defecation of his dog.

One of my friends had to chop down a fruit tree because the people ran over the garage roof all the time trying to reach the fruit. There is a pear tree out in the neighbor's yard there, and some of the kids run across my yard and crawl up on my garage roof so that they can pick the pears off

21

the tree. So the neighbor had to spend $600 to build a steel fence with barbed wire on the top to keep the hoodlums out, so he could preserve his property.

They moved Puerto Ricans into the building that the superintendent of the open hearth used to live in—down here on 36th Street back of the library, where people used to do their laundry—and some of the Puerto Ricans used to come down to the basement and steal the laundry out of the basement.

Now I bought a new bicycle because Paul Dudley White, Ike's [Eisenhower's] physician, said everybody ought to have a bike. And I've been reading a new textbook about how to prolong your life and strengthen your heart, and they say you ought to have regular exercise, so I bought a real pretty bicycle. Well, boys have been through my yard and around my garage and on my roof trying to find an opening down there so that they can steal my bicycle away from me. And I only had it about a month now.

Now I was walking up Grand Boulevard here about two years ago, and the Puerto Ricans up there had remonstrated with the Park Department to furnish them with some park benches to put along the sidewalk so that they'd have a place where they could annoy Whitey. So that Whitey'd be sure to move—those people hate Whitey so much—so that they could agitate them enough to have them all moved out, and they'd be pleased about that. Now these Puerto Rican boys were sitting on these park benches, their bicycles parked across the sidewalk, just to annoy everybody. So I says: "Whose bicycle is this one right in the middle?" They wouldn't say anything, but finally a guy says: "Mine." So I says: "Here it is," and I moved it off the sidewalk. And it wasn't five minutes before they started throwing rocks and clubs and bottles at me because I violated their civil rights. They have a right to park their bicycle exactly right in the middle of the sidewalk! I'm violating their civil rights to take up the middle of the sidewalk! Now that's the reason a lot of people move.

Now you probably noticed the rear end of my car that's all bashed up, in front of my house? All right. This happened about two or three weeks ago, about two o'clock in the morning. I had just spent a lot of time cleaning and sanding the bottom part of the car and fixing it all up so it'd last another ten to fifteen years. And this Puerto Rican fellow, twenty-one years old, drunk, driving a Cadillac that cost him $3,300 and which he owed money on, tore into the side of my neighbor's car and tore into my car. Neighbor's car is damaged to the extent of $900; my car is damaged to the extent of $750. This is the third time I've had a car demolished in front of my house. So, it ultimately gets so that the destruction is so great and the threat to your life and your property is so great that you simply won't put up with it any more and so you move.

They tried the fellow in court the other day for driving under the influence. He didn't have a safety sticker, he didn't have any insurance, and he left the scene of the accident. He had to be arrested by the police down in his home area, down around Parrish Street. So now he's supposed to pay all these damages back, but he only makes $326 every two weeks—he works for the city, he's a laborer over at the park, in the sanitary district. So meanwhile I've got to finance all the car damages and go to all the trouble of getting the bids and getting the car rebuilt that I'd already fixed.

So there's more reasons than race why people leave. When their property is subjected to endless depreciation and their life is subject to hazards, people simply will not stay. A couple of years ago, when I went to the Masonic Lodge over here—they had Past Masters Night—I came home about ten o'clock and I found that somebody had been in my house in the meantime. All the dresser drawers were open. So I went all around trying to find out what had happened, what was missing. And this fellow had brought a girl and had sex with her in my bed while I'm in the lodge meeting. There was sperm all over the bedsheet. And he'd broken my rear windowpane to get in.

Not just property, but life and limb were constantly threatened in the Harbor. Philip recalled the beating a roomer of his received from two blacks who attacked him as he was going to work at 6 A.M. When Philip went out the next morning at the same time he carried a revolver, saying to himself: "They're going to beat me up, I'll kill them." Nobody attacked him, but thenceforth whenever he left his house to visit a friend, even if only a block or two away, he carried a revolver or knife or gas pistol. This last weapon he described as resembling a fountain pen with a little gas cartridge that could be discharged like a revolver cartridge. He did not keep a dog because it was messy, had to be kept inside in winter, and could be stolen. According to Spalding, the rise in crime in East Chicago had resulted in large part from the type of immigrant entering the Region.

✦ The people who come here from Mexico are not the elite of Mexico. They're the peon type of agricultural laborer, and slum laborer. The people that live in the barrios and the shacks, and the pigs and the chickens all live with them. This is the kind of people we get here—the surplus people. Now the elite in Mexico are probably for their type of culture very fine people. But the surplus class probably couldn't make a go of it in Mexico, because Mexico is one of the fastest moving populating countries in the whole world. And you're talking about having a one hundred million population in Mexico, and it was only a few years ago that they had twenty million.

On the question of the blacks, Spalding felt that slavery had operated as a beneficent institution, that most southerners were "very generous, hospitable, capitalistic people," who didn't beat their slaves but tended to their needs, even after they became freedmen, treating them like members of their families. "If they needed medical attention the boss-man took them in the car downtown and got them a shot of mercury or bismuth, if they had VD—and most of them had VD." He continued in this vein, saying that the bosses would give their "niggers" (used as a friendly term) old clothes and food from the refrigerator, as he had personally observed on a visit to a southern plantation. "So the cultural differences down there were tremendously different from what they are here. I never hated any of the Negro people down there; we got along very well. And George Wallace and Lester Maddox weren't interested in hurting anybody; they were not sadists, they just wanted to preserve their way of living. Now up here we don't preserve our way of living; it declines every year. Thanks to the federal judges, who are already enforcing busing and forced integration and forced association with people, the racial lines harden, rather than becoming more flexible."

As the dangers around him multiplied, Spalding withdrew more and more from the outside world. Sometimes he never left home all day, but cleaned and painted the house, read books, called friends on the telephone, and watched television. When he did venture forth, it was only during daylight, and within circumscribed limits. Gary was off limits.

✦ Gary has declined tremendously; the crime over there is fantastic. I haven't been to Gary in years. I wouldn't go to Gary if I had an armored guard of marines to guard me over there. I have no reason to go to Gary any more, and I wouldn't go over there in any circumstances. I wouldn't go to Gary to the Lodge because I have to put my car in the parking lot and in half an hour it's going to be demolished. And I wouldn't go to Broadway. If I wanted to go shopping in a store and I have to ring a doorbell and a fellow comes and inspects me and I have to have a password to get in—like going to a secret lodge or to a Ku Klux Klan meeting—I don't want to do business like that, so I stay away. They closed up Sears Roebuck because of the fact that customers were being held up and hijacked in the parking lot. And Sears Roebuck lost incredible amounts due to shoplifting. And I don't like the city administration in Gary, so I don't go to Gary. I don't like Hammond very much better, because Hammond has been on a downgrade ever since they had the urban renewal. Every place you have urban renewal the place goes down. It went down here, it went down in Gary, it went down in Michigan City, it went down in Hammond.

Spalding then launched into an attack on federal bureaucrats with Ph.D.s in City Planning or City Financing or Real Estate Management who try to reorganize areas according to their own desires. Few places in the Region attracted him any more, and travel to Chicago entailed too much expense and worry.

✦ I used to go to a lot of parties at the University of Chicago and Northwestern; I don't go to them any more because I'm afraid of being hurt. And I belong to the Adler Planetarium and I'm afraid to go there for fear I might be hurt. And I used to belong to the Art Institute and I don't go up there because there's a lack of good transportation to go up there. And if you go out to the parking lot you might be hurt when you go out to get your car. Or if you come home here by train and you stand out at the station and call a cab and the cab doesn't show up, and then you pay a fellow about four dollars to bring you home. Then to go up there to spend the afternoon at the Art Institute costs you fifteen to twenty dollars by the time you get through with your lunch, pay your car and cab bill—so you don't go.

I used to go to the Chicago Symphony Orchestra and Grand Opera, and about the only way you can go to them is to hire a hotel room at seventeen to eighteen dollars a night and stay up there and come home the next day. Because we have no transportation to speak of. I think there's a train on the South Shore that leaves about 8 or 9 o'clock, and then the next one leaves about 12. And who wants to get stuck on the South Shore out here at 1:30 or so in the morning on a real cold nasty night when you don't even know if there is going to be a cab to pick you up?

So this once-active man, who had traveled extensively in the United States—and even studied Tahitian, thinking he might go to the Fiji Islands—now barricaded himself in his house. At the end of our interview he led me through his cluttered quarters, pointing out stacks of books with titles such as *Who Is Screwing the Average Man?* and took me upstairs into his bedroom, unabashed by an unmade bed and toilet articles scattered over a table. He opened a cupboard to display his rifle and ammunition and expensive Navaho jewelry set with turquoise stones, held up watches on the dresser costing several hundred dollars, and showed me a cudgel Lester Maddox had given him. On parting he offered to come and lecture to my class, apparently forgetting his vow not to set foot in Gary.

Philip Spalding, in spite of his extreme statements, fairly represents the class of embittered old residents in the Region about whom Dorothy spoke, a group that has suffered heavy financial losses as their homes depreciated. His bitterness keeps increasing because he is trapped in a deteriorating environment he loathes. Most of his fellow Wasps have accepted the losses, but made their getaway. Philip's string of personal-experience stories documents the harassments and dangers to which he sees himself subject every day of his life. For him the bright promise of the industrial Region has ended in a nightmare of crime, decay, and degeneration.

*Warner N. Babson, Jr., Hammond*

One evening I found myself in the opulent, southern-style mansion of Warner N. Babson, Jr., in midtown Hammond. We sat in a study crammed full of books and papers adjoining a living room the size of an auditorium, while he poured forth a stream of anecdotes about Hammond's history. A real-estate broker and lifelong resident of that city, a founder of the Hammond Historical Society, Babson was writing a short bicentennial historical account of Hammond. Powell Moore's *The Calumet Region* and an old Lake County history were open in front of him, but his recollections stemmed largely from scenes and incidents he himself had seen or heard about. Although the recent victim of a heart attack, Babson bubbled with energy and animation as he discoursed for ninety minutes on his home town. (He died some eighteen months after this tape recording.)

Our talk veered to the early days of Hammond, and Babson sketched out its beginnings.

✦ You may have heard of George H. Hammond, who came from Detroit. He was a leading spirit in a group of men, four of them butchers and retailers in Detroit. In 1868, I think it was, a fellow down the road from him, who ran a little fruit market, managed to ship fruit from Detroit to Boston by inventing a little freight car that would keep it iced up, and Hammond got talking to him. It was a successful adventure, so Hammond said: "Why couldn't we do this with beef? Beef is what's in demand." And they had tried various ways of getting beef to the market prior to this time, like they would pack it in cars and press ice down on top of it, but the ice would discolor the meat. The railroad employees refused to bring ice to cars, and if they shipped the animals live, they lost a lot of weight en route, because they wouldn't water them for one thing.

So Hammond said: "Why not slaughter the animals at the source?" Which would be out in the Midwest, because two-thirds of the beef is grown west of the Mississippi, but two-thirds is consumed east of the Mississippi. "We will get near to the Chicago stockyards." So they did. They located up in North Hammond on the south side of the river. They had about a forty-acre plant and they were very, very successful. They started with a $6,000 capital, and in four years they were worth two and a half million dollars. It just went over big. They couldn't build these railroad cars fast enough that they had invented back there in Detroit. Turn of the century they employed over a thousand men, but it was about the only industry we had in town. We had twelve thousand people here. If you look at the city directory, every other man was working at the G. H. Hammond Packing Company. But the plant burnt down. They never tried to rebuild it here. There is still a George H. Hammond Packing Company, but it's really not the original one at all. The only excuse for Hammond in being was the meat-packing company.

People conjectured that the burning of the plant meant the end of Hammond, Babson continued. Possibly the National Meat Trust of Swift, Armour, and other meat-packing companies wanted to force Hammond out in favor of Chicago, since they had to buy cattle in Chicago, ship them the twenty-five miles to Hammond, slaughter them there, and then ship the meat on again. Anyway other companies came to Hammond: the Straube Piano Company, "located about a block and a half from here"; the W. B. Conkey Printing Plant, which became the Rand McNally Company, "just about three blocks down, on Conkey Street here—you'd be surprised at the things they print; they have Encyclopedia Britannica, I know"; and scores more, giving Hammond, in contrast to the Region's other core cities, "over a hundred diversified industries."

The meat-packing company left one enduring, unwanted bequest. "This packing company is responsible for the railroad situation we have in downtown Hammond. George Hammond's idea was, 'I will build rather flimsy buildings, so I can say to the railroads, "Look, give me good rates or I will pull up and leave Hammond, I don't need you." ' Now his plant for almost thirty years, I understand, was the largest contributory income to the Michigan Central Railroad, which ran right by it. They were the original one. Then came the Monon and the Erie and the Nickel Plate, and he played these railroads against one another for rates that were favorable. And, you know, the railroad companies would come this way. And if you look at the downtown Hammond, you can see how he just kind of locked us in there, persuading railroads to go by his plant and pick up the business, and so we are left with the debris of a cut-up downtown."

Railroad crossings and interminable freight trains running through downtown Hammond doom shoppers and drivers to agonizing delays. I heard a story of a millworker driving home from work who, intolerably frustrated, climbed in the engine cab and shot the engineer and fireman of the crawling train.

The railroads did help bring industries to Hammond, where a good labor supply was available. Germans came as skilled butchers, and Poles followed to work in the meat-packing plant. "They settled on the north side of Hammond and in Calumet City. The Poles were clannish. I used to live right across the state line here when I was a kid, in Calumet City, and my grammar school was called the Sobieski School, named after King John Sobieski of Poland because of the heavy group of Poles over there. Calumet City used to be called West Hammond, until 1923. Right near us, a block away, was the St. Andrews' Catholic Church, which is still there, and they had their own school, which was heavily Polish. And, oh boy, every person around there was Polish, and it's almost still that way, very hard-core Polish people down there, good people, nothing against them at all. Their children move out to Lansing and Munster and Highland; there is just no room for them really. Few blacks settle in Hammond, and the 1970 census listed only 4 percent Negro, which is incredibly low for a northern industrial city, especially when compared to nearby Gary."

Here the speaker picked up a perennial Region topic, the decline and fall of Gary, and stressed the ominous implications for Hammond.

✦ Incidentally the county treasurer told us last week, told my son, that 60 percent of Gary is tax delinquent. Sixty percent! Now how long can this crazy city hold together, I ask myself. And I just don't understand it. That means that the mills must be paying at least 30 percent of the taxes, so how do you work out by running on 40 percent? How do they meet their payrolls and things like that. 'Course I know [Mayor] Hatcher from a long time back, and friends of mine who are closer to Gary over there tell me that Hatcher runs his life no different than before he was mayor. They don't think he is crooked in particular. But I was shaken down for a deal over there and it had to go right back to Hatcher, there is no doubt in my mind. The shakedown is common around here.

But this man [Hatcher], he is the wrong man for that city. He is the world's worst administrator. You know, he is out making big speeches all over the country and knocking off $1,500 fees and the city is going to pot. I took a tour of the city—I haven't been over there for about a year—and one of my associates is quite close to it, and he took me over there and toured the city with me. And I was just heartsick when I see how it is deteriorating, the very finest areas—boarded-up buildings, burned out—it looks like it's been bombed out; between 11th and 15th, right next to Broadway. Some of the finest residential areas, just heartbreaking really. They must have lost a lot of population over there. You know, they took ten thousand people off the registration rolls just for the last election. I think that was the most honest thing that was done in this county for forty years, in fact.

Inevitably the question arose as to whether Hammond would go the way of Gary, in terms of downtown degeneration and black infiltration.

Babson acknowledged the possibility, wondering a little apprehensively whether his grand home in the 160's block might not be engulfed by a black tide. But he drew a complex picture of white-black relations in Hammond, controlled until 1930 by the Ku Klux Klan and since 1930 by white liberals.

✦ Hammond knew what the Ku Klux Klan was in the twenties. When I was a kid about eleven, twelve years old, they used to sell the Ku Klux Klan newspaper on the streets in downtown Hammond. I can remember that, and I can remember the parade that came up on the street one night. They stopped in front of the Saint Ann's Old Peoples' Home, to light up their crosses in their white robes. 'Course I was scared to death, we lived right over here then. Dad walked me over there and we watched them. And I've heard men around here talk about, well, being pressured into joining the Ku Klux Klan. It was quite an eventful era in which to live.

When I was a youngster, I can remember that there was a great deal of antipathy toward the Catholics. I think it was really the foreign element like the Poles, who were heavily Catholic. It was an economic situation. They had all the businessmen belonging, and the Republicans—they were the strongest political party then—they wouldn't permit any Catholics to get into office very often. By the way, you remember the Grand Dragon in Indiana, D. C. Stevenson? Well, he took this girl, Madge to the Indiana Hotel in downtown Hammond here. He had been chasing out after her, and he picked her up and forced her to go to Hammond with him, and he raped and killed her. In 1926 I think it was. And that broke him and broke the back of the Ku Klux Klan in Indiana, when this was exposed what he had done to this girl.

In 1930 the situation changed, and the Democrats, with a different ideology, took control. Babson claimed that the low, 4 percent base of Hammond's black population aroused the ire of white liberals.

✦ They are all a bunch of whites that are doing it. They are just like maniacs! I call them modern Ku Klux Klanners, and they are a modern form of fascist. They are determined that they are going to turn this city into a black city, I'm sure is what they have in mind. Being a realtor we have to be careful; they [the blacks] are good people, we have no objection to them, but what our problem really is, is the Human Relations Commission. They have not been nice to us at all. They have tried to entrap us, in fact I think they were bridging over rights of freedom under the First Amendment, 'cause we can't tell people that this is an all-white neighborhood, or this is all black. And they have set out teams to trap the realtors, and they have trapped two of our boys. I think it is illegal for one

29

thing, it is practicing private detective work without a license. What are you going to do? They file suit in the federal courts, and it's just nasty; a guy can lose his license. Two of our good realtors have suits filed against them. There was a third one prior to that time but he got out on a technicality. But they [the Commission] just determined they are going to scare people into pushing Negroes, is what it amounts to. They would prove that a realtor denied a black the right to live where he wanted to live.

A friend of mine from our church told me about this. He lived in Gary, on the south side. He said there was one black who had moved across the street from them. He was a nice guy, he said. "We got along fine. But," he said, "five years later, I was the last white on that street." And they told me: "Whitey, get out." And they threw bricks through his window. And, he said: "I got out, and that was the end of it," he said, "for Gary, for me." He moved over to Hammond.

Babson drew the clear moral from this terse cautionary tale: "This is the problem, when they come in there is no stopping them." He continued with his analysis of the problems in Gary, told about a partner of his who at one time had an office in downtown Gary, and explained why he blamed the city's decline on white liberals.

✦ As a contractor he built mainly for colored people, and after World War II he made a lot of money over there, but now he can't go any further and the financing isn't available and he just doesn't want to get into it any more. His office girl, a white girl, was raped one time by a black. She was just going home at night and she was at the back door there, forced back into the building as she was leaving. They were on Sixth and Washington, and my partner moved clear out to Glen Park, which is way out, as you know. And they had been held up once or twice, and it was just time to get out. He left. He said: "I just can't make it any more." Who wants to go collect rents and be chased out of a neighborhood and bombed and stoned and that sort of thing? So really it's going to get to the point that there will be so many abandoned buildings that Public Service will have to cut off the service to whole blocks at a time, and they already have

Now a friend of mine who is a realtor over in Gary, spoke to our real-estate board one time and put it this way. When the blacks began to press for some impossible things, the city council in Gary went along with them, because the big power comes out of the mills, and all the executives say: "Yeah, yeah, give in to them, give in to them, let them have it, let them do what they want." Open housing was a new question: "Let's give it to them." But those fellows weren't living in Gary. They are living over in Flossmoor, Illinois, in all the lily-white neighborhoods, so they leave the poor Polish people and the Ukrainians and Croats to cope with the problem that they handed to them. And gradually Gary became known as a liberal place, and the blacks were just attracted there.

There's some mighty fine blacks, but, boy, they don't seem to care, and consequently now they are suffering, at the hands of their fellow people. It's pathetic. I know some Negro people that just don't go out of their house after dark any more. They [the lower-class blacks, often referred to as "the element"] have run the Mexicans out in some areas, and it's just been a lack of law and order basically.

Hammond could avoid the disastrous route of Gary, Babson believed, if its downtown struck bottom speedily and began rebuilding. He regretted that the Ma-and-Pa stores had disappeared, but some young people had recently opened shops of handcrafted articles, and his son had his eye on one called Pleasure Leathers. But downtown had no good restaurant, so midtown people like the Babsons slipped across the Illinois line to Riveroaks, for shopping, dining, and security.

Would Hammond go black, as Gary had done? "The whites here always have a tendency to panic the minute a Negro shows up, and I don't know how you can stop it. We got it now. There was a family moved in, they seemed to be a good family, over right near where I go to church, over there on 65th Street, up the street from my office; and all of a sudden there is three or four "For Sale" signs over there, right across the street from them. And I don't know what you can do. In fact, you know, I hear so many horror stories—what is going to happen—like this realtor told us over in Gary, 'If you own a home that is worth $20,000 or $30,000 or less, you will be in no trouble; you will be able to sell it.' But, he said, against that there were literally millions of dollars lost in the west side of Gary along 10th to 11th of Broadway, because there were no Negroes who could afford to buy them at that price. And when they did go black, why everybody lost money, practically."

I asked how he handled the situation himself.

✦ Oh, I am on guard, I'm on guard. If they are strangers to me, I'm on guard. If I feel I can't trust them, why I demand identity. I was used as a front for a team of Negro con artists here, about a year ago, couple of ladies. I don't know if you have ever heard of this old Drop-the-Handkerchief trick, where somebody finds a roll of money.

They found some money (they said) up there in the little store, it's a supermarket, about two blocks to the east of me. And they told this lady that they met—she was a white lady and she was stupid—"We will split the money with you if you show your good faith by putting up the same amount of money." Supposedly they had thirty-three hundred bucks.

And she went down and drew the money out. They told her they knew me, and they said they were dealing through me on this, and to prove it one of them stayed in the car with her, and the other gal went in to my office. She [the one in the car] said: "She works for Mr. Babson." And the gal came in to me, pretending she was looking for a place to rent. I was nice to her, but I'm on guard. She even named the place that she wanted, it was in east Hammond, which relieved me, because it was a black neighborhood. She seemed extremely nervous, but I gave it no thought.

Finally, at the end of the day, this old lady comes in. She said: "Well, I've got the money." I said: "You got the money, what for?" And I thought maybe one of my salesmen had said something to her and she meant she had money for a down payment. And she said: "Well, I live over on Park Place over here and I am a neighbor of so and so's, and these two Negro women met me up there and told me that they were working with you on the money thing" [laughs]. And instantly I said: "Did you give them any money?" And she said: "No, I've still got my envelope here." I grabbed the phone, called the police. She said that they had let her off in the parking lot, exactly where you parked tonight.

And she walked up from there, and they were going to wait for her to come back, told her that I would give her an envelope which would have the money. And so I called the police, and, boy, they were down there like that, because they [the two colored women] had even milked a colored man, a friend of mine, out in east Hammond a week before. I saw it in the paper. They got fifteen hundred bucks from him. So the cops were down there immediately and they took her in my rear office there and quizzed her and talked to her. And finally one of the policemen said: "May I see the envelope?" She said: "I didn't give them any money." And she showed him the envelope, and he opened it up, and nothing but paper! She had her thirty-three hundred bucks, that she had put in this brown envelope, and they had a matching envelope; and they had switched envelopes on her somehow.

Housing is probably the main concern of Region folk, and this is the perspective of a man who makes his living selling houses. Real-estate brokers as a group receive a great deal of criticism from Regionites who have sold at a loss and bought at a premium and blame brokers who manipulate whites into selling and blacks into buying. Dorothy had made this charge in an earlier interview. But here we have the point of view of a realtor, one with a deep attachment to his community and its traditions. As a local historian he cherished the landmarks that as a dealer in real estate he was obliged to commercialize. He blamed white liberals for allowing racial friction to infect the housing issue, charging agitators and con men with practicing entrapment on unsuspecting real-estate salesmen. In a surprising twist, Babson condemned the liberals as the ideological heirs of the Ku Klux Klansmen; both stirred racial animosities. His own son had come back from college to Hammond with liberal views; but after a couple of years in his father's business he had become even more conservative than his parent.

In contrast to the standard liberal horror tale of the single black family harassed and persecuted in the white neighborhood, Babson tells of the white homeowner engulfed and forced to flee from the black tide, and the white businessman driven out of downtown by the violent blacks who raped his secretary. Over the future of his beloved Hammond hung a pall, like the smog enveloping the Lake Michigan shoreline, in the threat of a Gary-like black takeover, with attendant crime and destruction. His very office had been used as a staging area by two black women fleecing a white lady out of her savings with the old pigeon-drop trick. In spite of the low black population in Hammond in 1970, Babson and his generation lived in fear of a black invasion, ending the pleasant traditions of meat-packing, railroads, Poles, and diversified industry that have given Hammond a special personality.

### Ed Zivich, Whiting

Smallest and most isolated of the core cities in the Region, Whiting, locked between Hammond and Lake Michigan, did not fall within my usual orbit. Dorothy had alluded to Whiting as dreary and stifling. To take its pulse I called on Ed Zivich at Calumet College. Ed, who taught an immigration history course there, was writing his dissertation on the Croatians in Whiting, his ethnic stock and home town. The college, located in Whiting's midpoint, 2400 New York Avenue off Industrial Boulevard, was housed in a tidy building donated by American Oil Company, which was phasing down its operation. Driving from East Chicago to Whiting past the oil refineries, I beheld flaming gas jets on tops of spires, forests of latticework, auto graveyards. The work force in the refineries had dropped from 20,000 to 2,000 as the companies became automated or shut down; Mobil had already closed its East Chicago operation, and oil no longer rivaled steel as a Region employer.

Ed was young and friendly, with a ready laugh, and emotionally and intellectually steeped in Whiting's history and lore. From his fifth-floor office he pointed out a commanding view of several landmarks: the Slovak Roman Catholic and Lutheran churches; a Ruthenian or Carpatho-Russian Byzantine Catholic Church; Number 12 Pipe Still, the towering spire of Standard Oil's refinery. Ed commented that Whiting was compact and well preserved, with architecture that reflected the turn of the century.

A week later Ed and his wife, Joan, invited me to a Greek-Croatian dinner at their home and talked Whiting and Region lore all evening long. Between them they merged three ethnic traditions, for Joan was Greek and Ed had a Croatian father and Slovak mother. Very few Greek families lived in Whiting, although the other three cities possessed large Greek contingents. "My Greek cousin went to Inland to work in the mill and learned the language they were all speaking; he thought it was English, but it was Mexican."

After dinner Ed spoke of the ethnic streams that had flowed into Whiting. The original German and Irish settlers fished, hunted, and farmed. Other immigrant groups began to enter Whiting with the construction of Standard Oil's refinery in 1889; the German schoolteachers, Ed believed, implanted in them a sense of inferiority. First came the East Europeans, with large numbers of Slovaks, followed by Croats and Turks. At one time the Turks enjoyed high visibility, through parades and receptions and coffee houses, but because they brought no women with them, most intermarried with other ethnic groups, and the Turkish community disappeared. The Slovaks typically gardened, tended their homes three hours a day, and saved their money; because of them, Whiting today is a very wealthy community. Ed's maternal grandfather had worked as a laborer in the refinery, raised five children, sent his daughter to business school, and left $25,000 when he died—a typical Slovak story. Because of the large families and the small area, the children had to move out of Whiting—to Robertsdale, Woodman, Highland, Munster—but they maintained the original immigrant home. Unlike other East European nationalities, the Slovaks did not revive their cultural traditions; at a picnic the week before they played no music and were content with barbecued ribs and bingo, and at their weddings they hired a polka band in place of their own violin, accordion, and bass fiddle. The Slovaks remained faithful to the Catholic Church, in contrast to some Croatian males Ed knew, whose anticlericalism dated from the immigration period. "My grandfather on his sickbed shouted, 'I don't want no priest in my house.' He lived to be ninety-one, a Camel [cigarette] and beer man." Each group of ethnics regarded other ethnics as "the Americans," and all the East Europeans joined in despising the native-born Americans who worked in Whiting— the blacks and "hillbillies."

✦ Outsiders consider our community very prejudiced. I heard a story yesterday about this. After World War II blacks got into Whiting's American Oil, Standard of Indiana, Lever Brothers, Federated Metals, but they could only stay in Whiting during the work day. For all the other plants they could catch a bus from the plant gates back to East Chicago, but for Federated Metals they had to walk through Hunkytown six blocks in downtown Whiting (now it's Hillbillytown, where they drive trucks, break up bars, drink whiskey, and brawl.) They had to walk down New York Avenue, only on the west side of the street, where there were fewer houses and more businesses, and get the next bus out of town—or else!

The hillbillies started coming in the fifties. The big push came in 1965, when they started moving into the old immigrant area. 119th is the Great Divide and the tracks.

Ed drew me a map showing the triangle of Whiting as it divided from Hammond. A Croatian tavern owner only opened from 7 A.M. to 11 A.M., to catch Croats coming from the night shift and avoid the hillbillies. Until 1955 workers lived right next to the refinery and walked to the plant. That year a great fire blazed for a day and a half when storage tanks ignited, set aflame adjoining processing units, and destroyed Stiglitz Park. Smoke hung over the area for a week, and drifted as far south as Crown Point.

After dinner Ed and I drove around Whiting in my car, with the tape recorder turned on. The intent was to record his comments about points of historical and folkloric interest and to acquaint me with Whiting. We drove past Forsythe Park and the two large factories of American Maize, manufacturers of Mazola Oil, and Lever Brothers, makers of soap products, on opposite sides of Indianapolis Boulevard. Going north and west we passed the Roby Tavern, an old Russian boardinghouse, which, Ed assured me, still served very good Russian meals. The Roby section once boasted a racetrack and amusement park and is known as Tobacco Row because cigarettes were cheaper than in Illinois, just across the state line by some viaducts a few hundred yards away. Since the Cook County, Chicago, commissioners had passed a special tax on alcohol, liquor also cost less on the Indiana side. Chuckling, Ed remarked: "Now both vices are cheaper here. So you got all the action moved over here. This area has had trailers in it for a long time. This is a southern white area. Hillbillies live in the trailers. So there's prejudice attached to trailers, 'cause that was the first housing available to southern whites in the community. So trailer equals hillbilly. Later they moved into the old Slavic neighborhood."

We kept driving down Calumet Avenue to Five Points, where five streets intersected, and Ed explained that this was Robertsdale, an older section that Hammond refused to allow to secede to Whiting, because it provided its only access to Lake Michigan, an access used by the Hammond Filtration Plant in Robertsdale. Children of immigrants, mostly Slovaks, moved to Robertsdale when they first left Whiting, in housing built largely after World War II. We passed a couple of bowling alleys, and Ed noted that bowling was the biggest single attraction for second-generation Slavic groups, especially the Slovaks. He pointed out a Sokol Slavic bar, a fraternal organization that operated its own tavern at 119th and Indianapolis Boulevard

We crossed the dividing line of Atchison into Whiting and turned east on 121st Street. On the boulevard we saw St. Adalbert's, a Polish Roman Catholic Church. At the turn of the century some seven hundred and fifty Poles, about the same number as the Croats, lived in Whiting and administered their own church and school. "I have friends who have had their entire first eight grades done in Polish." We came to New York Avenue.

✦ This is Federated Metals where the black workers had to walk straight down the street here, down to 119th Street, on the west side. We're coming up on Schrage on Indianapolis Boulevard, and this area used to be Sin City for the immigrants. They used to call it Oklahoma. A lot of the joints were torn down during Prohibition and the neighborhood became chiefly residential. Now we take a right here; this will take us into Oklahoma. This is the kind of housing that basically has been torn down in the other cities in the Region. Since this housing remained white, what has happened is that it's been allowed to stand. You can see Boarding House written all over some of these structures. They're much less attractive than the newer homes in Robertsdale. They're frame. You have basement apartments in every one of them. You can still see them, downstairs. And if you look to the back, they run all the way to the back. And there are outdoor porches. You'll see some structures, especially on corners, that used to be taverns. Like I say, in Gary or East Chicago none of these structures would be left standing.

They didn't have cars or garages. Remember they're living right on top of the refinery. As I say, this area is changing. There are still some Slovak families where one of the children holds the property. But they may be renting now to southern whites. This is one of the areas that has gone southern white. We're on Schrage Street. It was named after the little grocer, Henry Schrage, who sold cigars and work gloves to people who worked in the refineries, and he later got into real estate, handled Standard Oil's property acquisitions. Now over here there is a more modern development. These are a very small kind of bungalow-type houses. Mostly, I guess, these would be children of immigrants who didn't do too well economically. It would be people who were still refinery workers basically and couldn't afford to move into a more prosperous area. But again these people were living on top of their jobs. And if you open a [car] window, you can hear the refinery. If you live back here you can hear the noise. You can hear the units. This area straight ahead where the tanks are now used to be Stiglitz Park. Slovaks and a lot of the Byzantine Catholics lived in Stiglitz Park. It was a teeming immigrant community.

They [Standard Oil] made the mistake of having processing units right in the midst of the storage tanks. Apparently they had an electrical failure and the unit blew up and it blew up an adjoining storage tank. They started to blow up one by one. Luckily, only one person had a heart attack in the refinery and then one child was killed in the community by flying debris. Those are the only deaths. The fire lasted well over a day and into the next day, and fire equipment from Gary, East Chicago, Chicago in Illinois were fighting it. The public relations people told me that they would never build storage tanks near units again. So what they've done is to wipe out this neighborhood—buy it up I should say—then move all the storage tanks from the area on the east side of the street across to this side. These are post-fire buildings.

What I took to be a lighted high-rise apartment, Ed laughingly explained was a distilling unit complex. "For night photography this is a good place to get some shots. Exhausts give a nice glow off of those towers. The scenery and the smoke and the open flame back here is pretty phenomenal. Just astronomical. Surrealistic industrial."

We approached the entrance to Amoco Oil Company, Whiting refinery, Gate 13B on 126th Street, and Ed directed me into Dickey Road, a bumpy route leading east past the steamship funnels of the refinery to Indiana Harbor and the steel mills of Youngstown Sheet and Tube and Inland Steel. On the right the road ran past Marktown, a company-built enclave of European-style narrow cobbled streets and cozy homes facing the mountainous structures of Inland Steel. Delivery trucks and steelworkers driving to Youngstown honked at me testily. We passed a tomb-like group of buildings, the plant closed down by Union Carbide, its silent emptiness contrasting with the illumination and bustle around the active refineries and mills. After the dead spot we moved back into the stream of light and noise. "You can hear that constant hissing anywhere around the refinery at all times. It goes back all the way in my memory to when I was living in Whiting when I was young—always remember that hiss from the units. You could hear it all day and all night. It's just the burn-off, the operating noise. But it's a fond memory. But, see again, this is all the refinery. That's the pipe still unit, a backside view of it. Number 12 is the biggest—the tallest and widest. It's right there in the middle. That's the most fully automated refining unit in the whole place." In answer to my question, Ed explained that a pipe still completed the basic distilling process, from crude oil to finished product.

We drove through an old Croatian neighborhood and stopped to look at the church. "This is the church my grandfather helped to buy. This was the old German parish, and the Germans moved out when the 'inferior' East Europeans came in, ha, ha. But they left their church [building] behind, and it says very proudly up there 'Saint Peter and Paul's R Cath-

olic–Croatian.' That's about as militant as you can get. The priest is a
Slovak, John Halo, because the Croatian men had driven the Croatian
priest that they had out of the parish." The southern whites had pene-
trated this section too, and we passed a number of their trucks parked by
the roadside.

✦ The trucks may belong to a company. Not very many of the hillbillies are
owner-operators. Most of them work short and long hauls for other people. Make a left here. As I say, social class really shows in terms of the
housing. We'll be getting into the "better part," in quotes, The Village,
an area where East Europeans met with a lot of discrimination. As
in that whole story Joan was mentioning about my mother's parents
when they moved in here—about having German kids messing up my
grandmother's laundry, throwing mud on it and all that, because they
were quote-unquote Hunky. The term Hunky—I might use it joking
around but it really had a sting to it in the old days. Hunkies to the East
Europeans had the same kind of power as the word "nigger" to a black
person.

That was a problem my mother and her brothers and sisters had. They
lived pretty far from the Slovak school because they were living on the
next street up, on Sheridan, so they ended up going to grade school in
the German school; they encountered all sorts of prejudice from the sisters who taught there. Take a left at this corner here, I'll show you the
house they bought. Right here, on Sheridan Avenue: this one with the
white on top with the brick front. And they really caught hell for that
[putting on airs]. As I say, in these houses there's less frame and more
brick. And these are a little jazzier, to put it mildly. These families have
been here a lot longer though. The houses are further apart, they have
some yard. And this parish back here, Sacred Heart, is a German parish,
the group that sold their old church to the Croatians; they came over
here and built a new one. That's Sacred Heart Church there. This is typical for this side of Whiting. You can go in and out of all these streets,
Cleveland Street and all the rest of them here, and you'll see this kind of
big, more spacious, more attractive, more brick housing.

We came out on 119th, a broad boulevard, the Great Divide: Hunkyville to the south; the more pleasant, established part of town to the
north. "This is the main business district street. There used to be an
opera house here in the back, in Sherman's; you can still see the stage in
back of the store. This is the American Slovak Club here, this bar. And
then this whole hall on the corner is the Slovak home, Slovenskidom.
McHale's bar is about all that's left of the Irish in terms of their institutions. The Illiana Hotel there is from the combination of Indiana and Illi-

nois. Go straight ahead, and I'll show you some of the churches and then we'll go back into Hunkyville." We took a look at Saint John the Baptist, the Slovak Roman Catholic Church, largest in Whiting (technically in Robertsdale), and the smaller Slovak Saint Paul's Lutheran Church, and ended up south of 117th on Sheridan. "This used to be German, and what few Americans were here. And a few Slavic families moved here in the thirties, my grandmother's included, and didn't meet with a very pleasant reception. So there is the house they ended up with, the stucco up the street. They both died there."

As we discussed the animosity that Ed's grandparents had encountered from the Germans, he enunciated what might be called the Law of the Newest Arrival, a leitmotif repeated throughout his tour: *In a given area, the residents of longest occupation demonstrate hostility toward the incoming group.* In Ed's words: "It's inter-ethnic, not intra-ethnic. It's a classic thing, where the people who'd been here the longest hated the greenhorns the most. First it was the Germans against the Slavs. Well, now you get the same kind of process, where the Slavic groups, who'd been in this community since the 1890s, now hate the hillbillies. It's a never-ending cycle where the newest arrival is the fall guy."

We drove back into Hunkyville and stopped at a four-corner intersection with three taverns and a trucker's lunch stop, close by one of the main gates to the refinery. "This green-front building—I think it's now labeled 'Whiting Social Club' or 'Southside Social Club'—that used to be my Croatian grandfather's saloon. He was a bartender, bar owner, in the 1890s. He was run out of business by Prohibition. And my dad was born above this bar, upstairs." Ed pointed out a Croatian tavern on one corner, with a big sign, SELO (meaning "village" in Croatian) and across the street a Slovak tavern, named KLEN. "These would be premier locations. Look how big these buildings are. For boarders. These houses are right on the main gates for the refinery. The refinery is right in the backyard—look at that. Appalachian whites now go to those saloons."

Did the immigrants know anything about industrial work when they came over? "No. All the nationalities—Slovaks, Hungarians, Croatians, the others—all came from peasant families that had trouble because their land had been subdivided too much. And they didn't have enough land to feed all the children. It's one of those kind of weird offshoots of the Industrial Revolution, just beginning in eastern Europe. You had this gradual lowering of the death rate. This meant that more children lived longer. And it meant the family property, which was divided equally in eastern Europe among all the children, including female children, in one generation got divided up into nothing."

We drove down New York Avenue and into another old ethnic neighborhood, where a number of houses had been refronted and the porch stairways removed. Both sides of Ed's family had once lived here. "Another thing that was typical: as the family got bigger, you moved into bigger quarters. My father's parents lived in seven addresses in town, made seven different moves. My mother's parents made four, as far as I can determine. You could walk up and down these streets and never hear a word of English."

On the way to Ed's home we passed a Hungarian Reformed Church, which put Ed in mind of another "law:" *European enemies become friends in America.* "The Hungarian Catholics in town went to the Slovak Church. This is supposed to have been a real turnaround for them, a real putdown, because in Europe, Hungarians were trying to exterminate the Slovaks as a nationality. What you find is a lot of the antagonisms between these groups were not shared by the rank-and-file members. A lot of times nationalism in eastern Europe is the product of educated people in the cities. When it got to the villages it didn't have quite the same force. Peasants, you know, didn't have that kind of animosity necessarily."

On parting, Ed mused, "It's really strange, coming back here. It's really weird. You're educated, highest kind of degree possible, and still have roots in a place like this."

In this session I followed the strategy of recording a lifelong community resident asked to conduct a city tour. The idea is that the native guide can single out landmarks and people them with associations. Ed Zivich knew his town inside out. In the course of our drive, the several urban legends suggested by sites included the great Standard Oil fire of 1955 and the ritual walk on the west side of New York Avenue by black laborers after work. Folk attitudes and prejudices emerge from the guide's account of the neighborhood districting: the German disparagement of the Slovaks; the Slovak disparagement of the hillbillies. A Slovak stereotype takes form from the guide's scattered allusions, one of a thrifty, industrious worker tending his home, making a stake for his children, and, unlike his fellow-East Europeans, indifferent to his ethnic traditions. Clearly the older Whiting appealed to Ed, who identified with the Croats and Slovaks against the earlier supercilious Germans and the rambunctious newcomer southern whites. His imagination recaptured the earlier bustling scene when immigrant workers lived cheek by jowl alongside the refineries in sociable boardinghouses.

In these four conversations each speaker suggests a sense of place, a circumscribed orbit in which he or she moves comfortably. For Dorothy it is the milieu of wooded Marquette Park, the beach, dunes, lake, and quiet streets in her section of Miller, where black families live but no vendors and salesmen trespass and wild animals blend in with the landscape, that deeply satisfies her. She deliberately transferred her orbit from familiar neighborhoods in Hammond, where her parents and sister and high school friends still live, to this risk-laden territory within the city limits of Gary. Philip Spalding's orbit has shrunk considerably, from the golden days when Chicagoland, with all its cultural attractions, beckoned, to his present confinement within his own home on a street filled with Mexicans and blacks. When he ventures forth to a friend's house a couple of blocks away he arms himself. Warner Babson, in his palatial home in midtown Hammond and office nearby, has not succumbed to the siege mentality but feels threatened by white liberals and black homebuyers seeking to entrap him; he acts and talks cautiously. His hopes lie in a revived downtown, with specialty shops and good dining places that will entice Hammond's middle-class families back to the inner city. Ed Zivich's nostalgic affection for Whiting, a tiny industrial town frozen in its 1900s architecture of boardinghouses, saloons, and ethnic churches and restaurants, endures unabated. He roams through its streets like a caretaker, versed in the town's lore through the personal associations of his own and his wife's family, and his historical research. No signs of black or Latino invasion hinder his movements, but he does look askance at the alien hillbillies who have taken up quarters in old Slovak residences and bars and created some out-of-bounds zones for the old ethnics in Whiting.

Other profiles could yield wholly different orbits, but each Region dweller stakes out a particular turf and views the Region from its vantage point.

"It's known as a millrat, a fucking millrat. It's a slob
that goes out there and works for sixteen hours, goes
home for eight, comes back for sixteen, doesn't take a
bath for two weeks, sleeps in the goddam change
house. We call it a millrat."—a young laborer

# THE FOLKLORE OF STEEL

Six great steel mills ring the Lake Michigan waterfront, touching the
lives of everyone who lives in the Region. The history of U.S. Steel, also
known as the Gary Works and the Big Mill, parallels the history of Gary.
Inland Steel and its neighbor, Youngstown Sheet and Tube, pump life-
blood into East Chicago. To the east, in Porter County, rise the new mills,
Bethlehem and Midwest. To the west, across the Illinois line in Chicagoland, sits Wisconsin Steel. The mills' combined payrolls support seventy
thousand workers and their families. They run all day and all night,
seven days a week, to avoid the ruinous expense of closing down and
then refiring the furnaces. A haze of glowing smoke at points along the
shoreline marks their ceaseless motion.

Always they are called "the mills." When I first arrived in the Region I
lacked the vaguest knowledge about steelmaking and could not begin to
understand the intimate points of reference that steel people lived with,
such as the blast furnaces that made the iron and the open-hearth furnaces that cooked the steel. When millworkers talked about incidents on

the job, they drew pictures with their hands and on scraps of paper in an attempt to explain the mysteries of their occupational lives, but until I visited the mills I gleaned little from their verbal and visual efforts at instruction.

One does not just walk into a mill. The companies straddle the issue of accommodating tourists, torn between the urge to cultivate good public relations and the fear of injuries to visitors, mindful of the troublesome arrangements needed to prepare a tour, and wary of a negative image resulting from a firsthand view of the plant's innards. Only Inland Steel conducts regularly scheduled tours, booked months in advance, and provides elevated walkways, with well-marked stations and prominent floor signs explaining the processes for the information of viewers. And in July 1976 U.S. Steel reversed its closed-door policy, staging a bicentennial open house for a hundred thousand visitors.

In the end I managed to arrange guided tours to four of the mills on seven occasions. I beheld one cavernous structure of ugliness after another, each devoted to a single operation: the slabbing mill, the hot-strip mill, the cold-strip mill, the tin mill, the coke mill. Inside each I saw bulky machinery and steel products, but relatively few workers; these lilliputian figures seemed lost in the maze, and it surprised me that the mills employed tens of thousands. A hierarchy of three clearcut levels divided the employees: the laborers on the floor, bending, pushing, shoving, squatting; the blue-collar workers in the glass-enclosed elevated stations known as pulpits who watch dials and direct floor operations from on high in air-conditioned comfort; and white-collar managers tucked in offices close by the main action.

What fascinates the neophyte onlooker most are the processes to which steel is subjected. The whole sequence of mills, he comes to realize, is dedicated to the cooking of the mass of coke, slag, and iron ore into molten steel and the pounding, stomping, shearing, peeling, squeezing, scraping, trimming, scarfing, dousing, heating, reheating, rolling, coiling, and branding of the "heat" (as the ore is called) brewed in the furnaces. Rusty machines hammered, lifted, dropped, and banged at ingots, slabs, and coils. In the great tureens of the furnaces—the blast furnace that cooks the iron; the open-hearth furnace and the new BOF (Basic Oxygen Furnace) that cook the steel—the magic transformation takes place, the modern miracle of the mass, signalized by an incandescent halo above the furnace. Into the mammoth BOF bucket a phallic tube descends, carrying the oxygen piped in from Union Carbide in East Chicago; a sunburst glows over the bucket, the ore reaches its orgasmic climax, the bucket tips over and its contents pour out in a radiant river to the troughs below; then the bucket rights itself to resume the process.

"Cooking" is the word steelworkers employ to describe the heating of the ore in the furnaces and the addition of the various ingredients—silicon, dolomite, other chemicals—needed to bring the mass to the proper distillation. In earlier days the furnace men made the calculations, like chefs preparing a stew; today, although the human eye and instinct still play a part, they say, the computers have taken over.

From the furnaces the onlooker follows the heat as it is poured into ingot molds, and then sees the ingots dumped onto rollers that speed toward great presses. Coatings of slag peel off the ingots, like serpents shedding their skin, as the red-hot ingots clatter toward the hydraulic presses that turn them sideways, slice them to specified sizes, and release them to further mills where they are reformed into slabs and strips and coils. Second only to the furnaces in vividness of impression is the sight of a hot strip of new-made steel zooming along the rollers at frenetic pace, occasionally jamming in one of the presses and snapping in two on the rollway, whereupon the onrushing strip "cobbles" (coils back on itself into an angry roll) before the presses can be halted. Then comes the millworkers' task of banding the roll and hoisting it clear by crane before the next hot strip can course down the rollway.

A steel plant, with its twenty thousand employees working three shifts round the clock, takes on the character of a city, a one-purpose city dedicated to a single goal: transmuting nature's ore into steel slabs and tin cans. Ore boats unload at the docks, flatcars move ingots, mobile monsters called "slagaways" and submarine cars laden with misshapen metal crawl past mountains of coal and slag. The activities in some of the giant structures seem unrelated in any direct way to steelmaking: one plant recycled water; another, a "pelletizer," recycled dust; still another recycled oil, now economically feasible because of the rise in oil prices; two mills exchanged gases each generated and the other could use, through overhead pipelines.

In time the companies take on individual personalities. U.S. Steel, the Big Mill, is king. Creator of Gary, it sprawls along the lakefront and accounts for one-quarter of the total production of the United States Steel Corporation. Its guides spoke confidently about their property. The various mills of U.S. Steel covered four and a half miles of lakefront, and subsidiary plants occupied another mile and a half. The 160–210-Inch Plate Mill, named for the length of the roll, was the world's largest. One hundred and seventy-five miles of track lay inside the plant. Twelve blast furnaces had been built in a row before 1918, the longest string in the world. The newest blast furnace, Number 13, largest of its kind in the Western world (Japan had a larger one), produced eight thousand tons of molten iron a day. In seventy-one years existence the plant has produced more than three hundred million tons of steel, a record. The construction of the Gary Works was a feat equalled only by the building of the Panama

# The Folklore of Steel

Canal. While producing all this steel the company simultaneously, we were told, stressed reducing pollution, conserving energy, recycling, and safety measures. U.S. Steel made 86,000 products and was the third largest chemical producer in the world. The mill cost $167,000,000 in 1967 and would be worth half a billion dollars today. A steelworker's annual average wage—$14,000 to $15,000—was the highest in American industry.

Inland Steel in East Chicago enjoys the most favorable image of any of the plants, being locally owned by Jewish businessmen and catering to the community. Our tour guide said that Inland started as a junkyard when two brothers named Block bought a rolling mill in Illinois and moved it to Indiana Harbor. Inland took pride in relating to East Chicago and Chicago rather than to Pittsburgh and Youngstown. A person could go to Inland and buy an I-beam at reasonable cost, or place small-unit orders which no other company would take. The guide pointed out a patch of grass and forsythia planted in front of the slabbing mill, a brave little oasis in the wasteland.

In 1916 and 1917 Inland went to Mexico to recruit labor, hence the high percentage of Latins on its work force. Inland's guide, who conducted me on my 1968 and 1975 tours, spilled out facts to match U.S. Steel: Inland employed 22,500 people; met a $23,000,000 payroll each month; used a billion gallons of water a day, two-thirds of that of the city of Chicago; and made more steel in 1974 than the Big Mill—over eight million tons.

Youngstown Sheet and Tube suffered a reputation as being inefficient and sloppy. An engineer at the power plant said Youngstown was way behind Inland and that the place was a mess. So it seemed on our tour, led by an ex-advertising man hired two years before to improve Youngstown's image with the Hammond *Times,* whose kudos had gone to Inland. In contrast to Inland's neat elevated walkways, we groped our way on ground level amid the fumes on the oil slick floor crowded with great coils and cables, ducking giant cranes overhead, deafened by the thunderous roar. As a result we felt ourselves much more a part of the action. In the hot-rolled steel mill we saw a long thin strip of hot steel racing down the rollers break from the tension and cobble—rearing up like a wounded deer. The mill had to shut down while a foreman tied a chain around the jagged end, sizzling at a couple of thousand degrees, for the crane to haul off.

Bethlehem, newest of the lakefront mills, prided itself as being the cleanest, shiniest, and most modern. Its public relations man had actually called me and said they wanted to show off their plant. The tour guide, who exuded open friendliness, pointed out the "greenfield site" on the top floor of one mill, a control tower which he called "the most sophisticated conveyor-belt control system in the country, perhaps in the world." An older man sat at a panel board keyed to a semicircular row of small TV screens behind him which showed the operation of conveyors throughout the plant. We were told that when a second mill was finished, Bethlehem would have the largest plate-making capacity of any steel company in the United States.

Of the other two plants, Wisconsin Steel, in Illinois, seemed remote, and was known as old and somewhat antiquated; while Midwest, a division of the National Steel Corporation, lying close to Bethlehem, did not make steel but fabricated steel already produced.

All the producing mills took great pride and satisfaction in demonstrating the industry's newest technological advance: the basic oxygen furnace, which was fast replacing the open-hearths. The Inland guide told us that two BOFs have in the last twenty years replaced fifty-six open-hearths and three Bessemers. Inland built the last open-hearth in 1956. The BOF reduced the refining of two hundred and fifty tons of steel from six hours to thirty-two minutes. Gary Works personnel referred to the new furnace as the Q-BOP, standing for Quelle Basic Oxygen Process,* but the other mills referred to BOF.

In spite of this latest development, an executive described the steel industry as evolutionary rather than revolutionary, compared to aerospace, chemicals, electronics; the product remains the same as it was forty or fifty years ago. Nevertheless, fifty years ago the operation was 95 percent manual and 5 percent mechanized; the reverse is true today. Suppliers often made suggestions that led to technological change. Plants have adjusted to their customers, and Midwest mills chiefly produce wide, flat-rolled steel, both hot and cold, for Detroit automobile manufacturers. Mechanical breakdowns cause the mill superintendents' greatest headaches. They calculate that 19 percent of operational time is suspended for this reason, and their goal is to reduce "down" time.

Eventually I encountered many mill people who loved to talk steel. They included two steel company executives at a dinner party; the first black laborer to break the color barrier at U.S. Steel; a husband and wife at a university staff dinner in a restaurant, she from a family of English steelworkers; a tour guide for Bethlehem Steel; a union organizer at Inland who became a well-known state senator; a Birchite who had worked in the mills as a youth; a student in my class and his father, both employed at U.S. Steel; two other students, brothers, who gathered some millworker buddies in their home and sat around drinking beer and shooting the breeze: all animated talkers about incidents in the mills. In particular, the tape-recording of the socializing youths gives evidence of

* *Quelle* is a German word meaning fountain. Already the term is becoming folklorized; some say the initials stand for "quality basic oxygen plant."

performance skills, in the realistic use of dialogue, the mimicry of foreign accents of ethnic workers, the reproduction of mill sounds, the word pictures of mill scenes. Bursts of laughter punctuating the anecdotes or expressions of disdain at management policies indicate the depth of the listeners' reactions during the performance.

Young and old, black and white, East European and Latino, man and woman in the Region had tasted the mill experience, or knew closely someone who had. Anyone might turn out to be a teller of tales about the mills.

## THE OLD DAYS

One recurrent theme among veteran steelworkers deals with the earlier days of steelmaking, before the advent of unionism and computerized technology. In speaking of this era, thirty or forty years past, retired steelmen, or the sons and daughters who have heard their recollections, refer to "the old days," when workers felt loyalty to the company and pride in their job and played a greater part in the production process than they presently do.

In the old days steelworkers observed an unwritten code of dedication to the job and mutual support in time of need. A former secretary at U.S. Steel, daughter of a retired foreman, who worked in many offices around the plant and could keep track of absenteeism, told how the old-time mill laborers never missed a day. No matter what was going on with their families or in their homes, they came to work, even during the Second World War when everybody worked double shifts and seven days. "Dad was quite ill, but he wouldn't stop. And one day he just walked in the door after a double shift and passed out on the floor with double pneumonia. I think he went at least ten years without missing a day of work, and that wasn't unusual."

She recalled a worker in her father's shop who had tuberculosis but was not eligible for welfare because he owned a house. His doctors recommended six months in a sanitarium, but he would have had to sell his house to pay the costs. Also he had children to support, one in college. So the workers chipped in five or ten dollars each from their paychecks and supported the sick man until he could go back to work. This was their common practice with everyone in trouble. Most of the men were too proud to accept welfare anyway, and the East Europeans placed little trust in the government or in banks.

Although the laborers felt strongly motivated to work, the supervisor made sure that, whatever their attitude, they maintained a back-breaking pace. Thinking back half a century to his youthful stint in the mills,

# Land of the Millrats

Philip Spalding recalled that he worked fourteen-hour nights and ten-hour days in the open-hearth. One weekend he would get twenty-four hours off and the next weekend, when the shift changed, he would have to work twenty-four hours at a stretch. Sometimes during the long vigil he lay down on a pile of coke and slept for a little while, but this practice was frowned upon. Philip remembered a college lad hired in the coke plant or the open-hearth more recently, who, after working for two hours, decided it was sack time and climbed on a pile to go to bed. "That shows the difference between the attitude in the old days and the way it is now. In the old days nobody'd permit any type of conduct like that."

The bosses kept after the workers continuously. The timekeeper would mark as absent anyone he did not see on the job when he made his rounds. If the melting foreman or the pit boss or the electrical foreman noted anyone missing from his crew once too often, he handed him a pink slip, which meant he was fired. In addition to long hours the laborers worked in wretched and unsanitary conditions. A former union organizer remembered the lack of drinking fountains and the buckets of water carried to the work site. Such showers as were available had unprocessed water, and many workers contacted skin diseases from plant chemicals that seeped into the water.

The hand skills of the old days contrasted with the technical skills of the modern industry. A veteran steelworker mused about the considerable changes in his business since the early "primitive" period of the thirties and forties. In the old days everything was done on a hand-loading and hand-working basis. Today technically trained personnel push buttons, read dials, and operate an electronic data-processing system. "Why, we used to make sheet iron by taking a pair of sheets and pushing them through some rollers. You could measure the sheet when it came out, approximately how long you thought it ought to be. Now sheets develop from billets, which start out of a heating oven and run through continuous synchronous rolls. Each roll goes progressively faster as the piece gets longer, and then it's all wound up like thread on a spool." Mechanization has largely replaced human judgment and expertise.

In the old days casual methods obtained also in the recruiting of skilled workers. Here a young rigger recapitulates an account by an old-time rigger of how personnel were selected.

## The Old Way of Choosing Workers

✦ Joe: Mickey Thompson retired a year after I started [in the mill], so he would have retired in 1961. He was an oil rigger, Class A, and a gaining rigger, Class AB, and the top rigger, a feisty redhead. I guess he had worked forty or forty-five years as a rigger or as an employee in the mill all during the time he was there. Right practically from the day they opened the mill, I think.

He was telling about the "old days," in quotes, when, let's say, a few job openings were made open to a shop. Let's say a borer shop or machinist or something like this. They would interview like ten, fifteen, maybe twenty men who came in to see about getting a job. And of course they all had their stories about their experience and how much they knew about what was going on. The shop foreman or the gain rigger or whoever was going to do the interview would go out and listen to all this.

And when they were all done talking, he'd ask 'em to spread their hands out in front. And he'd look 'em over. And if, say, a few of the older men had missing joints on their fingers on one or both hands and they seemed to look like they might have had the experience, he'd take them with that. Their experience was showing there.

Joe added that the men had to have enough fingers left to at least hang on to a sledgehammer or pry bar or spud wrenches.

The same tale is told about railroad brakemen in the 1860s. Because of the hazards of the hand brake combined with the link-and-pin coupler, which required the brakeman to stand between two cars in order to steer the link into the socket and drop the pin, brakemen often lost fingers or suffered broken hands. John F. Stover, in *American Railroads* (1961) reports that yardmasters interviewing boomer brakemen for jobs approved old-timers if they could show a missing finger or two.

### The Union Shuts a Plant Down

Unions had to fight for existence in the old days. A retired steelworker and union organizer looks back forty years to recall his strategy in forcing the company to recognize the union's right to arbitrate points of dispute.

✦ We had the plant shut down three times, and this was actually how we got arbitration started in the steel industry. We couldn't get the companies to agree to arbitration. This was in the early years of the war. They were watching each one of us leaders so close that they would of fired us if they had caught us. I know that I had the locomotive engineers, which was very instrumental in shutting the plant down. We had two cases that we wanted to get arbitrated. We had talked about them at the union hall, and of course we had to be very careful that everybody at the company didn't know our strategy.

The first time we went into the plant, if we made any headway, then as soon as we walked out of the front door of the main office, there'd be people watching. We didn't see them but there'd be people watching us. As we walked out, if we didn't get a settlement I'd take my hat off and I would rub my hair with my hand two or three times and I'd put my hat back on. We'd get in the car and they'd take us out over the bridge and out of the plant. Well, at the time we was at the foot of the bridge, the engineers on the trains was blowing their whistles and the whole plant knew they'd had to shut down.

I'd get back to the office and they'd be calling. Of course they [management officials] was watching us. They didn't know the contact. They had police watching us really close. This happened three times, three days in a row. We shut the plant down three days in a row. The third day the company agreed to the arbitration.

There are several ways you can shut the plant down. I've been one of those types of people that was organizer. The locomotive engineers is a very key group to do this with. They can get mad and go home. Nothing moves. No steel moves anywhere. The hot steel won't move from the blast furnace to the open-hearth. Nothing moves out of the mill. The shipping floor is filled. Nobody moves the cars. The place is down. You just can't back up and have hot steel on the roads.

Or you can shut the plant down with the electrical department. Of course you have to keep electricity going to the mills. Somebody pulls the switches—that's the end of it. The company just can't have police and everybody watching everything.

Another group we'd shut the plant two or three times with was the cranemen. All we had to do was have every craneman walk off the job. The company had to have them. So long as you had it unanimous, and the cranemen all just walked off the job and walked down to the locker rooms and started changing clothes. They would have had to fire every craneman in the mill, and there was just no more cranemen. They couldn't afford to do that. If you didn't move nothing in the mill, the mill shut down. All I had to do was give the signal.

## DEATHS AND ACCIDENTS

Mill laborers, working among mammoth machines and volcanic cauldrons, know that a slight misjudgment or careless action invites disaster. Prominent signs inside the mills remind the workers to be cautious; signboards on the outside proudly announce the number of accident-free days since the last casualty. Yet accidents and fatalities do occur, in strange and unpredictable ways, and they become a staple theme of narration. Millworkers relate with precise details industrial accidents that have befallen them, or that they have witnessed, or that happened on their turn, or that they have heard others relate. They repeat them as cautionary tales warning listeners against ever-present dangers, and as true stories with dramatic and startling elements. Because they involve intimate knowledge of the technology of steel, these accounts often contain frames, asides, or glosses into processes of steelmaking.

The industrial-accident recitals of steelworkers contain the very stuff of drama. Their themes involve sudden death in grotesque forms, disabling injuries to every part of the body, narrow escapes, lucky recoveries. They are veritable encounters of men against machines.

## Personal Accidents

The personal experience narrative of injury at work, although it can never attain the dramatic finality of a fatal accident tale, carries a highly specific content. The speaker relates an incident that nearly cost his life, and he remembers and describes the moments with photographic intensity.

*Close Calls.* Here a rigger recalls how careless fellow-workers endangered his life on several occasions.

✦ I left the mill because I was tired of taking chances with people who didn't seem to care. I was afraid to continue. I had had a four-hundred-volt DC cable dropped on my head and watched it burn, weld to our railroad track, right under my feet, because somebody had forgotten to lock out a safety switch. And they assured me that they had.

Another time I was knocked off the blast furnace by a crane that someone had been playing around with. I turned around just in time to grab the hook, right out over the hole and back again. I was so scared I wet my pants. And things like that.

You don't even know what happened sometimes. Once somebody accidentally kicked a bundle of ten-foot, three-quarter-inch conduit pipes off the top of the blast furnace. Naturally it broke apart on the way down. They were sticking into the ground like spears right in between our rigging team. Things like that happen daily.

*Slipping on Grease.* A veteran Serbian millworker, a crane repairman, told me of a serious injury he had just received in spite of his experience and caution. He recounted the freakish accident, down to the position of his limbs when he lost his balance.

✦ Bosko: Well, I was working starting the gear slot on a charger, which charges Basic Oxygen Furnace, Number 4 BOF, Inland Steel Company. And I was coming down, and a fellow working with me handed me a torch. I went back up, handed him the torch. Then the hose of the torch was stuck. I went back, unhooked that hose. And I went up again, tried to come down. I had my right foot down and my left foot was on the motor. And my right foot start coming up, because I step in some grease, start falling. There was a rail, two by four, next to me; I grab myself by that thing, hold myself by that thing. The thing was loose, it was just not bolted down tight. When I pull on that thing, the thing went same direction I was going, on my back. I fell about four feet to the grease band, which protects the grease from coming down to the ground from the gears of the main arm which raised the BOF on the charger.

And I balance on that grease band, then tripped over my head right down to the ground. Landed lucky. I was lucky, landed on my feet. From my feet I went down on my knees. From my knees I went down to my arms. My arms gave way and then my forehead. I touched a piece of steel which cut my forehead. And I start bleeding very bad.

They took me to the nurse. Tried to stop the blood. Ten minutes the ambulance came and a doctor. They took me to the Saint Catherine Hospital in East Chicago. I stayed in the emergency room for seven hours. Took them about four hours to clean out the dirt in my wound. And the rest of the time took him to sew it and take X-ray of my forehead. I was released about 7:30 in the evening. Thirty-five stitches. From here all the way down to there [pointing to his forehead]. Wasn't painful because it just made a cut, nothing else. But thanks to God I was lucky: I land on my feet, I don't land on my head. I could be dead today. You wouldn't have nobody to talk to.

Bosko was given no time off because "this wasn't a disabling injury." It happened on June 23, and he was given easy work until his vacation started on July 4, doing "light duty to keep me where I don't have to wear a hard hat." I asked him where the fault would lie, since he had told of two other disabling accidents that day. He replied simply, "Well, there is some times, Professor, that you cannot help it. On my job I went that day maybe twenty times up and down. And finally you need just one time. I was careful that time as I was the first time when I went up, but there is some times that you cannot help it."

*Deaths Close By*

*The Laborer Who Fell into the Slag Buggy.* A most dreaded fatality deals with the worker who falls into the heat. Mill folklore claims that some laborers commit suicide by jumping into the heat. The rigger who patiently explained the following accident that occurred on his turn drew a diagram in my notebook to illustrate the physical relationships of the blast furnace to the slag buggies and the submarines. His statement on the vital process of "tapping" a furnace forms an integral part of the grim narrative.

✦ This happened in the Gary Works around 1960, in Number 4 or Number 5 blast furnace, on the turn that I was working. A big black man, about two hundred pounds, fell into a slag buggy.

[The rigger goes into a description of the process of tapping the blast furnace to explain the function of the slag buggy.] When the heat is ready to be tapped, the workers blast a hole in the furnace with a small dynamite charge that blows a hole through the taphole, which is covered up with fire brick and fire putty. It used to be a manual job. A series of ditches or submarines lead away from the tap, about three feet deep, for the iron and slag, which comes out in a solid stream. It has to sit there for a short period for the iron to settle. In the furnace it is being churned up by a lot of hot gas and can't separate. There are several ways for the molten mixture, for the iron and for the slag, to go from one submarine to another and into the slag buggies. The trainman moves the train of buggies up to a channel. One heat is six to eight hundred tons. Each slag buggy would hold thirty-five to forty tons. One submarine, which transports pig iron from the blast furnace to the open-hearth, holds two to three hundred tons. The laborer standing on the edge of the floor overlooking the slag buggies is breaking up the solidified slag to maintain the flow into the buggy. He was actually outside of the superstructure of the mill, of the blast furnace itself.

Most of the laborers in the blast furnace are strong, very strong. They have to be because it's very heavy work. This fellow was a very tall man. And the edge that he was working on is just a floor that's jutted out from the building, because it was unsafe to even walk up there. They had tack-welded a little half-inch steel pipe between the columns that held the mill up, just as a warning to keep you from walking off the edge. It was a twenty-foot drop to the ground. On occasion these laborers, when they were breaking the slag away at the end of the ditch, would lean on this. The metal tube was strong enough to prevent you from walking off, but not strong enough to lean on. And he was leaning way out to break off the slag, and evidently had rested a good part of his weight on it, or maybe the weld just broke. I don't know. But it broke, and he lost his balance and fell down, about eight feet, spread-eagled-like, into the half-filled buggy slag bucket.

The slag is rock—you can't fall into it—the heat is about 2,000 degrees. There is just a burst of flame and the body is cinderized. The people who were standing there said you couldn't see anything had fallen; the slag kept pouring in. You couldn't shut off the furnace or it would blow up.

I was working in the furnace at the time, as a rigger moving heavy machinery. A rigger had to climb a hundred and fifty feet up, stringing up chains, changing motors and wheels. We saw people running and ran over to see what had happened. We all felt a camaraderie. Plant protection was there, and the police, and an ambulance, but there was no way to detect the remains. The old story was that the widow could get a part of the heat.

*The Lad Who Was Crushed.* The panic that follows a fatal accident is recalled by a veteran steelworker employed in the 84-Inch Hot Strip Mill in the Gary Works, where steel slabs were flattened, elongated, and rolled into coils.

✦ William: About a year and a half after I went to work in the Sheet and Tin Mill (now the 84-Inch Hot Strip Mill) a young lad got crushed by a slab. And it was a trying experience—I mean, I didn't know the lad personally; I'd been in the army so I wasn't worried about somebody being dead or anything like that—but what really tore me apart was the people, the crew that worked with him. They just about went out of their heads.

And I had orders from the safety man: the body wasn't to be touched, the slabs weren't to be touched. I had to pull a gun on a craneman to keep him from taking the slab off of the man until the coroner got there.

Dorson: Why did he want to take the slab off?

William: Well, he thought he might be alive yet, but there was no possible way. The man's head was about two inches thick. And there was no way the man could be living. It might save somebody else's life, I figured. I thought I was justified in what I did.

*A Vessel Tilts.* Rarely does the worker actually see the fatal accident, since few men are grouped together at any one time, and constant safety precautions reduce the number of deaths. But the observers quickly relate the grim details to others on the turn who immediately gather round, and the story spreads. In only one instance among the many I heard recounted did the speaker witness the fatalities. They occurred during the tapping of a furnace. A longtime steel man and union organizer reports the episode.

✦ The worst accident I saw was an old Bessemer. The Bessemer is a lot like the new BOF. The pressure of the air would blow the impurities out of the iron. The dirt and everything would go in the air and it would hold the steel right up in the air. That was how great the pressure was.

Well, this vessel was not tilting like it was supposed to tilt. The people that work on this vessel usually sat down in the bottom of this building, not directly under the vessel but over to the side. As soon as they'd tap

# The Folklore of Steel

out, why they've got to go up and see that the mold is moved up. They was waiting for this vessel to tap. It was a hot day and they was back under the building against the block wall where it was rather cool, sitting.

This vessel wasn't tilting, and the electrician was down on the board trying to get it to work. For some reason or other the proper switches wasn't pulled. He was working the board. Somehow he short-circuited the current to the vessel, so that the operator had no control of it upstairs. And he tilted this vessel. There was no molds under it, and this hot metal came out on the ground and splashed on the wall and splashed back and burnt seven men up, just killed them. That was the worst accident that I had seen. I was right in the vicinity at the time. I went right there immediately to see if I could help in some way.

*Hit by a Freight Car.* Cranes overhead and ore- and scrap-laden freight cars moving constantly but irregularly, sometimes in semi-darkness, can deal instant death. A young laborer descibes this situation.

✦ When you're working down a track, you have a long track—some of them tracks are almost a mile long. And, hell, they fill them up with so many cars sometimes you can't see the engine on the other end. Especially working at night, it's so dark. And about four months ago they had some guys down there working with the cranes. And this guy was a crane switchman. And there was a couple of cranes working down there. And this other crane on the other half of the track didn't know he [the switchman] was working down there.

And he [the craneman] kicked a car down there on top of him [the switchman]. It didn't cover him completely but it smashed his right side. We were just getting ready to start the turn. I was working the eleven o'clock job. And they told us about ten minutes after eleven—no wait, I had already been there—he told us at about a quarter to eleven. At ten minutes after eleven they told us he had already died.

And that's the way it happens. Especially with them new cars. They have ball-bearing rollers. And they're silent, and you can't hear them cars going down the tracks. And sometimes it gets foggy as hell out there in the wintertime, and if you're not careful you kiss your ass goodbye. I've walked down the rails where something, just instinct, man, told me to step back. And all of a sudden, whoossh! right on through the night a car goes whizzing by. And it's very difficult to stop sixty or a hundred ton rolling by you.

*In the Acid Pit.* An accident that was no accident is the subject of this account. A southern redneck vents his spite against a hippy with a dastardly act. Again the relating of the narrative requires a close description of a mill process in which the scene is laid.

✦ Ben: When you work in a pickling bath, over in the galvanizer, you'll see it's an acid bath. Were you ever down there?

Arthur: I've heard stories.

Ben: Everything's brick man, brick. It's like a brick pool. It's where they have coils sitting out, you know, they get rusty. They run them through this acid bath, man, they come out spanking new on the other side. So they can store them forever and they come out looking new.

So we have to go down there and clean it sometimes. And they have flames over the top of them. This heat and this acid takes care of that corrosion. And they never turn off those gas flames shooting above it, so it's hot. And they drain the acid out. Now what you do is, when you go in there they don't give you anything special, just rags. And they hose you down. And you go down and replace the brick. And you better be wet. And there's one thing I can tell you, with the atmosphere that's down there, if you have any skin exposed, for even a few seconds, that skin is gone, burnt.

Paul: Is that because there's acid flowing through there, besides the heat?

Ben: Yeah. They just drain the tank, and you go down there as the last bit of it goes [makes slurping sound] down the tank. [Makes clapping sound], you're down there! They don't hose it down or nothing. They're very cheap. When you're peasant labor—we were transient labor, working the yard department—that means this mill says, "I need so many laborers because we need this job done." Well, if you're moving around to whoever wants to take you, that means you get the shittiest jobs, because people are going to take care of their own.

All right, so the acid pit is a horseshit job. And this one guy—I don't remember his name, his first name was Bill though—he had hair down to his ass, beautiful blond hair. And he'd wrap his hair up and tick it under his helmet. Well, we had to climb in and out by a ladder, and he's climbing out of there and this old redneck motherfucker kicked Bill's helmet off. And I'll tell you something: his hair fell out, but his hair disappeared before it hit the ground, and it was only a six-foot drop. Bingo, he was a bald motherfucker! Eyebrows, moustache, beard, everything gone. And he sat down and literally cried, and I could see why. And they had him in the hospital because he had small minor burns on his face and head.

And we tried to find that fucker that did that. And if we would have found him that day, we would have stripped him down and thrown him in the acid pit.

# The Folklore of Steel

*Hot Metal Spills.* Cooking the molten iron and steel in the blast furnaces and open-hearth furnaces, and transporting the heat in ladles, buckets, and slag buggies from one part of the mill to another, and from one mill to another for processing, constitute the central stages of steelmaking. If the hot metal escapes from its containers, it runs amok like volcanic lava. Here are three instances of how such a castastrophe could occur. In the first the teller explains the technical process of cooking the ingredients in the open-hearth furnace at much greater length than the accident itself. The same teller then recounts a similar case in which no lives were lost but the runaway ore greatly damaged the plant. In the third accident a young laborer barely outraces the flow.

✦ One time we had a case in the open-hearth furnace where they caught a hot-metal ladle [interrupts himself to explain]. A hot-metal ladle is a ladle that is filled with pig iron that's dropped from the blast furnace and put in what they call a hot mixing machine and then kept under a certain number of degrees, about 1,000 degrees or so. And they put it in this mixing machine and pour it out of there into the ladle, and then the ladle contains this hot iron at about 1,000 or 1,200 degrees. And then they pour that through a spout into the door of the open-hearth furnace, and this is what they call a recarbonizing process. Because the carbon content of the pig iron is many, many more times than the steel in the open-hearths, in what they call the open-hearth path. When they would have the steel in the open-hearth furnace for a certain number of hours, the test piece which is drawn out and examined would show a certain amount of carbon, a certain amount of manganese and phosphorus and other items that they wanted to have in the steel. This was according to the heat specifications. Well, they would figure out how much of this hot metal, which is liquid pig iron, and they knew the analysis of pig iron, and so they figured how much pig iron they ought to put in with these various component elements—add it to the component elements in the open-hearth furnace, which would result in a certain finished steel, after taking into account for oxidation of certain of the elements due to the fact that the heat in the open-hearth furnace was about 2,800 degrees, you see.

And so then, one time they're taking a carrier of this hot metal down the open-hearth floor. And the bottom of the open-hearth container had a large casting piece where they could hook a chain hook on it so they could use that to tilt and pour it out better. And this got caught on the top of a boxcar and spilled all the metal on the floor and burned up about fifteen guys right there on the floor.

Now I never experienced any of this but this is what I heard.

## Land of the Millrats

✦ Another time we had a situation in the open-hearth where the melters had been off on Thanksgiving holiday, and they were drunk and they shouldn't have been working. And so they weren't paying proper attention to the operation of the open-hearth furnaces, and so some of the heats got out of control.

Now if they had what is called a boil on the bottom or a boil on the top hole, it means that the steel is actively eating the bottom out of the furnace. It's just like an acid that you put in a pot, in an aluminum pot, why it eats a big hole there. And that's what was happening.

And so we have five hundred tons of steel go out on the bottom of the floor and run down through all the control mechanisms and go down through what they call the soaking, the pouring pit, and so forth. And all this steel was lost. It burned up all the car tracks. We had a tremendous loss there because the only way you could do to clean this mess up was wait until the steel had all hardened, and then you had to take a crane down there and hook it on with some chains and pull up all the tracks and railroad ties—what was left of them—and then pull it all out. And then take it up to the scrapyard and break it all up with a big steel ball that was out there just for that purpose.

And then they'd have to break it into scrap and put it into scrap cars, and weigh it in so that you'd know the proper charge, and figure out what the estimated component elements of the steel were, such as carbon, manganese, phosphorus, sulphur, and then recharge that into the furnace. And then you have to melt it up all over again. And some of those furnaces used about eight thousand gallons of oil in a twenty-four-hour shift, so they used a lot of oil to compensate for the fact that they had lost all the steel out in the pits, you see, through the accident.

✦ Paul: You told me about one time they poured the steel in the truck and there was water already down in the bottom.

Mike: That was Keith's cousin—second cousin. And what he'd do is he'd drive a semi out to the BOF. They'd pour the molten steel into these buckets, these big ladles, which they had mounted on the semis. And he was sitting in the semi while they were pouring the steel into the ladle. And there was water in the ladle already. And so when this steel hit the water in the ladle, it exploded—it busted the ladle open.

Paul: I heard that just before it was ready to explode; it was getting really hot, and the window that was right behind him melted. As soon as it started melting, he got out—he says he was getting out of the truck. What happened then?

Mike: Well, it blew up, and he was already on his way out of the truck trying to get out. And all this molten steel went all over the floor and he slipped on it, and he burned up his hand, and his face, his neck, his feet.

Paul: Well, he was in the hospital for a long time and had to have every part of his body, almost, bandaged up.

Mike: Yeah, they sandwiched him between two boards, so they could turn him over on his stomach, or turn him over on his back. He couldn't turn over or roll over because it would break open his skin, tear open his burns.

Paul: His whole head was burned, all his hair. And his hands, they became like a web.

Mike: They had to wire 'em open so they wouldn't stick together.

*Heroic Surgeons.* Some tales of industrial accidents in which a machine or piece of metal cruelly mangles a laborer end happily with heroic acts of surgery. For the mills the ambulance and the surgeon are ever-ready. The speaker in the first narrative heard it from his father, chief surgeon for Inland Steel back in the 1920s. The teller of the second account is a youthful laborer who heard it from the injured party.

✦ I heard that one time a chap was in what they call the continuous-rod mill, which is a series of rolling mills that are in one line and produce sequential diminuation of the diameter. In other words, the rod goes into the first roll for the first pass and it may be, say, two inches. And then by the time it goes to the next roll it's one and three-fourths, and on its way down until maybe it's a half-inch or so way down the end, you see. They had chaps in the old days who used to catch these rods as they were coming through. And they have a very high peripheral speed. And so they had to aim those tongs to catch the rod when it's coming right through, so it wouldn't wrap itself around them, or so it wouldn't wrap itself up in a great kinky coil like a hose gets wrapped up in every once in a while. So they had to be very careful; it was a very dangerous job.

Well, in this particular case this fellow was a little careless, and the rod went right through his head. And I understand my dad patched this fellow up, and even with the rod going through his head his brain wasn't destroyed. And my dad got an honorable mention in some medical journal about how he patched this fellow up.

They didn't have very many safety inspectors, and the compensation laws weren't very strict in those days. We had no paramedics or medical assistants. My dad was the whole medical department.

✦ Ben: My cousin got his arm ripped out in Number 2 blower. He was lucky. I don't know the name of the surgeon, but we got one of the best bone surgeons in the world working for Inland. He sewed his arm back together, and the guy can play the drums again. And the accident only happened six months ago.

My cousin was a hooker and he had his arm severed, ripped off. Because his craneman was drunk. He was illegal. He was an illegal Puerto Rican, they found out later. But he was drunk. He [my cousin] tries to hook up a chain and the guy pulls him right up. And he's hanging up like that in the air. He was using an angle iron, and it slapped against the wall. Cut his arm clean, right at the joint.

Paul: Right off?

Ben: Well, no. It was hanging by just a little bit of meat. But everything else was cut off, bone and everything else. Clean severation, all the ligaments and shit. Matter of fact, they wanted to amputate his arm, but that bone surgeon happened to be there.

But here's the thing that my cousin told me. Now he fell down, he don't know how. But he looked, and he seen that if it wasn't for his clothing his arm would have been somewhere else. But he held his arm, and he was bleeding like hell. And he said he was conscious, and he walked; he tried to get to the office. And a guy seen him and freaked out and ran screaming running the other way, wouldn't even help him. He said he fell down. He said he didn't pass out, but he was laying there, looking up, just wishing to God somebody'd come and help him.

Finally somebody—I guess a guy ran off and told someone. They came and picked him up and put him on a litter and took him out to the ambulance. And all the way to the hospital, and all during the time they were telling him "we've got to amputate" he was conscious. 'Cause your body has certain mechanisms that keep you alive. Now if you can't tell me that that wasn't a brain fry.

After they took his shirt off and seen his arm almost completely off, they said, "Well, we might as well take it the rest of the way off." But the reason that bone surgeon said he'd take care of it was because it was a clean cut. No bone was broken, nothing shattered. It was a clean sever, man. So he [the hooker] said he wanted a chance. And it took six and a half hours for that operation.

*Feet Crushed.* Sometimes, however, the most heroic surgeon can do nothing to repair mangled limbs. A steelworker talks about two crippled fellow-laborers.

✦ That was a fellow he lost his four toes. I went to visit him in Saint Catherine Hospital. He's a man who have sugar diabetes and his wound wouldn't heal up. He's in very bad shape. He was a mobile mechanic working on the forkhigh lifts—fork with the two fork, you know—and he was repairing them. And the chain which they were tied to, it broke, and then seven hundred pounds of that steel fell on his foot. Cut his toes off his right foot.

# The Folklore of Steel

There was two disabling accidents in one day. Puerto Rican fellow by name Julius, high lift ran over his foot. That's about three thousand pounds. I went to see him too, in the hospital. He's in very bad shape. His foot swelled up like that, you know. They couldn't do nothing; they cannot operate or set the bones in the foot unless swelling go down.

## Deaths Heard About

*Murders in the Mill.* According to the lore of the mills, accidents do not just happen; they may be deliberately contrived and take the form of covert murders or criminal assaults that result in disabling injuries. Two young millworkers talk heatedly about these supposed acts and the company cover-ups.

+ Ben: And we've had fights out there. We've had guys, I ain't going to mention no names, but a foreman was killed because he was fucking with a guy so much. From two floors up he dropped a seventy-five-pound air hammer on top of him.

You can use anything and say it's an accident, man. You get some guy, you go over there and kick him down the stairs, you push him in front of a charging car, push him in front of a train, anything in the night, man. And when it's dark out there you can wipe anybody. Knock him over with a brick on him, run him over with a fucking forklift. There's juicy ways, and people do get killed. And they write in the safety reports, "So-and-so accidentally did this." And everybody's saying, "Your ass." And you know it's bullshit.

Paul: They got a lot of stories going around about . . .

Ben: Oh, you wouldn't believe. You know, there's a lot of people killed every day out in the mills, and they never publicly admit it. And they applaud themselves when they get "U.S. Steel Gets Best Industrial Safety Award for 1975" or some shit like that. I'll tell you something: I seen the ambulances go by every day. I'm only out there for eight hours. I wonder how many times they go by in the whole twenty-four hours.

And I'll bring home an Inland paper, and in there all the time they have guys who are dead, mostly retirees. But there's three or four in there who were working at the time they were killed. And this is every fucking week. That's a lot of people. And that isn't including all the ones who get mangled.

*Killed While Eating Lunch.* The rule in the mills is: always stay alert, never relax your guard. Three young millworkers reflect on this caution in the wake of a senseless fatality.

## Land of the Millrats

✦ Arthur: One time, I think it was my first year at the scrapyard, in Bethlehem, there was a guy killed. They got these big cranes that go across. I think there are about three or four in the old slabyard. And they [the cranes] come up and they'll get the slabs and they take them over to different areas. There was one guy, *he was just* eating his lunch. I heard the thing came by, smashed the shit out of him.

Paul: They have a lot of cranes. They're always supposed to have a horn blowing off on the crane when it's moving, isn't it so?

Ben: Well, sometimes though they'll just beep it a few times when they get going. That's to let you know: "Hey, something's moving." It depends on how the safety program is.

Paul: But you're always supposed to be smart in the mill, to watch the ceiling as much as you watch the ground, aint't it?

Ben: If you're inside a building, yeah. That's one thing, it's almost like if you're going to be driving a car, to be a good driver you got to have almost 360-degrees vision.

Paul: Yeah, the mill's crazy.

*Beer as a Cause of Death.* Death in the mills may come not from overhead cranes or molten metal, but from failure to take simple dietary precautions. The speaker's father had been the plant's physician.

✦ In the old days many times the chaps that worked in the sheet mill would be a little careless with their personal living habits. Many were big drinkers, drank a lot of beer. And many of them would go out there and work under these very hot steamy conditions, and they'd come out and they were overheated. So they'd drink beer and get cramps and then they'd die.

Several cases were like that.

*The Guy Who Died on a Pusher.* Death on the job may occur in inexplicable ways. In the following unusual death-tale, such a nonaccidental death embarrassed the plant personnel.

✦ There's one story that I'd like to tell you about a guy who died on a pusher. A pusher is as big as a freight car and charges coke into the furnace in the coke mill.

Now the maintenance men hide a lot of times. They'll go over here, they'll go over there, as long as the machines are running and they got their work done that they were assigned to do. I mean they're usually assigned something, but a job is either gonna take five minutes or an hour, and one can't tell how long. So if the job gets done quickly, they hide out. Hence the friction between production and maintenance workers, each claiming superiority to the other.

So the maintenance guy has gone over to the pusher operator. The pusher guy is a real big talker. He's saying, "Ah, the weather's no good" and all this. The maintenance guy's sitting there not saying a thing. And the pusher operator turns to him, says "Hey, why don't you say something? You look kinda blue." So he went over to this fellow and felt his pulse, and the guy was dead.

So the pusher guy called the foreman and said, "What shall I do? This guy is dead next to me." And blood started coming out of the dead fellow's mouth. And the foreman said, "Well, hold him and I'll come up there." And he went up on the pusher and he says, "Well, leave him there. We'll call the coroner out. Just keep acting like nothing happened."

So the dead guy is sitting down there and the pusher goes down this set of rails and the rails are bumpy. And the guy's bumping around, and they were afraid he's gonna fall over on the floor. The pusher operator told me, "What they did was they took a wire and they wired him so he wouldn't fall over. Finally they came and got him and took him away." He said, "I think he was on the pusher—now don't quote me—for an hour and a half after he was dead."

He had a heart attack or something. It wasn't anything that made a lot of noise.

*The Man Who Was Coupled.* Most mill fatalities are mercifully quick, but in this gruesome narrative a worker dies lingeringly and agonizingly in full view of the entire work force on his turn. Three young millworkers, usually callous and caustic about goings-on in the mill, turn somber in recapitulating his agony.

✦ Mike: Out in the yard, outside the fab shop at Bethlehem, there was a guy that was switching cars. And the engineer thought he got the signal to move the cars back, and this guy was in the middle of two cars, and he was crushed by the couplers, the couplers just closed in on him, but he was still alive when that happened. And this guy eventually died, 'cause everything in the middle was just squished.

Ben: You're working out there with guys that are drunk, engineers especially. And if they move, you got to work fast. There are certain ways you have to open up knuckles and drawbars of railroad car couplings by your hands. And you have to walk between train cars a lot of times. And you're supposed to make sure that nothing's coming either way. If you're working—sometimes you've got a busted pin, and you're changing a knuckle or something—you're standing right there in between them damn cars. You're supposed to get twenty foot of space, but I'll tell you something, you're lucky if you get twenty foot, 'cause things are so damn crowded.

## Land of the Millrats

So the guy is in there in between the cars, working. And this hogger wasn't drunk, but the brake slipped. And the car rolled back and coupled this guy up, coupled him up right in the middle. It didn't really cut through him because it's very blunt. It just coupled him. So they got a hold of the cops and the ambulances, and everybody come over to where he was.

And the guy knew he was dead, and everybody knew he was dead. But his last wish is that he could talk to his family. Well, we couldn't get him to a phone before he died. So what they did is they hooked a phone through a radio. But unfortunately that radio went to all the radios in the mill, and all the trains through our radios. Everybody heard it. They cleared the lines, just telling us about the trainman who got caught between the couplings and was calling his wife on the radio. So the only way he could talk to his family was to talk to the radio and connect it to this phone line. And so everybody stopped all work; everybody stopped, man. And a lot of guys got off the train. But there was an outside speaker; no matter where you went, you still heard it. And the guy just got on the phone and weeped; it shook everybody up. Guys went home sick, almost the whole damn crew. And that's over two hundred guys on that particular shift. The yardmasters let 'em all go. So anyhow, he had to explain to his family the condition he was in, I guess about thirty minutes or so.

Paul: He lived that long?

Ben: He lived longer than that. They figured in his condition that he would live, before he would lapse into a coma, about sixteen hours.

Paul: How long did they have him that way?

Ben: He had been that way three and a half hours before they could get the hook-up of the telephone. And by that time he had enough of his shit together where he could rap to his family. So he explained to his family, I guess about thirty minutes or so.

Paul: And then, finally, he just said: "Go ahead and pull the car."

Ben: Well, yeah. After he got done talking and whatever, and said his goodbye and all this good stuff, he handed them back the radio. 'Cause he still had movement in his body—part of it anyhow. Maybe the spine was severed. He had movement in the upper half. And they wrapped sheets around his body. They pulled the pin [makes a slapping sound], and he said goodbye. That was it, you're dead. Just like that. He exploded. Because of the pressure.

I didn't hear him myself. I'm glad I didn't. I wasn't working switchman then. But my father told me about it. This was in seventy-two, early seventy-two, just about when we got our hand radios in. That's the last major death—well, I can't say the last, but that's the first and last time they did anything like that.

3. Basic Oxygen Process (BOP) shop at U.S. Steel.

4. Railroad siding at Hammond.

5. The 84-inch Hot Strip Mill.

6. Not only workers, but many objects pass through the plant gate.

7. Refinery towers dominate the skyline.

8. Railroad tracks leading to a refinery in Whiting.

The Folklore of Steel

## A PIECE OF THE HEAT

One of the most persistent legends in the mills concerns the disposition of the molten metal, the heat, into which a laborer falls. Since no remains can be salvaged, what is the grieving widow to bury? Out of respect for the dead the heat presumably should not be processed, but what then should be done with this expensive mass? Steel people on every level, from pit labor to top management, repeat stories of what happened to the fateful heat. In two versions—one in the Mexican tradition, the other from a nonethnic maintenance worker—supernatural agencies provide fitting memorials.

✦ Kenneth: Then they had cases where fellows had fallen into one of these ladles, and I understand the first thing you see his shoes are floating on the top; he's burned up. His shoes float on top for a minute, then they burn up too.

Dorson: Oh my God! How could he fall in?

Kenneth: Well, he might be up working around some electric wire and he wasn't very careful about his footing, because a lot of this footing was covered with ash and with sand. Slippery, and he could fall in. Some chaps, I understand, jumped in to commit suicide. It's a real easy way of committing suicide: you just don't know what happened, just like that. It's almost instantaneous, because the steel is about 2,800 degrees hot, and a fellow burns to a crisp in no time at all. I understand that when people burn up it smells like roast pork.

Dorson: So these people become pieces of steel?

Kenneth: Well no, they don't become pieces of steel. There's just nothing left; they're just burned up. They might become a few pieces of carbon, or something in the steel. But that's all that's left. Although I heard that one time that they had buried one of the ladles out some place. And then they finally decided they had given it a respectful burial, so they went and dug it up and brought it back and melted it up.

✦ Bosko: I heard this story that happened in Number 1 Open-Hearth. A man fell in the ladle when they were dumping heat out of the furnace. They dumped that heat right by the furnace. It was staying there for long time.

I don't know how true is that story, but I heard it from the old workers which told me about that steel. And I believe that they would do the same thing. They wouldn't use the steel. They would just put that steel on the side. That steel would stay.

Dorson: But you wouldn't see anything of the man in the steel?

Bosko: No, you wouldn't, because that steel is started out at 2,700, 2,800, 2,900, maybe 3,000 degrees. And you know it's a matter of seconds that a big chunk of steel is melted down. Human flesh wouldn't last maybe two, three seconds if it was burned down to the ashes. That's too much heat for a human body to stand.

✦ John: This story circulates. You're talking about a story which is associated with the Gary Works. A fellow literally, the story goes, fell into a ladle, which is what you're calling a heat of steel, and it is in fact. So the ladle is a quantity of steel which then can be taken somewhere. That's the story I recall. The whole ladle from the open-hearth was taken into the lake and dumped.

Lot: Dumped, buried. But you're talking about possibly one hundred and fifty tons of steel that's being dumped from the ladle. That's a large quantity of steel. Nowadays the federal government wouldn't permit you to dump that into the lake. You can't do it. So what do you do?

✦ Mike: I've heard stories about, like, if a guy falls into a vat of steel, they'll take the steel out to the lake and they'll dump it into the lake, kind of as a remembrance to him. Instead of using the steel, they'll dump it, as a memorial to the guy.

Paul: How many tons of steel do you think that is, man?

Mike: It's probably just enormous, because these are, like, two-hundred-ton kettles.

Ben: Well, they used to bury the whole ladle, years ago. But now that's too damn expensive. When you go in, when you hire in, they measure your exact weight. And if you fall in a ladle they pour out the exact weight, and they ship that out and they bury that. They bury an ingot. They tell you, "Well, this must be him." You may not even be in that part of the damn mold, man. But that's what they do, they pour it to the damn ounce, if they can.

✦ This happened over at Inland. A laborer fell into the steel pit—hot molten steel. The family was notified, and they requested that the company produce the real body, the natural body. The company could only produce a piece of steel, molten steel, assumed to be that of the body. The widow put up a fuss, said she didn't want any hunk of steel, she wanted the body of her husband.

Evidently the undertaker persuaded her not to view the remains, and as a result she never did see the remains. He told her not to look in the casket. So they buried the steel, and planted it as an individual, and identified it in the burial service.

## The Folklore of Steel

This was told by a black steelworker in his fifties at U.S. Steel. "I heard it from my nephew who worked at Inland, who heard it around the union hall, from a fellow named T.J."

✦ I had a conversation with my nephew at his house Sunday, and he said where he worked at Inland Blast Furnace Number 28 this one fellow fell into the melting pot that goes into the furnace, and they shut off the furnace for a few minutes. Well, the following year on that particular date the furnace shut itself off for ten minutes.

This was told me by Luis Valdez, my nephew.

✦ One of the boys told me that the story in one of the plants at Wisconsin Steel is that most of the time when they pour a ladle full of steel, a face appears on the top of the steel, and this face is a result of a man who fell into the ladle and died. And they weren't able to get him out of there because of the hot grip that lines the ladle. That happened about ten years ago. It was a Polish laborer.

So now when the steel fills up, this face forms on the top of the steel.

### MILL THEFTS

"I just steal what I need from the mill."—millworker's
philosophy

A continual battle of wits ensues between the working force and plant protection. Every class of steelworkers—laborers, foremen and supervisors, top management—takes part. Thefts range from flashlights and monkey wrenches to an entire mill. Working in a vast arsenal of mechanical equipment and valuable metals, with no visible proprietor save the impersonal corporation, mill people could easily adopt the attitude that they were only helping themselves to materials that they owned jointly with their employers. The code condoned taking for one's own needs, but condemned theft for resale or personal profit.

Beyond the desire to purloin objects, millworkers seem also to have stolen from a sheer sense of derring-do and bravado, even at the risk of losing good jobs. All the maintenance and production people with whom I spoke agreed that their jobs paid well. But many added that the job offered no satisfaction save the money. Mill thefts added excitement and drama and ego titillation in soul-shriveling work.

In the broadest terms, tales of mill thefts fall into the categories of the trickster-thief who gets away with his stolen goods and the one who gets caught. We see here the classic folktale confrontation between the trickster, the outlaw, the picaro, on the one hand, and the authority figure, on the other. The spotlight shines on the millworker and his strategem, while his adversary, the security guard or plant protection man, never assumes a personality. Often the uncovering of the deception is no more than an anticlimactic coda: "He was caught and fired." All of the tales are told as true, but an apocryphal fiction occasionally slips into the corpus.

The borderline between taking and stealing may not be all that clearly defined in the minds of some millworkers, particularly those of an earlier day, as the following observations by a longtime union organizer reveal. Note that he does recognize stealing, but considers it a distinctly different act from openly appropriating certain articles.

### Helping Oneself

✦ When you say "theft," I think of that as stealing something to sell on the outside. There was only a few people do this. I think most people felt they was part of the steel mill, if they wanted a piece of steel. I never even thought about it as stealing. I used to get into the open-hearths, get in the stainless steel. We would take this and we would lay it on a railroad track. We would mat it together. I don't know but what my wife may still have some of it. But we would make jewelry out of it. We'd make bracelets, we'd make knives. We'd bring the jewelry home. In fact I think I have a knife now that I made in the steel mill. This was no secret. You didn't hide it. I mean the superintendents and everybody saw us in our spare time making this stuff. I think when you speak of little articles being taken out, I don't think the company ever really cared. I used to enjoy making knives. We gave knives to some of the soldiers that they took with them to the service during World War II.

There was some stealing. Of course some of the employees would take nickel or brass if they could get to it and throw it over a fence, and then after they got out of work they would go by and get it. But those people I think were about all caught. Because we had guards that would watch the nickel bins.

### Getting Away With It

Nowadays no millworker takes objects out of the mill in broad daylight, while supervisors beam. Plant security keeps an eagle eye out for all smuggled articles and metals. Yet, in one case a worker did walk out in broad daylight, unmolested. This is the classic folk legend of mill thievery.

## The Folklore of Steel

✦ *The Wheelbarrow.* John was an immigrant laborer from eastern Europe who worked in the mills. And every afternoon when leaving work he trundled out a wheelbarrow with his work tools, covered with straw. The gate guards were suspicious of John, and they always examined the wheelbarrow carefully, poked under the straw, but never found anything except the tools, which clearly belonged to him. So they had to let him go through.

So this went on day after day, year after year. Finally the day came for John's retirement. He had worked thirty years in the mill. So, as he is leaving on his last day, trundling out his wheelbarrow, the gate guard said to him: "All right, John, we know you have been stealing something. This is your last day; we can't do anything to you now. Tell us what you have been stealing?"

John said: "Wheelbarrows."

Sundry containers and ploys are used to sneak coveted items past the security guards.

✦ *The Tarpaulin.* An old fellow was carrying out some heavy tools in a tarpaulin. He was all bent over from the weight. The gateman asked him what he had in the tarpaulin. "Dirty clothes."

✦ *The Lunch Bucket.* Gary and I were talking the other night. He works for Standard Forge; and he also has worked for a number of the electrical firms; and he's been in and out of the mills.

And he was telling me about one of the men he worked with had a lunch bucket that the handle and the locks were reinforced, so that he could cut million cable—which is very large copper cable and the wire is very big, and you can cut maybe ten, twelve, fourteen, fifteen pieces of that about ten or twelve inches long—and it would fill a lunch bucket up. And it would probably weigh thirty or forty pounds.

And this guy would cut this cable, put it in the lunch box, and then he would practice carrying the lunch box so that it looked like it was empty. He would swing it back and forth and carry it so he could walk right in stride when he went out the gates, so it wouldn't look like there was anything at all in it, so he wouldn't have to tuck it under his arm or anything. [The speaker swings his shoulders and arms in a jaunty way to simulate the carefree worker going home with the empty lunch bucket.]

✦ *The Clothes Bag.* Mike: Whenever you leave work they can have spot checks where they stop your car and check everything in your car—the contents and stuff. One of the tricks I used was, I wouldn't carry nothing out till the end of the week; and whatever it was I was carrying out, I put it in my sack of dirty clothes, 'cause like you wear these clothes all week, you know, and they get to be pretty stinky and dirty, and your socks were *bad* [laughter]. I mean they smell really nasty.

Paul: Especially like you sweat in 'em for five days.

Mike: For eight hours a day, for five days a week, and the *same* socks. And so, like if I was going to take something out, I'd stick it in the bottom of the bag of dirty clothes, and I'd put my socks on top. Then I'd roll it up really tight, you know, so it'd keep the air in there, and then like I figured, if anybody's going to stop me they're going to open this bag up, and they're going to get a big whiff of these socks as soon as they open this bag up. And the guy's not even going to think twice about looking, and they'll just close it back up.

✦ *The Gym Bag.* Roland: Hey, this black dude I used to work with, Arthur, I used to work with him in the tin mill, and we used to work in this room where they made galvanized steel, man. And we used to make the money there. Oh God, oh yeah! A hundred dollars a day there sometimes. Just unbelievable money. I used to bring paychecks home, I'd just freak out, you know. But the thing about it was, we never did nothing. The place was, like, so clean, man, that there was just, like, no grease on the floor. The wood walks that they make the floor out of—they have, like, four-inch by four-inch wooden blocks everywhere that were made out of pine, and they got like creosote on them. They were, like, *clean*, everywhere. And usually you can't even see 'em, because of the grease.

But anyway, this dude. We were making all kinds of dough. And there was, like, this spare parts room, and it was covered up with barbed wire and a fence, but it was inside, inside the building. And so he climbed it, and he got in, and there were, like, these *big, big* brass bearings, man, that weighed about twenty, thirty pounds apiece. And he had a gym bag that he used to bring his clothes in and out with, and he used to take those out of the mill. He never got caught, you know. And then he'd take 'em downtown to this place where they buy metal, and they used to give him dough for that.

Bill: Yeah, that brass sells, man.

✦ *The Overcoat.* Mike: And, like, there were stories about guys who steal hoses for torches, you know, so they can do some burning at home and stuff. They'd steal the gauges and everything they could get that had to do with burning. They'd steal like forty feet of hose. In the wintertime especially, they'd take this hose, and they'd wrap it around their belly, and they'd put on these big heavy coats.

Paul: Did they need to have anybody help 'em?

Mike: Yeah [laughter], there's two guys—

Paul: One guy's turning it while the other guy was wrapping it.

Mike: Yeah. And they'd get it all layered up real nice and then they'd put on their winter coat and zip it up, and then they'd walk out the gate with it.

✦ *A Foreman's Truck.* The foremen made a mint when the company was building the 84-Inch Mill. The guards checked the workers' bags, but not the foremen's trucks. A coil of stainless steel and a truck were missing. One foreman has stainless steel gutters and paneled half his wall with stainless steel. When they took inventory six weeks ago, half a million dollars worth of supplies were gone. The foremen could ask for anything and get away with it, like an order of two thousand screws and bolts. They'll take mercury lights home. The other day a foreman showed me a pile of batteries and said, "It's Christmastime, here, take some for the kids." And he'd tell me, "Take the soap, but don't get caught." I have to wash half a dozen times a day; I need a strong soap.

✦ *A Supervisor's Car.* You can just about get anything out of that mill that you could possibly use for anything. Plumbing supplies, electrical supplies; if you know the right person, you can just about get anything that you need, I would say. I have personally gotten five-gallon gas cans of gas and put them in a supervisor's car.

Oh yeah, yeah. They have more access to it than anybody else. They can drive in the mill; I couldn't. He told me, "Go get five gallons gas." Well, he poured it in his car. You get two five-gallon cans of gas, you've got a half-tank of gas. And I did that a few different times. In return, I might get something from him if I wanted it.

✦ *A Cherry-Picker.* Then you have the obvious theft. We had one at Wisconsin Steel. I don't think they've found them yet. They stole some magnets. You know what a cherry-picker is? A cherry-picker, it's like a truck, and has this boom on it and can pick up heavy objects. You know what a magnet is? It's attached to a crane. Well, they took the cherry-picker and they lifted the crane magnet actually over the fence and were trying to load it on to a flatbed truck on the outside. Well, the guy who ran the cherry-picker apparently knew how to start it, but he didn't know too much else about it, so he tipped it over. It fell over onto the fence.

It was at that time that the guards realized that something was going on at the fence. The guards came over there; of course by that time the truck was gone. All they could find was the cherry-picker tipped over, a couple of magnets, some still inside, one on the outside. Apparently the truck has been loaded with two magnets because two magnets were missing. We made a big search.

## Land of the Millrats

✦ *A Flatbed Trailer and a Forklift Truck.* We used a chain link fence in some of our plant locations to separate our plant, Bethlehem Steel, from the town, Portage, which is practically inside our gates. In this instance three coils eight-feet high of chain link fence disappeared from inside the factory in one night. They were located near an area of the fence that was about to be replaced; the fence had been torn there because a truck had gone off the road and ripped up the fence. Nobody saw the coils leave from any gate. And it required a flatbed trailer and forklift truck to load them and transport them.

They were not observed leaving the plant. And they were not in the plant the following morning. That's a fairly good example of organized theft. Majority of stuff that leaves the plant does not go out at night.

✦ *The Twenty-Year Cadillac.* A fellow in the mill stole piece by piece everything that went into a Cadillac, over a twenty-year period, beginning in 1955. So it represents the features and parts of a Cadillac between 1955 and 1975. He announced it after he built the car.

They made a big public relations deal out of it.

(Johnny Cash celebrates this feat in a song hit.)

*Getting Caught*

Some of the mill theft tales about the trickster apprehended can be seen as variants of those of the trickster successful. Both sets of thieves use similar means of carrying out the stolen goods, but bad luck or carelessness spoil the getaway of the losers. In some instances the purloiners made little attempt to conceal their thefts. My friend Larry, a welder at the Big Mill, told, with a laugh, of workers, even foremen, who were fired because of tools discovered in the luggage compartments of their cars when plant security phoned the gate guards. He continued:

✦ *Flashlights and Power Tools.* Look under any bar in the area and you will find a flashlight from U.S. Steel. One fellow who got caught had just bought a new house; and the flashlight he stole didn't even work.

I said to him, "Joey, why did you do it?" He just shrugged his shoulders. Four foremen were fired for stealing power tools, worth about one hundred and fifty dollars. One put a tool under his shirt. It was silly of them to jeopardize a good-paying job that way; you practically had to commit murder to get fired.

✦ *Copper Wire.* There was a guy at Inland who stole copper wire. He had a very clever way of doing this. He did this for quite a while too. And he was caught rather strangely also.

# The Folklore of Steel

He used to take copper wire and wrap it around his body, fifty feet. He did this every day, wrapped his body with copper wire. And he'd walk out this way. He'd have his clothes over him. He was fat. You know copper weighs a few pounds; he probably added fifty pounds to his body weight whenever he did this. One fine day in the wintertime he slipped and fell on the ice. And it happened right in front of the gate. And the guard, being such a nice guy, walked over to pick the man up.

He couldn't pick him up, this guy weighed so much, he was so dog-gone heavy. This guy said, "Out of my way; I don't need any help." But he couldn't get himself up either. He was so heavy he couldn't get up himself. So the guard got another guy to come over there. Both of them pulled at him and they finally realized there was something wrong with this man. So they brought him inside and they asked him, "What's going on?" Of course they started to feel his body and they recognized that he was solid. So they stripped him and they found he had all this copper wire on him. And they investigated and they found he had been stealing copper wire for some time.

+ *Tin Ingots.* There's a story, supposedly this happened in the Gary Mill, where a guy carried home these little tin ingots from the tin mill over a period of twenty years, solid tin. And the reason he did that, about two years after he started working there, some supervisor really hacked him off. And in order to get even with the company he started stealing. But all he ever took were these little tin ingots. And he took them in his lunch box. Little lunch box, every day at lunch. He worked in the tin mill. He'd put a tin ingot in there. He did this over a period of twenty years, did not get caught.

And the way it happened that he got caught was he kept all of these things in his basement. He had walls lined, like you got bookshelves, you know, with tin ingots worth a fortune. Well, one day he had a party and he had some people down there and he was showing off these tin ingots. And I guess one of the people there blabbed it to somebody else, who blabbed it to somebody else, and it came to the attention of some Gary Mill big shot. And they sent out the police. And, sure enough, there were all these ingots. I don't know how much they were worth, but it was quite a fortune. This is how the guy got caught.

+ *A Stepladder.* There's a story about a fellow who was about to paint his house. He needed a stepladder, an extension ladder. There were a lot of them at work. He couldn't figure how he could get one of those ladders out of the plant, home. Twenty-footer, you see. So he finally rigged up a deal with his buddy. He says, "I'm gonna push your car out; you pretend that you're broken down. I'm gonna push you home."

He tied the ladder under the two cars. They caught him.

Can you imagine the length that some people will go to get something like a ladder out of the plant?

*Plexiglass.* This cautionary tale combines the themes of the mill character and the mill theft. The teller's sympathies are for once against his fellow-worker, because he is so unpleasant a character.

✦ This one fucker where we worked, his name was Ray Johnson. And everybody called him Johnny, and he was a big fat guy, hillbilly. And he was a bullshitter, you know. And he used to down-rap everybody, just cuss at everybody, and he never said a good word about nobody.

And the superintendent came through the mill one day, and this Andy guy had taken a can of spray paint, so he could spray on the floor where the floor was fucked up, where he wanted to weld, to reweld it again. And he went around spraying, and he snuck up behind the superintendent and he sprayed his *shoes* all white. He was a real fucker, and he just *fucked* with everybody all the time.

And one day he stole a piece of plexiglass and he took it and he put it in the back of his pickup truck. And he was riding out the gate and they stopped him and they found this plexiglass. And they said: "Man, you tried to steal this, you know. You're fired." And, like, the guy was making twenty-two grand a year.

And he tried to get his job back, and nobody'd help get it back 'cause he was a real fucker. And we came into work one day and the general foreman came up to me and he says, "Hey, I saw Johnny out at the gate today." And I say, "What was he doing out there?" And he says, "Ah, he was out there trying to sell plexiglass" [much laughter].

✦ *Alloys.* This worker was going on vacation the following day, and he brought his trailer all hooked up to his passenger car preparatory to leaving on his trip that day after work. A guard asked him why he drove it in all hooked up. And he said he had worked all evening to get it hooked up and he really didn't have time to disconnect it. And besides he was going on vacation. Couldn't they just let him park it out of the way somewhere? So they allowed him to go in, contrary to the rules.

That evening when he pulled his travel trailer out of the gate, one of the guards noticed that his tires looked kind of flat. Seems he was very heavily overloaded. And when they stopped him at the gate and decided they'd better examine this car, they discovered that he had covered the floor with a very valuable alloy that he was exporting illicitly. Unfortunately there's a very ready market for valuable alloyed metals on the outside. If you get it out of the plant you're pretty well assured that you can sell it.

# The Folklore of Steel

✦ *Tires.* There was all kinds of theft that goes on between suppliers coming in. This was another one at Inland, where a supplier of tires came in with tires and would leave with tires. Same tires. And he would charge the company for having delivered the tires. And he would make out another slip said he had old tires for recapping.

He'd come in and out with the same old tires. He had to deal with some clerk who would sign for having received the tires. This guy would come in and out and when he went through the gate going out, the guard would get the slip that said "25 recaps."

It was all done very cleverly for years. Finally he got caught. Eventually they do catch you.

✦ *Crane Brass.* They were shooting a movie at U.S. Steel based on *Boomtown.* So the guards held back the men coming out of the gate at quitting time because the shooting was still going on. The men thought it was a check to see if they were carrying out any stolen property.

The most precious thing one can take out is a brass bearing for crane ropes: "crane brass." So they began emptying their lunch buckets, their clothes bags with their work clothes; and bearings and tools clattered all over the ground with a great bang bang.

✦ *Scrap Metal.* When I was out at U.S. they said in the mills where they make steel, they'll have, like, fifty- to a hundred-pound scrap pieces of metal: various metals, like brass, copper, nickel, stuff like that. And these guys would take some of this stuff, brass or copper or whatever, and melt it down. Then they'd pour it into these cigar boxes that they had outside in the sand, and they'd let 'em cool. And then they'd stick 'em in their bib overalls or their lunch boxes and carry them out with them every time they left. I find that hard to believe, because if you pour molten anything into cigar boxes, it'll burn.

And they had a big racket going. There was supposed to be all kinds of people involved, like foremen and laborers and some of the guys that were the security guards out there, so they could get through.

And finally they busted the whole ring.

*Cable.* Getting caught does not necessarily mean punishment, as this tale illustrates.

✦ This is a true story now. Standard Forge had closed down. Or at least they reduced their staff by about a thousand people. They're down to about a hundred now. They're in East Chicago. And they used to be a large forging plant with a lot of hammers. Now they concentrate on making railroad axles only. And they have all modern equipment. And they've moved into just one building, rather than the whole hammer shop. Inland Steel rents some of their space for warehousing.

In the old hammer shop area they have a lot of large cable that used to feed the building. Recently on the night turn the security guards caught some guys out there stealing the cable, cutting it down. So when the guys were seen they took off running. So the security guards decided they would try to set a trap for them.

The guys had had the cable over by the fence, pulled over toward the gate. There is a large railroad track which separates Standard Forge from Inland Steel's old cast armor plant, which is to the west side of Standard Forge. There's a drive that you can drive a car or truck down. And the guys were trying to get this copper wire over there. They had it lined up over there. And these guys had actually gone in the hammer shop area and cut all of this cable up into little pieces. Hauled it and drug it out over the gate. Thousands of pounds of copper.

So the guys took off, but the guards were sure they'd come back. So the next day the guys did come back and they managed to get the stuff. And the Inland police got 'em and held them till the city police came. And they had a shoot-out with the police. And because of the shoot-out the plant management people at Standard Forge refused to press charges against the guys, 'cause they were afraid they'd come in and shoot the place up.

So even when they do get caught, they manage to get away with some of the things that happen. So these guys actually were caught; they had the goods on 'em, and no one would press charges against them, even after the police had been involved in the shoot-out and had risked their lives. The company wouldn't press charges.

✦ *Brass.* A foreman in the yard department drives everywhere all over the plant with a company truck, which makes it easy to steal things. An electrician told him about some brass in one of the merchant mills which was down for a week for repairs. A security man saw the brass under a stairway and spotted the foreman attempting to steal it in his truck. The foreman admitted to the theft and the case went to arbitration. The electrical man took it to arbitration.

At the hearing he told the identical same story as he had before, but the electrician had large gaps in his story. It turned out that the guard who caught the foreman had reported the theft to the lieutenant of the guards, who said, "Put the brass back exactly where it was."

The guard then went to the captain, who then had to fire the lieutenant for trying to cover up. So three men were fired: the foreman, the electrical man, and the lieutenant of the guards. This happened at Wisconsin Steel over the Christmas holidays.

# The Folklore of Steel

✦ *Plumbing Supplies.* Some years ago they had a case that went all the way to the general superintendent over here at the Inland Steel Company. And the whole management was suspect. And one chap, who worked in the plumbing department, his whole basement was stocked with plumbing supplies. He stole from Inland. He'd take things out in his lunch box, take it out in a tool box, or anything at all, drive his car into the mill and fill up the trunk in his car. And perhaps the plant guards were getting a certain percentage of this. And fraud sometimes goes all the way to the top management, as it happened to go in this case, because they had a lot of steel that was going out through the plant that wasn't billed out; we had a big shortage. And some of the top management of the plant over here was selling it on the gray market.

✦ *A Whole Mill.* There was a story about some supervisors out at U.S. in the late sixties. These supervisors had outfitted this whole mill that they were building in Texas. They were building a finishing mill in Texas to finish steel, and they had built the structure.

Paul: Didn't you say that they'd get the ore—the boats would bring materials into the docks, and they'd just reroute them all the way down to Texas?

Mike: Yeah. When they'd get supplies in for U.S. over there, some of the ore boats'd bring it in. And what they'd do is rechannel everything and make it look like it was supposed to be shipped to Texas, 'cause U.S. Steel's got mills down there. As far as people knew up here, it was going to Texas, but people down in Texas knew nothing about it going to Texas.

And they'd have it shipped down to their mill. And they said they were just, like, they only had this one machine to go to finish their mill. And they got caught. They busted all these guys and threw 'em in jail.

*Workers' Pay.* In one unusual piece of roguery, a foreman ripped off his work crew. Foremen play a central role in mill tales, as the immediate authority figures over the labor gangs. They report on absenteeism and incompetence, pass on recommendations for transfers, and assign duties. A reminiscing old-time steelman declared: "The foremen were kings or dictators and even helped themselves to the workers' wives." A Wisconsin Steel executive tells about this trickster foreman.

✦ There are all sorts of schemes where people do steal from the mills. Here was a scheme that I thought was clever. This happened at Inland Steel, where this guy was a maintenance foreman in the mechanical shops; he assigned maintenance at the 76-Inch Hot Strip. Apparently for some time he was taking five dollars per week from every maintenance man who wanted to work midnights. And this was special dues to the supervisor. I guess he made out the schedule. Now I supposed these guys wanted to work midnights 'cause there was very little work to do, and they could just sleep on the job. And most of the people had second jobs during the day. They'd work during the day, and they'd come there at night and sleep. Really nice deal. This man was not discovered for many years.

The way he got discovered was sort of accidentally. A relatively young worker, he was a foreigner, filed a grievance with the griever, which is like a steward, saying that he protested that the company raised its dues. And the griever was a rather stupid individual. He didn't know what this guy was talking about. So he went through the grievance procedure. The company became aware of this, said: "Well, what are you talking about, protest what dues?" Said: "Joe Schmoe came and filed it, why don't we talk to him?" And the guy tried to tell, "I been paying five dollars to XYZ for several weeks now. And he said we just got a raise, we gotta pay ten dollars; it's not worth ten dollars to me." "What's not worth ten dollars to you?" "Well, I gotta pay to the foreman ten dollars."

This is how it came out, through the back door. This foreman, he made—I don't know how much money he made. He had twenty-five people working for him. You figure for years and years he was being paid five dollars times twenty-five, one hundred twenty-five dollars a week from the people. Then he got a little bit greedy, tried to raise it to ten dollars.

The reason they didn't complain, it was obviously very satisfactory. They wanted the midnight shift. Not only that, they wanted to be left alone. He was the foreman, you see, who was on that shift. And he never bothered them. The only time he'd ever ask them to do anything was when he absolutely needed them, you know. The rest of the time, say he needed a five man crew generally, there were twenty-five people on the crew; that meant twenty of them could sleep. He'd pick five of them, he'd say, "Monday is your night to actually work." They'd rotate it off.

*A Special Case: Alleged Theft of Tires*

In one instance, here related by a management official of Bethlehem Steel, the seemingly clear-cut theft case proved other than what it first appeared.

✦ That's one of my most unfavorite stories. Last fall I located a pair of tires, which were appropriate for my three-quarter-ton pickup truck, at a local gas station. I inquired the price and learned that the tires were available to me for twenty-five dollars apiece, which meant that I could buy two brand-new tires for just about the price that I would expect to pay for one identical tire. I was curious as to why the reduction in price. And learned from the man that he was going out of business and that he was trying to reduce his inventory. Be obliged if I could take them off his hands.

So a short time afterward I paid him for his tires and picked them up. Took them home. And before I had a chance to mount them up on my truck I noticed that they were branded "B. S. Steel Corp." That means Bethlehem Steel Corporation. On the side of each. On each side of both tires. I suspected that they were our tires and had been stolen, so I approached our purchasing department and plant security people and learned in fact that this was our brand. And they proceeded to gather a statement from me. And immediately thereafterwards arrested the individual. And seized the remaining tires in his stock which were similarly branded. They took him to the police station and asked him to produce a receipt for the tires.

He said: "Well, if you'd asked me at the gas station I could have done it. Now that I'm here, you'll have to escort me back to the gas station to get your receipt." They drove him back to the gas station. He produced a receipt showing that Bethlehem Steel had in fact sold these tires at auction since they were a size that was obsolete for the current rolling stock in the plant. And they were in fact legitimately for sale on the open market. And he charged me exactly what he'd paid for them. He made not one penny on the transaction. So it doesn't always pay to be suspicious of everybody. Things are not always what they seem.

He said Bethlehem was going to finance his trip to Hawaii. He's gonna sue us for false arrest. His very words.

### Management's Philosophy

"There must be a million stories how thefts have gone on and how they're finally discovered."—steel company executive

A humane executive, systems coordinator for one of the mills, explained management's tolerant attitude toward smaller thefts.

✦ In big industrial complexes it's virtually impossible to keep the employees from stealing. I think in a way, I can't prove this, but I think the philosophy that the management has, is they will permit a certain amount of thievery. Because I think they believe it's a kind of catharsis for the employees. This is a way where they let off steam. Not the big stuff. They go after the big stuff. But the little things they wink at.

They permit it to happen because they know working conditions aren't always what they should be. Many employees steal simply because they feel this is how they get even. And the management lets it go on, permits it. I guess it's kind of a permissiveness 'cause they feel, well, "If the employees do this and we don't go after them, then that solves many other problems." Because they will vent their spleens doing that rather than destroying expensive equipment. It's much easier for the company to let a man steal a little bar of zinc or whatever, you know.

## CANTEEN RIPOFFS

### Demolishing the Coke Machine

One of the great legends of the mills describes a confrontation between a worker and a coke machine, with the man ultimately triumphing. In its wake a full-scale fracas may ensue and a wildcat strike erupt. I first learned of the episode from a folklore collection in our archives turned in by a student who had worked summers in U.S. Steel in 1969 and 1970 and reported how a crane operator got mad at a coke machine that didn't work and smashed it with a three-thousand-pound coil. On inquiring into this curious event, I discovered that various millworkers in different mills over a span of time had presumably perpetrated this deed. In other kinds of industry the same vendetta occurs, and is filmed in *Blue Collar,* a 1978 release starring Richard Pryor and depicting scenes in a Detroit automobile factory.

Of the five accounts that follow, the first three come from solid citizens of the mill hierarchy, who chronicle the affair with a close memory of the facts and an objective view. The last two proceed from young rebels of the present generation who delight in ripping off the canteen themselves, thereby becoming "mill heroes." In their eyes the canteen has been ripping them off all along, with its stale food and unreliable service. Vengeance on the canteen provides the same release as do torturing rats and goofing off in the millworker's battle against boredom and degradation.

✦ Fred: That happened when I was shop steward in the coke plant [of Youngstown Sheet and Tube] in 1954 or 1955. The guy put his money in the coke machine ten times and couldn't get either his money or his pop. So he grabbed a forklift and drove through the washhouse [the locker room, where the coke machine was located] and took out a couple of courses [rows] of bricks, because he couldn't get the forklift through the door. Then he picked up the coke machine with the forklift, and backed outside through the hole he had smashed. He raised the lifting device, the fork, so the coke machine tipped over and broke. Then he took the bottle of pop and nothing else.

The company tried to fire him. They were perfectly justified; it was wanton destruction of property. As shop steward I argued he had a just grievance. The superintendent—who has a hearing aid he turned off when grievances were presented to him, so he could rattle the grievance committeeman by saying "speak a little louder"—insisted on the five-day letter, which discharged the worker and gave him five days to present his grievance. We tried to get him to make a quasi-legal contract proceeding out of it and to give a reprimand instead of a suspension. But he wouldn't, so we shut down several units, such as the machine shop and the labor gang—a work stoppage, not a strike; it lasted two or three hours. Then they reinstated the guy, just took some of his time off.

✦ Larry: That happened in 1959—no, 1961—where I was working in the Gary Works. A guy, a colored fellow, kicked in or broke the coke machine when he couldn't get the coke out, and they were going to fire him. The assistant grievance man for the union was John McLaughlin, and he discussed the case with the company superintendent, whom he claimed spat in his face; so he punched him in the nose. Then the company fired McLaughlin (who had forgot to take himself off the company payroll and put himself on the union payroll when he became grievance man, by telling the secretary to make the change). When the company fired him, the men went on a wildcat strike, since a union man had been sacked. There is a stipulation in the contract between the company and the union that no union business can be done on company time, so the company felt justified.

Some workers wouldn't recognize the wildcat strike and tried to cross the picket line, and the strikers prevented them from entering. The company brought TV cameras to the gate and took pictures of the fights, and company superintendents identified their men who were picketing, and nine or thirteen of them were fired. McLaughlin was suspended for a year, and the matter went into arbitration. All the men were reinstated and given back their seniority, but they didn't receive retroactive pay.

Jack McLaughlin is the top grievance man now.

✦ Lot: Inland Steel has excellent labor relations, but they almost had a strike about four years ago [1972] in the 80-Inch Hot Strip Mill because of the fact that some guy had literally demolished a coke machine. I mean he just, like, he took a great big hammer (he was a millwright), and he took all of his frustration out on the coke machine. He just hammered the coke machine to death, totally, you know.

Well, so the company shut all the machines off. And the new crew came out and they were incensed. And they said, "By God, if you don't get new machines out here, we're gonna walk out." And ARA was the service at the time—I guess they still have the contract—and they brought new machines out the next day and they averted a strike. But you see what happens, these machines take such a beating and some people attempt to steal money. This is how the machines initially get beaten up. They will try to take money out of a machine, and if a machine stops working, so the next honest guy who comes in puts money in the machine, he gets cheated. So he kicks the machine, you know. And the next guy comes around, he gets mad, he takes a hammer, starts beating and before you know it—. There was a little warehouse that Inland Steel had, I saw approximately a hundred different machines stored in there. I mean the service life of a machine at one of those steel mills probably isn't any more than a year. That's pretty bad. The workers really get mad at those machines.

Vicki: That's all they have, just coke machines? They don't have a whole automat?

Lot: Well, at Wisconsin Steel we just put a new service in. And those machines I think will last pretty long. We have one in my office area there. We've given one of the secretaries change money in case the change doesn't come out; there's a big note that says see so-and-so. So the machines, nobody has beaten the machines. But I remember a guy got mad and kicked in a part of a wall by one of the previous machines by my office. He really got incensed. First he started to beat on the machine and he hurt his hand so he stopped doing that. Then he started kicking.

John: What about machines being cut up with a torch? I heard a story of someone stealing an infra-red machine out of one of the canteens, also. I personally know a fellow who devised a hook that he stuck up the shoot where the food comes out. Now, I've seen this personally. You stick this hook in there, it has a certain little bend in it. You touch a certain lever in there and it would dispense the hot dogs out. And he'd rip off the hot dogs out of the machine. The machine would give a little click or buzz.

Lot: Did he sell them?

John: No, he would do it for his friends. You'd hear this little buzz and click and it'd drop the hot dogs. And he'd dispense them among his friends. I was in there personally and saw that.

Lot: Were you one of the friends?

John: I did get a couple free hot dogs. Right. It was only done now on the midnight shift. There weren't too many people around.

Lot: Few supervisors.

John: He wouldn't do it in daytime.

Lot: Midnight is when much of the damage is done because you have fewer supervisors around.

John: There are fewer people around. But you know hot dogs came out freely when he was around. And not only just hot dogs, whatever sandwiches were in there.

# The Folklore of Steel

✦ Roland: We ripped off the coke machine once, and we busted it open in this roll shop, me and these two other guys. With a hammer and a bar [laughter]. We opened it up to try and get the money box, but that was even harder to get at. But we got into the pop and all. It was on a midnight, and all these people started coming out after we had it opened. And we were throwing pop out to everybody—we were the mill heroes [laughter]!

Bill: Hear it for the pop-man [laughter]!

There was this guy named Rocky that works out where I work. He used to rip off the milk machine every week. On midnights he'd go over to the other side, and everything would be shut down. And he'd just take a crowbar and open the machine up. And one time they caught him, the plant protection guys.

Roland: Oooh, that's bad.

Bill: And they caught him and they took his picture and they dusted for fingerprints and they fired his ass.

Roland: Once plant protection gets ahold of a man, there's nothing that anybody—a foreman, management, anybody—can do, 'cause plant protection is like, they're like police.

Bill: They're tough fuckers, man.

✦ Mike: The canteens are a ripoff. The food is shitty and it costs you a lot of money, and you only eat there because you're hungry and you haven't got any lunch. And a lot of times you just get tired of taking a baloney sandwich to work with you all the time. So like, you know, if you get a chance to pimp over a canteen machine, you will.

And, like, I learned how to break into the milk machines at Bethlehem and U.S. You just had to reach up in there and bend your arm around a certain way and grab whatever flavor you want. Chocolate and regular milk and orange juice, and tea sometimes. And not more than a month after I learned how to break into both of those, they put on these new doors so that you couldn't put your arm in there.

And a lot of times you always hear stories about there were these guys out in the fab shop that broke into the sandwich machine once. And they stole all the sandwiches and turned 'em onto everybody. And between the four of them, they split the change that they got out of the change machine.

Paul: How'd they get into it, do you know?

Mike: They pried it open with a crowbar. There was a lot of times they'd just come up with a hammer, you know, just go *whack* you know, and they beat it, you know. And like they're [the company] really worried about their machines out there, because it's supposed to be kind of like a privilege to have food machines out there. But you always put your money into 'em, and you never get nothing out.

Paul: But didn't you say like some guys'll just eat for free because they'll go to the change person at somewhere else and tell him they got ripped off?

Mike: Like out at U.S. they got hot canteens where you can go and order food from these ladies who cook it up. And a lot of times you ain't got no bread so you go over there and you tell the lady, "Well, I, uh, I lost a dollar-twenty in these machines." And she gives you this little ticket and you sign it and you fill it out, and you take your dollar-twenty and you go spend it on whatever you want to spend it on [laughs]. Go eat whatever you want to eat, you know.

And you do that because you figure all the time you're out there, every time you put money in there, the odds are you're going to lose money everyday out there, in one of those machines. And they're really worried about their machines. They say: "Don't kick the machines! Don't hit the machines!"

But, like, a guy'll put his money in and he'll look both ways 'cause nothing comes out you know, and he'll look both ways down the aisles to see if there's anybody around, and he'll lean up against the pole and he'll kick the machine as hard as he can [laughter]. And you always see these machines with the faces all caved in and stuff, you know. Like, they had this candy machine out there that these guys were breaking into all the time. So they put this steel mesh grid on it, like the stuff you walk on on floors out on the mill, and they put this on it. And then you're suppposed to *guess* what candy you're picking 'cause you can't see the candy, you know [laughter].

They had all the lights turned off so you couldn't break into it. And they're always putting these big heavy padlocks on it, put 'em in places where you can't move 'em, because a lot of times, you know, if there ain't nobody around some of the guys get really hostile. And they'll go over there and they'll pick up with a fork truck, and just take the thing and dump it somewhere. And you hear stories about guys going over there with a crane and just hooking it up with a crane and ramming it into the wall, or just picking it up and dropping it—and just *pssshhhooo*, you know.

Canteens are always ripping you off.

## GOOFING OFF

"I just try to get away with as much shit as I can up
there."—a young millworker

Many youthful laborers regard the mill as a bunkhouse and a play-
ground. In complete contrast to the work ethic of their fathers, they take
pride in and boast about sleeping on the job and indulging in horseplay.
As one of their number explained it, they already have cars and stereos
and a chance at a college degree, and the union provides job security, so
neither the carrot nor the stick moves them. Pranks and practical jokes,
sometimes ritualized as "Horseplay Day" on Friday afternoons, sometimes degenerating into senseless vandalism, occupy their minds and
energies during the interminable turns.

*Paint Sticks and Pigeons*

✦ Roland: Tell 'em that story about how guys took that chalk and threw it
on the steel.
Bill: Oh, yeah. We were fucking around at work one day, you know.
There was nothing to do. We didn't feel like working. So we walked up to
this like stairway, up to this crane. And we found this door. And normally
this door is locked, but the door was ajar. So we walked through there.
And there was like a little passageway that led up to the roof of the mill.
It's like about seven stories high. Way the hell up there, you know.
Roland: You see, the steel comes like a coil from the bottom, and it gets
heated, and it goes *way* up in the air.
Bill: And it goes through about seven miles worth of steel, you know,
just getting washes.
Roland: It goes up and down, getting washes.
Bill: We're up there, we're watching this shit going on there, and we
have these "El Marko" paint sticks; we had about three or four boxes of
'em.
Paul: Are they paint?
Bill: No, they're paint sticks; they're like crayons.
Roland: Big crayons.
Bill: And we threw 'em in there, and it fucked up the steel, and got
white shit all over, you know. So they had a *big* investigation [laughter].
And those dudes were all investigating, you know. They had all these
fucking chairmen of the board, guys who make two hundred and fifty
grand, investigating this thing.

And they determined that the reason that the steel got fucked up was because of pigeons: pigeon shit [much laughter]. And so they had a big program to exterminate all the pigeons.

Paul: How'd they do that?

Bill: They were going to set poison out for 'em. Yeah, poison—peanuts or something [much laughter]. All because we fucked those guys over. 'Cause we had about a million tons worth of steel with white shit on it. And they couldn't figure out why. And they deduced that it was pigeon shit [laughter].

*"Horseplay Day"*

✦ I worked in this line gang. The line gang is a group of electricians that do this mill construction. They work for the mill but they do construction work. Then they do the high power line work in the mills, put up new cranes or overhaul old cranes, or do any kind of major repairs in the mill.

And there were a lot of us that were about the same age. And we used to do all kinds of mischief. Friday afternoons after dinner, that was horseplay day. No one worked Friday afternoons. You always tried to work exceptionally hard in the morning on Fridays so that you could spend the time horseplaying.

One of their favorite tricks was kind of nasty. They would urinate in coffee cups. And then they would tie these coffee cups on everybody's lock to their lockers, with the lock hanging in the coffee cup. And we had one guy who was especially bad about this. That was his favorite trick. He used to like to dump the coffee cup on fires in the wintertime and make it smell.

And so one day he had a big paint can on the roof. No one knew this except him. And he'd go up there and he'd urinate in this paint can that was sitting up on the roof on this electrical control house that we were building. And it had quite a bit of urine in it. Well, it rained, and it filled all the way up to the top. And he and another young fellow got to horseplaying on a Friday afternoon, and for some reason this young fellow went up the ladder and John Mohee went up right behind him. And when that young guy got to the top of the ladder, he spied this bucket full of water. Well, as far as he knew, that's all it was. And John, the guy behind him, this is the guy that had filled it up.

And Bill grabbed the bucket and dumped it on John. Well, as soon as it hit John, John knew it was one-half urine. And he really got upset. And so they were running through the building, and John grabbed another bucket he saw to throw water on Bill. He let the bucket go, and it turned out it was water only on top, and green paint the other half down. And it hit these new control panels, which were hundreds of thousands of dollars worth of control panels. It hit the control panels. Well, then they knew they really had trouble. And they both had green paint on them. And they knew that if the boss saw the green paint, that he was obviously going to know who it was. So here are the two guys that had been fighting and horseplaying a few minutes before they dumped the water on each other, are over there scrubbing each other's neck and back, and washing each other's hands so they could get the green paint off.

But they did get caught, and they did have to go back [to the control room], and they spent several days in there just scrubbing down all those electrical panels getting the paint off of them.

Horseplay is common in the mills, especially among the line gangs and the guys that move around a lot.

## Fourth of July in the Mill

✦ Mike: And we used to do stuff, like, if there was nothing to do, we'd go to the top of the crane and take a whole bunch of paper up there with us. And we'd just sit up there and throw airplanes off the top. Paper airplanes, just shoot them all over the place. And once we took some bottle rockets out there with us and shot 'em across the shop.

And one time—that's how they sent us all home one day—it was the Fourth of July and nobody wanted to work, so everybody brought out fireworks, 'cause, you know, it's against the rules.

Paul: Didn't you say that happens every year?

Mike: Yeah, every year, it's kind of traditional in the fab shop. Every year everybody takes out fireworks and tries to get sent home. And we were shooting bottle rockets across the shop and guys were lighting off firecrackers all the time, and the foreman would come out and bitch. And as soon as he walked back in the door to the office, another firecracker would go off. And we did this about four times, and he finally sent us home.

## Sleeping on the Job

Cranemen hold a special, celestial position in mill lore, as they hover over the proceedings taking place below. They can sleep with impunity.

✦ You're working midnights, and, like, you might not have a load for three hours, so you just sack out. And there's been plenty of times when cranemen have been up in the mill, up in the cranes, sleeping. And the foreman'll come because he can't wake him up. And nobody can wake them up because they're just *sound* asleep, and the foremen can't get to them because they're out in the middle of the floor and there's no way you can get to the crane from there.

And a lot of times when you're sleeping in the cranes, guys would throw shit at you, just to wake you up. Pop cans—whew!—you can hear the shit bouncing around and off the walls and sail over your head. And it wakes you up.

Several mill themes appear in the following anecdote: sleeping on the job, ethnic characters, and aggressive rats.

✦ Roland: You know, Holman, when he was a janitor at U.S., he had this washhouse. And adjoining the washhouse was, like, this storage room. The storage room was really big, you know, and it had these big steel plates—well they were like shelves, but they were really wide, like bunk beds. And to us, that's what they were—at lunchtime [laughter]. We used to take clean mopheads, you know, and take, like, five or six of 'em and then wrap 'em up in a clean rag and then that'd be your pillow. And we'd lay on these things, and if you didn't get there in time, you wouldn't get a place to sleep [laughter]. We'd sleep there from like ten-thirty till about one-thirty, you know. We'd just hide out.

And this one dude, Francisco, he's from Puerto Rico, and one time he got there and all the beds were taken. And he says "Aw, fuck!" you know. So he takes this piece of cardboard, he lays it on this dirty floor, he lays on the cardboard. I mean he's just *beat,* and he lays down on this cardboard. And he's leaning on his arm like this, and he said he felt this like little "beee-e-e-p" on his fingertips [laughter], and he opens up his eyes, man, and there's, like, this rat, you know, this *thing,* and it's like nibbling at his fingertips. Like licking the salt off his fingers.

Bill: Maybe he had some fried chicken or something [laughter]. The rat wants some fried chicken.

Paul: Wow! That's pretty heavy. What'd he do, just jump on up?

Roland: Yeah. I was just sleeping and he gets up. He goes [imitates Latin accent] "Hey, man! There's a rat, man! He bit one of my fingers!"

Youthful sleepers-on-the-job get their just deserts from a foreman witih a sense of humor.

✦ Well, Dave Frank, labor foreman at 84-Inch, was telling me one time he had in his gang some college students for the summer. And usually they're happy-go-lucky—because they're only there for three months and they're gone, you know. It's an experience for them, to really realize how big a place it is and how it works and everything.

And these guys were on day turn. It's kind of hard to stay awake on days certain times, and there's places you can hide. And these guys went to the washhouse. And I guess they'd been doing this a couple times, you know. And so the foreman finally found out where they were hiding. (The foremen sometimes just go around, look in all kinds of places where people hide and go to sleep. Then they'll find them and write them up.) What the students did over there was, they were laying down on the benches that the guys sit on to change their clothes. And one was laying on one bench and another was laying on another bench. And so the foreman went over there and he took a snapshot of them. I guess an Instamatic job. And then he went back and punched their cards and laid their cards on top of them.

Then when they woke up, they actually came down to him and they laughed about it. They didn't grudge and cuss and all that. It was unbelievably funny to them.

So they just went home early, I don't think they got any time off. In other words, like they fell asleep at one o'clock. He punched their card at one o'clock. So they didn't get paid for the last three hours.

### Sleeping on the Toilet

With the emergence of the union some workers spent most or all of their time not making steel but negotiating grievances of the labor force. The union organizer; the president of the local; the grievance committeemen; the griever, who first hears the complaints and carries them to the committee; the editor of the local's paper—all take their places among the mill personalities. A lore springs up around confrontations, from grievances to strikes, between laborers and managers.

Grievance procedures minimized the risks of sleeping on the job.

+ This one fellow in the mill used to sneak off to the men's room and go to sleep on the toilet. So one time the supervisor looked in and saw him there, with his head on his knees, under the partition (which is required by state law). And he called him by name, three times: "Joe." But the fellow never answered, so the supervisor fired him for sleeping on the job and not responding when he was called back to work.

The fellow took the case to the arbitration board. He denied being asleep, and claimed that the position of his body was not indicative of his being asleep, and that the name Joe could have applied to other workers with that first name. So the board voted in his favor not to fire him.

But privately he admitted he had been sleeping.

### The Breakdown Game

The workers sometimes deliberately slow down their output so they can lengthen their jobs, whose time periods for various job classifications are set by industrial engineers. But on certain occasions maintenance men speeded up their work—to afford themselves greater leisure.

✦ That set of rules sometimes is put by the wayside though. Like on a midnight shift, the breakdown game, waiting for something to go wrong. It's all they're doing is just waiting. On a bad day you may have eight hours work and sometimes work overtime. But usually on a midnight team on a weekend there is nothing, because hardly any of the mills are working, so there is not really much that can break down. But on occasion it builds up on one shift and overflows into the midnight and you wind up with a lot of extra work.

There was one especially cold night we—all six of the gang—wanted to stay in the shop and play poker because there wasn't anything really urgent. But because of the slack that was left from the afternoon shift, the boss had left word that it's got to be cleared up. so he made a deal with us. He said: "If you go out and take care of this work"—X number of jobs—"we'll sit down and play poker the rest of the night." And we had to change one wheel of a skullcracker, which is an outside crane; fix one cable in an open-hearth; and move some trash buckets somewhere in some other plant. And each one would have taken on the day shift about, let's say, three to four men, for four or five hours. We had only six men and we were done in two hours with all of it. And we played poker for the next six. I lost eighteen dollars.

*Vandalism*

Although goofing off is passive and horseplay is humorous, vandalism can be vicious and destructive. It may take the form of fouling up the works for malicious pleasure or of wanton destruction of property, even to the inconvenience of fellow-workers. Goofing off, horseplay, and vandalism all shade into one another, reflecting the same attitudes of indifference and hostility toward the company.

✦ Roland: It's really hard to get fired from the mill. You know, it's really hard.

Bill: You have to go up and hit your foreman in the mouth to get fired.

Roland: This guy didn't want to do this job, and the job was banding these tubes up. And if the bale tags said "No Tags" on it for production planning—where it comes from [that is, the office deciding on their disposition]—you wouldn't wrap 'em up, you could set it [leave it]. So what he did was, he wrote "No Tags" on all of 'em himself. And they caught him, and they *still* didn't fire him. You see, they couldn't prove that he did it.

Paul: What did you say? Like he'd do one a week, or something like that?

Roland: It's this way. I do the same job. He works the turn ahead of me, and I get maybe one or two bales—there's like fifteen or sixteen pieces in a bale, whatever a customer orders—and I may be getting lucky and not have to band maybe one or two bales a week. But this dude had like eight or nine bales in one night that he didn't do. And they caught him, but he just denied it, and there was nothing they could do. They couldn't prove that he wrote it 'cause he wrote it with a big crayon. Just had the chalk marks for evidence. Anybody can write anything on the slabs.

Bill: Well, you can fuck the company over a million ways. You could just take all the IBM cards and throw 'em away.

Roland: Sure. You can go around, and they have these tags, you could switch tags. That'd fuck everything up.

Paul: Don't guys always bust their machines?

Roland: Oh hell, yes. We take big bolts and just throw 'em in the gears. We take pennies and put 'em in the fuses, blow everything up. We do anything. Yeah, and you go and take this big chain that's along the wall, and you pull it, and this whistle goes "Ooooooh." You pull it like four times, and this little old greasy man'll come over and you go [laughter] "My machine's broke, man. I don't know what's wrong with it." He'll take like two or three hours to fix it, while you're eating at the canteen, taking a nap [laughter].

Paul: They don't ever hassle you about that either.

Roland: No, I do it two or three times a week.

Bill: They can't, man. 'Cause there's so many; the union can fuck 'em back so many ways. See, a lot of the guys just don't care.

Roland: I call off probably sixty days—sixty times in the last half year. If I don't work today and I call off, they'd probably give me a day off, if I didn't wake up feeling well. If I was going to a funeral, to the hospital, or something. If I just said I was sick, that meant "OK, write me up and give me two days off." OK, and I went to my doctor and I said, "Hey, I was sick." And my doctor looks in my throat and finds something wrong, an infection. OK, I take that back to the union and I show them, and I say, "Hey, I *was* sick." They wrote me up and gave me two days. OK, they have to pay me that time even though I wasn't there.

Paul: Do black guys do that too?

Roland: Oh sure. Black dudes, man, in the wintertime! My grandpa's a foreman in the tin mill. He's got this black chick that she'll go on sick leave all winter and just work in the summer, you know. She just works it that way every year. "Well, it's time for her to go away. Time for her to be sick."

## Land of the Millrats

✦ They got these air hoses that they used to hook up to machines, they work off the air pressure, just for blowing dirt off of stuff and junk. And what these guys used to do was take welding rods and stick 'em in the air hoses, kick on the air hoses. And they used to shoot 'em at each other and have battles in there. And these rods would go really quick. There's a lot of places in the tin on the walls where they just shot 'em right through the tin on the walls.

✦ I was witnessing one fellow. I came to clean my glasses and there's glass-cleaning water [at the place], it was provided by the company in agreement with the union. You squirt the little pump on your glasses. Then you have paper and dry your glasses, clean your glasses. He unscrewed the top of that and threw the pump in the garbage. Then the next man come, he wants to clean his glasses. He couldn't clean them because the pump is gone.

And I asked the fellow why did he do that? He said the company would put another on.

I don't believe it's right.

✦ Well it's happened in our shop. We had the telephone in our elevator which was put there by the company for our own good, because that elevator is operated automatically by pushing buttons, and it could anytime break down and get stuck between the floors with you or a bunch of people inside. And that phone was there to ask for help, and call the fire department to get us out, or notify our foreman that we are stuck in the elevator. That guy's cutting off the receiver of the telephone, taking it away. It's happened a few times in our shop.

And company's painting, for instance. They paint elevators, they paint restrooms; people don't care, just spread grease and dirt over the nice clean paint in washroom or elevator or locker room. Some are people who really do damage. It's very hard to deal with, you know. And it cost money, lots of money. Company have to pay the man who paints that. And the company have to pay for the paint. And it's for our own good. But people are just like that and they destroy.

### Lunch Buckets

A subtheme of horseplay revolves around lunch boxes or buckets. Young millrats bent on mischief find them inviting targets—visible, often untended, and highly prized by their owners. In the unrelieved tedium and jangle of mill life, the lunch break looms as the one oasis in the day—hence, too, the importance of the canteen. The contents of lunch buckets, particularly those belonging to ethnics, astonishes the more conventional eaters. "One Italian always brought dago red [a home-made wine] and hard-boiled eggs in his lunch basket," marveled an observer. A scatter of little anecdotes report the trickeries perpetrated on carriers of lunch buckets.

✦ One of the favorite tricks at the mill is to put a dead mouse or rat in someone's lunch bucket. The lunch buckets often are lined up, so they are easy to get at. Sometimes the workers put them in lockers, but in other areas they don't because the lockers are too far away from where they work.

Another trick that ran its course was, one man—the man who started it evidently—acquired a sanitary napkin, poured ketchup on it, and put it in somebody's lunch box. And so this popped up, say, for a few weeks. Just like boys will be boys. And you had tampons being used the same way. You had prophylactics being found in lunch buckets. And ladies' scanty panties, and things like this.

✦ There are a lot of things that people do to other people's lunch boxes. The electricians used to have a habit of doing those tricks. The guy wouldn't notice what we had done because the worker's wouldn't usually check their lunch box before they would leave the plant. We would take the cap off the thermos bottle and use this heavy industrial rubber tape and tape the whole inside of the cup and the cork and then put the cap back on. So the wife would always end up getting stuck with the mess when the guy got the lunch box home.

And that same kind of thing goes to a story one of my buddies told me. Where his dad works they put a sparrow in the guy's lunch box. And he didn't know it, and he took it home, and then his wife opened it up to clean out the lunch box. Out flew the sparrow and scared the hell out of her.

✦ One time my old man was working with this one hillbilly dude, out at U.S., named Waltie. And this dude had four big raw meat sandwiches in his lunch. And my dad sent him over to this bin. And my old man went over there and he tore this guy's bag of his lunch open and pulled a little bit of bread out, and he said. "Well, I hope that rat over there didn't get into any of them lunches" [laughs].

This Waltie dude goes "What!" And he runs over there, and he looked in his lunch, and it was just torn open. And he threw the whole lunch away. All those sandwiches.

# Land of the Millrats

## RATS

Steelworkers in the Region are not dubbed "millrats" without reason. In the older mills—and all except Bethlehem and Midwest are aged—rats abound, and so do stories about their size and voracity. Laboring men and ravenous rats share the noise, dirt, and danger of the mills and interact in enforced intimacy. Rats take on human characteristics, and workers come to feel like trapped rodents.

The appeal of the mills for rats, as explained by a maintenance worker, lies in the scraps of food left lying around and the storage places and shelters from the weather available. In the mills, far more than in homes, the rodents can find places to burrow and hide with relative ease.

Only a portion of the mill people I spoke with told rat tales, and these were all the younger ones, in their twenties, save for a forty-one-year-old electrician. To them ferocious rats fit naturally into the scene of ugliness, tedium, and unrelieved desolation they associated with their jobs. Rats offered some diversion, as topics of conversation and as targets for ingenious methods of killing, some of which backfired. In this respect, rat destruction belongs with mill thefts, goofing off, and demolition of the coke machine as pastimes that make bearable the monotony and gloom of millwork.

Descriptions of the size and savagery of mill rats fall into a tradition dating back to colonial times, of "true" tales concerning the gigantic character of American beasts, such as the Big Bear of Arkansas and Moby Dick. Ratón the rat catcher follows in the wake of Davy Crockett the b'ar hunter, in a somewhat less noble setting.

### Size of Rats

✦ One time I'm going down the rails at Inland. And we're going pretty slow. We usually don't go over four to eight miles an hour. Why kill the job? As soon as you get done you have another fucking job to do. And one night, this is no shit, I see this shadow go over the rails, and it came over one rail, and over the other rail. And that damn rat, as his front paws were going over the second rail, his tail was still coming over the other rail.

And a guy's got a rat tail out at work, too, that's four-foot long. It's about an inch in diameter at the base. Now if that isn't a big goddam rat, I don't know what is!

✦ Paul: How big would you say those rats stand?
Ben: They ain't super huge—

## The Folklore of Steel

Arthur: Super mean.

Ben: Yeah. Their bodies are not all that long, really, but they're bulky. The rats are no longer skinny little things running around. They're built like damn bulldogs.

And there's a couple of guys have got heads of rats that are as big as dogs. Well you know my dog Pomeranian; there's rat skulls a lot bigger than that damn dog's head. He's a little dog, but you assume he'd be bigger than a rat.

And some of those other guys, they got rat tails. There's the one they got hanging up at Number 6 dock. That guy, I guess he just found the tail. It got run over by a train or something. The damn thing's almost four-foot long.

✦ Roland: The size of a rat depends on how clean the mill is. Naturally it depends on the environment they have, the quarry to eat. Like at U.S., there's just bullshit everywhere, you know. So they've got a lot of places to run, they've got a lot of food to eat. But like at Bethlehem, I hear they're really scrawny.

Bill: I've never seen any rats there. But this one guy I knew worked down by the docks at U.S., and that's where they've got a lot of 'em, 'cause they go in and off these ships. This one guy down there said the rats down there, some of 'em were as big as dachshund dogs.

Roland: Whew! That's pretty big. Is that those sausage dogs?

Bill: Yeah, those little wiener dogs. Yeah, as big as those.

Paul: My brother told me they're a lot bigger than cats, the biggest cats you can find.

✦ The only rat I ever saw at Bethlehem was a scrawny, puny rat, looked like he'd never eaten, you know. You could see the rib cage and stuff.

You always hear stories about mill rats out at U.S., about how some of these rats are as big as small dogs, you know, and you always hear about three-legged cats and stuff. One cat comes back with his leg chewed off. Or they never see the cat again, you know. And then you hear stories about dogs being let loose out there, and you never see the dog again.

✦ Roland: The rat problem is so bad at U.S. Steel that the company got this real bright idea, that they're going to bring these weird little rodents from Australia, to eat the rats. But it got all screwed up because they made it with the rats at U.S. They mated with them. And their babies, their offspring, they were—

Bill: A hardy bunch [laughter]!

Roland: They were like twice the size of regular rats. They were like the size of these rodents, plus. I guess the genes, the chromosomes in them just made them that much bigger.

Paul: How long ago did they do that?

Roland: That was like in the thirties or forties. A long time ago.

*Ferocity of Rats*

✦ There was a guy, he was bit. He had the top part of his shoe torn off by a rat, 'cause he refused to give the rat his lunch. It was Julio Santos. He was running away, it grabbed him just above the ankle, the top of the shoe, and he kept going.

Here's the thing that's odd. You go out there some nights, and you're working midnights in a dingy hole. You're supposed to shovel this pile of shit from here and move it over there, in the open-hearths. I'd be sitting there one night eating my lunch, and these damn rats, they'll walk up to you like a fucking dog and look at you like "Hey, buddy, you better give me some food or I'm going to try to bite your ass off."

✦ Johnny Gardner knew a guy out in Inland who was sleeping on the floor, and a rat came up and bit him on the lip. And like he's got a big scar. He grows a mustache, you know; he doesn't want people to see his scar.

✦ Arthur: When we used to work out at U.S. they used to have this one shanty where everybody ate. Around lunchtime, this huge, fucking rat would just sit there and look at you. And no matter what you did, you just had to give it to him.

Paul: You had to feed him or else, eh?

Arthur: Yeah, really. There's just no way about it.

Paul: I heard about that.

Arthur: One day, one guy was just sitting out eating his sandwich. And he looked over, he seen this huge rat. And the other guys looked at him and said, "You might as well give it to him. He's going to take it anyway." So he threw it to him, man. That thing grabbed it up and scampered off somewhere. He called him Vito. They had a name for him, Vito the Rat.

✦ On the bottom of our lockers we got this steel, almost like a fencing, or it almost looks like a screen. It's pretty heavy steel screen. We had a couple of them one day were eaten through, and the rats got to the food. Man, no shit. It's too low at the bottom for a guy to get up underneath there into that hole. And if you punched holes in the bottom, the thing [screen] would be bent out. But the stuff was bent up and *in*. So something came through the bottom. And it chewed up on the shoes and everything, man, really tore it up.

## The Folklore of Steel

✦ Them rats, they're really bad news out there. I remember one time down at 6 Dock we took in—we weren't supposed to—but we snuck in eighteen stray alley cats and locked them up in our shanty, where the rats would go in. Kept them all there. And this is no shit. By morning when we came back, about sixteen hours later, there was only two cats left alive, man. And they were up high.

Them rats shredded them cats to pieces. And there was some damn good-sized cats. Some of them cats were literally brought in in bags. Mean as hell, man. We just threw them in there, scratching, tearing each other up, just playing like, some big as dogs. But them rats just tore the shit out of them, tore them to pieces.

### Fear of Rats

✦ Paul: What did they do about the rats? Like at Inland, did they finally just quit trying to exterminate them? Did they just let them go, or did they have a rat clearance?

Ben: Well, there's not much you can do. You see, we used to be able to carry guns when we went out. That's 'cause people are always trying to rip off trains. They don't even bother to think what you got in there. If you got a boxcar they figure you got gold. Most of the time you got an empty boxcar, a bunch of bricks, or some shit, 'cause you're taking her to the steel mill. But they also used them guns for rats. And a lot of times they go down to Number 6 Dock, which the guys working there consider the bad areas, the foremans are allowed to carry guns, to shoot the rats with.

We went out in Plant 2, by Number 3 Open-Hearth. It'd be Number 2 Mull Yard, I think it is—mull foundry, it'd be on the west side of that. We had a bunch of scrap out at Double-E Yard out there, by the beanery. There's always rats out there by the beanery. People stopped going to the beanery, there were so damn many rats. And one day we were out there, they had cranes to move the steel; they were loading the scrap in the cars. And a craneman lifted up this big piece of scrap like a ladle, he lifted the thing up, and there must have been a thousand damn rats.

And them rats don't run any more. Some of them, damn, they'll charge a man. When you corner them, they'll charge a man. 'Cause we have had guys who have gotten bit by rats out at work. They had more balls than brains and wanted to kill the damn rat 'cause the rat scared them. And the rat turned around and tore their ass out.

✦ And one of the funny parts about that [the rats] is when I was working out at Number 6 Dock, the labor of loading steel on the barge. Everybody'd be down on the barge working. And they had these really tiny ladders that were angled in the corners, and you couldn't hardly get out of them barges.

Well, if you really wanted to shake up the Mexicans down there in the barge, you would yell, "Look out! There's a rat!" And fifteen mother-fuckers there are trying to climb the side, with their hands, teeth, whatever. Beating the shit out of each other to get to that ladder, man.

And it was surprising, man. Guys would say, "Hey, there's my brother there." You get down there stuck in a hole with a rat, man, they're not going to give a fuck who you are.

✦ There was a nurse where I worked, and I was electrician, and one night when we were out there upon a Sunday night—we used to start the mill up before the Monday morning shift—we told the nurse that if she would sit in the chair and watch out toward the oil cans, she could see these barge rats that we had been telling her about.

And so while she was sitting there, I slipped over to the electric shop and took a roll of friction tape and kind of rolled it across the concrete. From where she was sitting she couldn't see me. And I rolled it across the concrete, and it rolled up along the chair where she was sitting. And just as it got to where she was sitting, to where she could only see it out of the corner of her eye, I hollered "Rat!" And she jumped up and she wet her pants.

She never quite forgave me for that experience.

And that same thing happened to her two or three years later, except that it was a real rat that scared her. She always worked midnights. And the guys had chased a rat into the entrance: the dispensary had a double Dutch door that went into a locker room on one side and went into the safety office and nurse's station on the other side. They had chased a rat out of the locker room into the area between the nurse's station and the outside in this little alcove, and someone opened the door accidentally and it ran through the nurse's station. She jumped up, again wet her pants.

This time I was her boss. I was not an electrician now; I was plant safety supervisor. And she called me up at about two in the morning screaming over the telephone that I had to go to her house and bring her a pair of dry pants.

*Killing Rats*

To kill and torture rats became for the millworkers not so much the elimination of a pest (a near impossibility), but a form of entertainment. A college student who worked in the mills in the summers of 1969 and 1970 saw fellow-laborers throwing rats into cinder ladles, grease pits, open-hearths, acid baths, and betting on how long it would take a rat to dissolve in the acid. He reported that some workers acquired celebrity as rat stalkers, waiting thirty to forty minutes behind a stack of wood or a barrel and then pouncing on the rat. One stalker threw a stick a great distance and killed a rat pushing a bottle across the floor. Another rigged up a rat-catching device by placing bait on an electric plate filled with water and connected to two electric wires; the rat flipped three feet in the air when given a 220-volt charge. Other accounts follow.

✦ Oh, I've seen a number of times when they would catch and somehow try to torment a rat. Whether it be by fire or trap it somewhere where it couldn't get out. Try to burn it to death or throw things at it to try to kill it by stabbing it or shooting things at it, you know, maybe with an air gun shoot pieces of rock or steel or anything they could find that could actually torment the rat. Steel mill rats get rather large.

✦ Roland: Your brother Mike works in Bethlehem, you know, and he told me this story about when he used to work in the slabyard, the 80-Inch, at Bethlehem. They used to herd the rats down to one corner of the building. Then they'd have a hot slab in the crane, about five inches thick and about six, seven feet long, and they're about four, four and a half feet wide—they're really heavy too, they're solid steel. Anyway, those'd be hot, and they would herd all the rats down to one end of the building and then drop the slab on those rats.

Bill: When I worked at U.S., weekends when I was in high school, I knew a guy, Chris Williams, who ran a forklift out there, and he'd pick up these big steel plates with it. And the rats would be hiding behind them. And he put it [the forklift] a couple points forward, and he'd just drop it and smash it on these rats. And he'd pick it up, and these rats would be limping around [roars of laughter].

Mike: In the slabyard a lot of the rats would have their babies in these kettles, and I don't know why *there*. But they said they [the millworkers] used to walk over there, and they'd pour gas in these kettles and torch the rats up.

✦ Ben: One Mexican, he's about not much bigger than a rat, and he's the rat-killer. Really.

Paul: He goes around the mill killing rats?

Ben: Yeah, he's got a special thing that looks like a harpoon he got off one of the ships. We used to load steel on the ships.

Paul: They got a nickname for him or anything?

Ben: Yeah. I think he's just called—the Mexicans call him—Ratón, which means Rat. So everybody calls him Rat Fink, Rat Face, because he's like a weasel. He doesn't speak any English. He just goes around smiling all the time. And that's his job out at Number 6 Dock. He's kind of off his nut. So it's just to keep him happy.

They were going to get rid of him. But the guys say, "No, let him alone. That sucker goes out and kills a lot of rats, man." So he spends his whole shift out there. Doesn't even hardly come in for lunch; he takes it with him. He's out there sneaking around. You look and say: "That's bizarre! Look, what's that fool doing out there? He's out there chasing rats and killing rats." And he's got a lot of rats racked up.

In this moralistic tale the rat torturers, not the rat, suffer.

✦ That happened probably fifteen or twenty years ago in Inland Steel, where some men were going to kill a rat by gassing it. They trapped the rat in a pipe, and so they decided they would cover the end with a large piece of glass, and then they would fill the pipe with acetylene from a torch. So they had the end blocked just so they could put the torch in there, and began to fill it. Men were watching through the glass to see if the rat would die.

And for some reason that no one can really explain, except that there may have been some grease in the pipe and the oxygen may have been hit, but for some reason the pipe exploded. And it killed one man, and the glass shattered and severed the leg off another man. And it had long-range results, because horseplay with rats in the steel mills is very common. The guys trap them and torment them and things like that.

## CHARACTERS

Anecdotes about odd local characters blossom in American small towns and urban neighborhoods, constituting a major, though little recognized, genre of American folklore. In the mills, too, characters abound and little stories cluster about them, but they take on a different coloration. Because of the mobility and turnover of the labor force and the conditions of work in the mills, close relationships rarely develop, so cycles of anecdotal lore such as prosper in close-knit communities do not form. Rather the single vignette capturing a physical or mental trait, sometimes encapsulated in a nickname, enters the mill traditions. The older mills with the senior laborers possess the most characters. They fall into extremes: the ugly and the tidy; the wily and the dim-witted; the blasphemous and the pious; and the shadowy oddballs.

# The Folklore of Steel

*Wart Man*

✦ Bill: U.S. has most of your foreigners. Bethlehem has mostly hillbillies and [laughter] niggers and hippies, you know.

Paul: Yeah. Like Bethlehem's pretty young, you know.

Bill: Yeah. Like the average age is about twenty-seven, or something. But out at U.S. everybody's a character. You got eighty-year-old men, you know.

Roland: Did I ever tell you about Wart Man?

Bill: Wart Man? Oh, the guy with bumps on him?

Roland: Oh yeah. This guy's foul. This guy—God, this guy's bad!

Bill: He's got bumps on his head or something?

Roland: He's got 'em all over, all over his hands too, you know. He's real little, and carries these pipes on his shoulders. And he's got these bumps, man, that it looks like something Hollywood would make. They're just all over his face, and all down his neck, and all over the side of his face, and all over his hands, I guess, and all over his arms; I've seen them on his sleeves.

Bill: Do you call him Wart Man?

Roland: I heard somebody call him Wart Man.

Paul: You say people just kind of freak out if he walks by?

Roland: Yeah. When he walks by, you know. People'll be talking—like, we walk through this tunnel to get to work. You don't have to walk outside; like, you walk in this gatehouse and get in your car—you go down this tunnel. And they just repainted it, because there was so much graffiti and [laughter] shit like that, and they got tired of looking at it, so they painted it. And he walks through this tunnel. Everybody's talking, and all of a sudden he walks by and everybody just gets real quiet [whispers to indicate how crowd quiets down]; they just don't say anything when the Wart Man walks by.

Bill: Wow!

Roland: That dude is just so ugly, I feel so sorry for him.

Bill: Really? Man, the guy must have a hell of a time.

Roland: He had a brother, I heard, that went to Mayo Clinic and had some set of warts taken out. Yeah, he had some injections and all kinds of stuff.

Bill: So his brother had it too?

Roland: Yeah, but this guy won't do it. It's really weird.

*Clean Mr. Tucker*

✦ In our department we've got this guy named Mr. Tucker. And the dude runs a cog machine, the same thing I run, at the Tube Mill. And I get just *filthy* greasy. And this man could wear a white shirt out there all week, the same work shirt all week and not get it dirty. And it's really weird, 'cause everybody in the whole department has *so much respect* for this man because he is so clean [laughter]. They call him "Mr. Tucker" all the time. His name is Gene Tucker, and they call him "Mr. Tucker." "Hi, Mr. Tucker." Yeah, even the foremans have a whole lot of respect for the man because he stays so clean [laughter]. That's a hard thing.

### Mudmill Charlie

✦ Mudmill Charlie worked in the coke plant, the dirtiest, hottest, meanest job in the mills, and stayed there for fifteen years because he made good money loaning a dollar for a dollar interest. On payday the coke workers would blow their money on whiskey, or broads, or gambling and come home cleaned out. They could tell their wives they had spent twenty dollars, but not all a hundred and eighty dollars, so they had to borrow from Charlie.

He never had to ask them to pay, because he carried the biggest old .45; he would just put his hand in his pocket. There were fellows who never got caught up, because when they paid off the old debt they would be broke and have to borrow again, so there were guys who owed Charlie for fifteen years.

### Manoodle the Banker

✦ Paul: Did you ever hear anything about guys who would lend money out there, collect interest off of it?

Ben: Yeah, the bankers. There's one guy, I think his name is Manny Dominguez. We just call him Manoodle. And he's a high-time gambler too. I don't know why the hell he works at Inland Steel.

Paul: That's probably where he gets all his turkeys, out there.

Ben: Now when I go in there at night I sometimes play cards. I take in three or four dollars. I don't mind that. But I go in there, they want me to get into a card game. And this is no shit. I walked in and there was sixteen hundred dollars on the table. There's eight guys playing cards. And when these guys walk in and say, "Let's play cards," they whip out stacks of money that are about four inches deep, and they ain't all singles either.

And so one guy run out of money. And Manny took him out there, and have them be going toward the john. I seen them go in there. He goes in his locker, he opens this little box, and he hands the guy two hundred. You see this a lot. And everybody—they don't say it or prove it—but everybody's got an idea that he's the banker out there.

# The Folklore of Steel

## Hard-Luck Herbie

Herbie is the classic hard-luck, sad-sack, schlemiel folk character—the born loser. He furnishes anecdotal fare for the raconteurs, and often the two types live and work together in a symbiotic relationship.*

✦ Yeah, I think that almost every job that I ever had, there has been one or more of the famous storytellers, or the guy who can always top you; no matter what you've done, he always has a topper. Jim Ingram was probably my favorite character who was like that. Jim was from just over the Kentucky line. Oh, he could tell you stories about almost anything. He could tell you stories about some of the people in the mill.

We had a fellow that worked with Jim before I came here. His name was Herbie, and I can't remember his last name. And Jim used to tell a story about how Herbie was hired by Standard Forge because his uncle got him the job. He had been fired from the railroad—at least this was Jim's story—he was fired from the railroad because he got one hundred and twenty-five points in one day, and you were supposed to have fifty points in a year, maximum. You would get points for absenteeism, or for doing something dumb that cost the company money.

And the story Jim tells about Herbie was that it was a winter day and Herb had one of these handcars loaded with tools. And Herbie brought the handcar to a shanty closest to the place where he was supposed to work. And he left the handcar full of tools on the track and went into the shanty to start a fire in the little potbellied stove that was in the shanty so he could warm up when he had a break on the job he was repairing.

And while he was starting the fire in the potbellied stove he heard a loud noise and a big banging and crashing. And he went outside and found out a train went through and hit the handcar. It had demolished all the tools.

So he was all upset about that, and he was going about cleaning up the handcar and picking up what he could find in the way of tools and trying to make excuses, when he noticed that the shanty he had been in was burning down because he had left the door open in the potbellied stove.

## Motherfucker

✦ During a strike, one known only as Motherfucker would do two things: get drunk, and load his pistol and threaten to kill anyone who came near.

* On the very first collecting trip I ever made, in Wilton, Maine, in 1944, the local story-teller, "Slick" MacQuoid, led me to the local town character, old John Soule, and pointed out the frail little man weeding a garden, then told me two tall tales about old John's fragility. See Richard M. Dorson, "Maine Master-Narrator," *Southern Folklore Quarterly* 7 (1944): 280.

# Land of the Millrats

One day a U.S. Mail truck came through, and Motherfucker was so drunk, he shot out two tires—a federal offense. The fellows had to collect one thousand dollars to keep him out of jail.

## Fuckface Jones

✦ Ben: They take out their frustration at work. Like this one guy we got out there. His name is Fuckface Jones. The first thing he says when he sees you: "Hey, Fuckface!" So we call him "Face." He's an engineer on our railroad.

He went down to a real little town in Tennessee. This other guy named R. C., who also worked at Inland, he told me about it. He said that he's down in this little town in Tennessee, his home town. And he goes into the post office. Now the post offices are like county post offices; you know, two or three towns use the same post office. He said he's in there trying to pick up some mail. And all of a sudden somebody yells out of nowhere, "Hey, Fuckface!" And it was Fuckface Jones.

R.C. was visiting his family in another town, and he wandered in and saw Jones. And right out there in front of God and everybody, women and kids and the postmaster.

## Preacher Hughes

✦ Ben: They got this guy, he's a preacher. And he's working out there as a switchman with all these other clowns. He's really pious, man. So they call him Preacher Hughes, and he going to give us a sermon. And one day he got juiced. And so it was on New Year's Eve, and I'm out there working. And all of a sudden he blocks out all the radios, talking on the radio. And he had a revival, singing "Rock of Ages" and all this shit.

And my old man (he worked in the mill as a train engineer) and them were saying they can't use the radio to call in their moves. He's trying to break in, you can hear him faintly in the background, "Get that fucker off there!"

He won't gamble, this guy Preacher Hughes. At first they said, "Wow, this guy's really bizarre!" But then, he was really mellow. I seen him in the minutes when the spotlight wasn't on him. There wasn't anything hypocritical about him. I could tell at times he was a little peeved, because everybody's always playing cards and stuff. So he's a loner. And they harass him all the time, saying "You going to have another prayer meeting this morning, Preacher?" After that one time that he got juiced.

He had a problem with that booze. But he tried his best and he licked it. So that's where he got back on the wagon. I never heard him cuss anybody out. He's never really talked against somebody. If he would say something about somebody, he says, "Yeah, well he's kind of that way." But he never brings it up himself.

Paul: Was he a real preacher, though?

Ben: Yeah, he was a preacher. He just retired as a preacher, or a pastor, one of the two, of some church, a Baptist church. And he's a far-out guy. It's just that sometimes he seems a little too pious. But it's not phony; it's the way he is.

### Cecil the Corn Popper

✦ There's a guy his name is Cecil and he pops popcorn all the time. And we have an intercom throughout the mills: all you have to do is call up Cecil about a given time during each shift—we work shift work—and you can hear the popcorn: BING! BING! BING! BING! you know, and it transmits over a hundred and fifty stations.

### Overtime Worker

✦ At Bethlehem there was a time when there weren't a lot of people out there, so there were all these doubles [double shifts]. Like, in certain parts of the mill you can double almost every day if you want. This guy he had a camper and he lived there. He'd sleep eight hours and work his eight-hour shift and double over for eight hours. So he'd work sixteen hours a day, then go back to his camper and sleep out in the parking lot.

And they said this guy did this for something like six months, sleeping in that camper like that.

### Nicknames

Little stories behind or explanations about nicknames form a subgenre of the character anecdote. Mill society is rich in nicknaming lore, as these testimonies bear witness.

✦ The people from the south never heard of a lot of different nationalities we have. Usually any foreign element is a "Hunky." This took everyone in; where maybe some of themselves were in the category, they were calling others "Hunkies." Of course almost everyone had heard of a Polish person, and a Russian, but a lot of 'em hadn't heard of a Serbian or a Croatian or Lithuanian—well, who is this group? So almost everyone in the steel mill goes by a nickname, especially if he was on one of the jobs that you had to refer to: Big Red or John or Hillbilly or something of this name. You could more or less symbol a person by that name than you could anywhere else.

# Land of the Millrats

✦ Ben: Most of the people you meet out at the mill, you're not really friends, you're job friends. And when you leave the job you forget each other. Unless you maybe might see them out somewhere say: "Hi, hello." That's about it. You don't ever invite them over to your house, rarely. Unless you work with a guy long enough to where you're compatible. And a lot of guys out in the mill, you know them for years and never know their name.

Paul: Just know them by a kind of a nickname.

Ben: Yeah, like Fuckface Jones. Nobody remembers his first name. A lot of guys I know out at work, like Shorty—I don't think there's one out of a hundred of them damn switchmen that knows that his real name is Jorge Rodriguez.

Arthur: I know Shorty.

Ben: Yeah. Stutters: du-du-du-du-du-du-dut [makes a clapping noise] "Talk right, you motherfucker!"

But a lot of those guys, like Ron Berry out there, we jive him. His father works there. We call him Old Man Berry or Elderberry [laughter]. It really is bizarre. Whenever they call up Berry they always say, "Hey, Boisenberry," or "Strawberry," or "Beri-Beri."

And, like me, well, they call me Glassburn, the Mexicans do. But most of the guys call me like they called my old man, Juicy. Juicy Jack Glassburn. 'Cause that was when things get in a real bind and everything's all fucked up, there are about eight trains tied up . . .

Arthur: I've seen him in action, man.

Ben: . . . and cars off the rail, and everything is just all screwed up, and nobody can move them. The whole railroad is shut down in the plant. They'll tell him. He'll just say, "Well, that's just fucking juicy" [laughter].

Arthur: I seen him do that. It's great!

Ben: So they call him Juicy.

Paul: Those guys'll say that.

Ben: Yeah—"That's just juicy, you dumb motherfucker." He'll say, "That's just juicy; That was a real Mexican move," and crap like that. So they call me Juicy Junior, or they call me Jap [Glassburn is of mixed Japanese and Scottish ancestry] or Glass Ass, whatever the fuck comes to mind. Or "Hey, Glassy," stuff like that. So a lot of those guys, they don't know my fucking first name, and I've worked with them for years.

And nobody knows their name. Like this guy named Cozio, we call him Cozy. Another guy's last name is Cook, we call him Cooky. Nobody knows their first name. And we got another engineer out there named Bob Shabe. And he works with this guy named Wolinsky. Then they got this other guy, I don't know what the hell his name is, a Mexican. But they call the crew Shake, Rattle, and Roll. And it's funny as hell. But it's real. It's bizarre out there!

And, well, there's the Whale. His name is Dan Whitey. We call him Whitey the Whale, 'cause that guy is so big, man. And this Whitey the Whale makes the rest of the world look that small.

Paul: He looks like he's nine hundred pounds, eh?

Ben: Well, he's an engineer. When you see him leaning out the window, his fat by his shoulder blades hangs out in a roll. Now that's fucking fat, man [laughter]. And he ain't got no neck, either. He's a far-out dude, but he is such a fat fucker, Jesus. He can't hardly get on and off, man.

We got another guy, nobody knows, everybody's forgotten his name, but we call him Smiley. He's a little Mexican hogger, man, that looks almost like that James Coco or whatever, that's on TV. He was partially bald, he had the bushy eyebrows. We used to call him Smiley, 'cause he's got this big as hell smile all the time.

The next speaker combines an account of how he got his nickname, "Crazy Joe," with a separate story formula, "My First Day on the Job." Because of his experience as a rigger and cable splicer in the Navy, Joe easily demonstrated his skill in a comparable job his first day in the blast furnace, and thereby earned his sobriquet.

✦ Dorson: How did you become a rigger, Joe?

Joe: Well, I can tell you in a very few words. I had a nickname when I was in the mill. They called me "Crazy Joe."

Jill: Everybody has a nickname.

Joe: Yeah. "Big Mike," "Little Mike," "Toledo Slim," "Crazy Joe." I got that by climbing in the blast furnace.

When I was hired, Carl Schoonover was the manager of our shop. He told me when I interviewed that "You have to climb a rigger." He said, "Are you afraid of climbing?" I said, "Not at all; it's never bothered me." "OK," he said, "now I mean climbing high." "No," I said, "it doesn't bother me." He said, "OK."

Well, we have, I think, a six-week probationary period before I could belong to the union, and then I would be in. He said, "If in that period we see that you can handle it, well, that's OK."

My first day on the job, they sent me to the blast furnace, and we had to move a fan. I think it was not a very big fan, but we had to have a cable hitch up high so we could swing it out of the way of the furnace. There was no way to get there so I crawled up a channel iron. I think it was about twenty feet up in the air over the edge of the furnace. And I put this cable hitch on, and I crawled down.

And old Carl Schoonover came over and, to put it in his words, he kicked me "right square in the ass." And he said, "If I ever see you do that again, I'm going to personally kick you out of this mill."

And I asked him, I said, "I thought you wanted me to climb?" He said, "I didn't expect to see you doing it the first day on the job!"

And then Toledo Slim started calling me "You crazy, crazy Joe." And it stuck, too.

## TALES OF THE MILLS

These mill stories fall into the categories of personal experience narratives and repeated anecdotes. Only rarely does a given narrative prove to be apocryphal, of long antiquity and wide dispersion, like The Wheelbarrow, or do legend variants emerge, such as a Piece of the Heat, or the Demolishing of the Coke Machine. The large majority of the tales appear to rest on a factual basis.

Folklorists are beginning to accept "true" stories, personal narratives, and conversational dialogues as grist for *their* mill, on the premise that all kinds of impromptu storytelling deserve attention. The orally told tale is, after all, a prime concern of folklore scholars, so why should they decide a priori what kinds of tales the folk should tell for their consideration? Still, before opening the door too wide and calling any kind of narrative a folktale, I would impose some restrictions and ask for evidence of a corpus of oral stories. By corpus, I mean a coherent, connected body of narrations with consistent themes. The steel industry has generated such a corpus, which belongs to a larger all-embracing corpus of industrial narratives whose outlines we are just beginning to perceive.

One message that comes through clearly in these tales is the hatefulness of industrial work. This sentiment is amply documented in interviews with factory, office, and service workers published by Studs Terkel in *Working* (1974) and Barbara Garson in *All the Livelong Day: The Meaning and Demeaning of Routine Work* (1975). What Terkel reports from dozens of scattered working people, and Garson from several unlike factory systems, the present chapter intimates within the setting of one industry in one location: the revulsion of the industrial worker against the job. Terkel and Garson use the method of the direct interview; I have arrived at the same conclusion through folklore.

Why do millrats stay on jobs they loathe? A couple of sayings indicate the answer. "I am tied by the golden handcuffs" refers to the pension, profit-sharing, and insurance benefits that induce workers to remain in the mills. Many take a mill job as a temporary measure, planning to leave as soon as they amass a stake, then become too dependent on the high paycheck to make the break. "If you buy a second pair of safety shoes, you'll never leave the mill," steelworkers say ruefully. Each new laborer has to buy safety shoes; when he wears these out in his "temporary" job and purchases a second pair, his friends tell him: "See, you're never going to leave."

"I married the wrong GI."—Moroccan woman in Gary

# 3

# A SPECTRUM OF ETHNICS

Ethnicity has grown into a major academic pursuit, as one discipline after another—history, political science, sociology, anthropology, literature, folklore—attempts to determine the components of ethnic behavior and their effect on American life. Folklorists feel a special interest in ethnic populations, since they come in large part from European or Asian peasant stock. The peasantry that never took root in the United States in its formative years streamed into the republic during the post–Civil War decades.

Most early folklore studies of immigrant-ethnic groups, chiefly doctoral dissertations, concentrated on retentions in the new land of Old-World customs, beliefs, and expressive culture. A shift in emphasis dates from the 1970 dissertation of Robert Klymasz, who observed Ukrainians in western Canada and turned from preoccupation with retentions and memory culture to examination of ethnic lifestyles as they unfolded in the new setting. Klymasz smiled at the lachrymose students of immigrant folklore who bemoaned the loss of Old Country tales, songs, and festivals; he encouraged them to consider the wealth of ethnic cultural phenomena spread before their eyes. Whether or not ethnic celebrations in North America departed from Old World practices, the celebrants still called themselves Greeks or Filipinos or Mexicans. With the renaissance of ethnic pluralism in the United States in the 1960s and 1970s, signalized by the activities of civil institutes and public fetes heralding America's diverse stocks, children and grandchildren of immigrants chose ethnicity over assimilation as a goal.

In my quest for ethnic folklore in the Region, I was troubled by the lack of an organizing principle with which to appraise the field data that came my way. How did the possession, practice, and assertion of ethnic traditions serve their carriers? Should one generalize or particularize about the many discrete ethnic groups on the urban scene? Eventually I did perceive some distinctions that helped make sense out of the welter of ethnic folkstuff in the city. I separated them into the presentational, the historical, the communal, and the esoteric traditions of the ethnics and associated them, respectively, with their public, civic, social, and private selves. These categories represent a descending scale of involvement with the nonethnic world, from the geared-to-the-general-public face of the presentational traditions to the intensely private nature of the esoteric traditions.

Public performers advance the image advocated, promoted, and advertised by the ethnic bloc to the urban citizenry. This image may take the form of a monoethnic festival, or participation in a multiethnic festival. On a national scale, the American Folklife Festival, held annually in Washington, D.C., on the Mall of the Smithsonian Institution since 1968 and attracting hundreds of thousands of visitors, represents such a public display, in which ethnic and other performers are featured as musicians, singers, dancers, and craftworkers. In fashioning this public image, members of ethnic groups put their best foot forward, before a responsive audience that delights in this kind of entertainment, perhaps with embellished commentary by a presenter.

Another ethnic face emerges in public view from time to time, the historical-civic, aglow with pride but often of a militant and contentious mien, seeking not so much the approval of audiences as the backing of government and the courts. These are the embattled ethnics, whose Old Country loyalties and hostilities still dominate their emotions. When American Greeks seek congressional reprisals against Turkey, or factions of American Serbs resort to litigation over the property of the Serbian Orthodox Church, or a Latino coalition of Mexicans and Puerto Ricans lobbies within state government for bilingual, bicultural education programs, the ethnics are taking public action. But this action differs considerably from attempts to regale fellow-Americans with folksy costumes and dances. These ethnics are fighting for cherished causes and convictions bound up with historical traditions little known to other Americans.

A third face of ethnic behavior in the United States turns away from outside contacts to the confines of the group. The observance of communal rites, such as baptisms, confirmations, weddings, funerals, holy days, saint's or name days, and such special occasions falls within this category. Performances on stage in the great hall by singers, musicians, and dancers, followed by spirited traditional dancing of the audience on the ballroom floor, also belong with communal traditions. These performing bands and dance troupes frequently appear in public places or before outside patrons, clubs, or organizations, so that the public-presentational and the social-community traditions intersect.

Fourth, esoteric traditions sustain the ethnics in their daily lives. Here we enter the spheres of folk medicine, folk belief, and folk religion; of home decoration, domestic folk arts such as embroidery and egg-painting; of musical-instrument-making; of household rituals. Members of ethnic groups may share these esoteric beliefs, narratives, and customs with sympathetic outsiders, but they do not parade or exhibit them, and usually one group knows and cares little about the folk concepts of another. Mexicans realize, for example, that *susto* is a psychological ailment affecting only them and requiring antidotes known only to Mexicans. Private beliefs in the evil eye—surprisingly pervasive in the New as in the Old World—black and white magic, specters and ghouls, and creatures of the night are found in this division.

These four categories, though they crisscross in American ethnic folklife, serve different functions for their carriers and hence need to be distinguished by the folklorist. All help to reaffirm ethnic self-confidence and vitality in the midst of the mainstream culture. Presentational traditions take on the character of what the German folklorists call *folklorismus,* the exhibition of consciously staged folk music, dance, and craftsmanship for the entertainment of tourists. In Gary I learned of the extraordinary support for the Gary Junior Tamburitzan group, but it turned out that the youthful members came from mixed backgrounds, not the pure Croatian represented by the music, dance, and costume. Sweetness, gaiety, and the smiling aspects of ethnicity come to the fore in presentational traditions, which deliberately court public approval.

A darker side emerges with the historical traditions of religion, language, and past glories. These bring to the surface long-smoldering rages and enmities, folk hatreds, as it were, against Old-World neighbors or factions within the ethnic group. But they also engender pride in heroic figures and cultural distinctions of each group. In the United States ethnics struggle to accommodate their inherited historical traditions and symbolisms to those of the new fatherland, to balance a dual allegiance and patriotism.

With the communal traditions, the ethnic group expresses its inner solidarity and cohesiveness in the alien land. To see Serbians, young and old, dancing the kolo in the great hall or on the picnic grounds; or to witness a Greek island band playing in their great hall to the island's Gary society; or to observe Lithuanian language instruction in the Saturday school of their isolated inner-city church—all give a sense of the powerful reinforcement members of ethnic groups derive from their inward-looking observances.

Esoteric beliefs and practices fill yet other needs, enabling ethnic individuals to cope with fears, crises, anxieties, and dangers from evil spirits and ill-wishers, and to derive satisfaction from shared secret lore. In the face of sickness, threats, and mysterious portents, ethnics resort to inherited folk wisdom or folk magicians for succour and relief. The deepest layer of ethnic folklore underlies the belief system that regulates their universe. Yet it, too, comes to the surface as in the evil-eye amulets and the sexually potent elixir sold in Greek and Yugoslav stores. Private traditions also provide psychic comfort in knowledge of prized foods, tabooed jokes, proverbs and expressions in the mother-tongue, and similar ethnocentric matters.


## FESTIVALS

Regionites do not conceal their ethnicity. In September 1975, early in my sojourn, I visited Hammond's International Culture Festival; in July 1976 and July 1977 I attended the Gary Festival of Ethnic Music and Food. Both affairs represented broad community efforts to provide their nationalities with display cases in the way of exhibit space and performance time. I enjoyed the color and gaiety of the International Culture Festival as I wandered in the bright autumn sun among many hundreds of weekend visitors, eyeing the tables and booths set up around three sides of the James A. Howard branch of the Hammond Public Library. On the fourth side, rows of chairs faced a raised platform where ethnic musicians and dancers performed. Eastern European groups dominated: Romanians, Hungarians, Greeks, Serbians, Poles, Lithuanians, Croatians, Ukrainians—all rivaling one another in the splendor of their peasant garments and the appetizing odors of their foods. The other event, scheduled as part of the city-sponsored Gary Founders' Day celebration, was held mainly indoors, in the Marquette Park Pavilion in Miller, a scenic setting amid woodlands and sand dunes, but with only one central area on the upper floor of the two-story building for exhibits. The ethnic musical and dance presentations took place outside, and ranged from a black choral group to an Egyptian-style belly dancer.

Two points struck me about the ethnic content of the Hammond and Gary festivals and similar occasions. First, the more the ethnic groups asserted their identity, the more alike they appeared. One table or one dance troupe seemed indistinguishable from another, since all the ethnics dressed in bright costumes, displayed dolls and dishes and clothes from traditional handicrafts, prepared traditional foods, and sponsored young performers who sang folksongs and demonstrated folk dances. At one table I ate Romanian stuffed cabbage and at another Hungarian stuffed cabbage; the lady from Hungary explained that her dish was tastier because the rice was precooked. In standardizing the ethnic blocs, community sponsors hid varying degrees of ethnic consciousness, smoldering animosities between and within ethnic ranks, and differing emphases on aspects of expressive culture. The public saw homogenized packages of shiny ethnic wares.

Second, the public was misled at these festivals by marginal and fringe groups who seized the chance to gain the spotlight. At the Hammond event a militant red-power speech was broadcast over the stage microphone by a Catholic Ottawa from Canada, who denounced the establishment's shabby treatment of Native Americans. His charges of neglect and discrimination neatly outflanked the blacks, the Mexicans, and the East Europeans, whom he lumped together in the power structure. His part on the program was labeled "American Indian Folklore." But only a transient group of Native Americans taking an industrial training course passed through the Region.

At the Gary festival I encountered Filipinos, Moroccans, Ethiopians, West Indians, and Assyrians. They gave a distorted picture of Gary's ethnic composition. The Serbs, largest ethnic stock in the city, had the leanest table in 1976 and no table at all in 1977, nor did the Romanians, Hungarians, or Czechs. Two olive-skinned sisters and their eighty-two-year-old mother at the Moroccan table constituted Gary's total Moroccan population. What had brought them there? "I married the wrong GI," the elder sister chuckled. At the Assyrian booth I tentatively asked if the Assyrians shared with the Greeks the belief in the evil eye. A patriarch responded:

✦ I believe in that. Because of what I have experienced. I have seen it, and I believe that there is something in it. I can't explain it, but there must be some kind of evil radiation that damages, hurts, or even kills something. Some kind of a mental radiation, that could be a noxious poison.

One report, one example: There was some beautiful Arabic horses on display in Teheran. And one of the rich people liked one of the horses so much, he wanted to buy it for himself. He said, "Ah, what a horse!" without using the word *mashallah*. Mashallah means "May God protect you." And the second round the horse choked up and died of this radiation, this pollution. That's the truth.

And also I had a sister who had beautiful eyes, beautiful. So some Armenian lady said, "Oh boy, what beautiful eyes!" just like that, without saying mashallah. My sister had her eyes operated on twice, and almost went blind afterward.

He gave the words for evil eye in Assyrian as *ayma bishta,* literally "eye evil."

Individual ethnic groups as well as community sponsors promoted public festivals to make a splash, and the splashiest of all has come to be the Grecian Festival, a five-day-long affair in 1976. I had been warned in 1968 that the Greeks were the most clannish, secretive, and withdrawn of Gary's ethnic groups. At that time a Greek friend invited me to a downtown coffeehouse, patronized only by Greek males, whose own wives could not cross the threshold. There they sat, reading Greek-language newspapers and eating Greek pastry, insulated from the non-Greek world outside. Now eight years later the Greek community had dedicated a resplendent Hellenic Center in Merrillville. The Center housed the Saints Constantine and Helen Greek Orthodox Church, a spherical structure capped by an immense golden dome and connected to a spacious hall used for dances, bingo, and social occasions. For the well-publicized Grecian Festival the organizers used the indoor space of the hall and the outdoor space of the adjacent grounds. Visitors coming through the courtyard entrance into the archway connecting the church and the hall found themselves facing tables piled with Greek pastries, spinach pies, and honey cookies. A list advertised: Tiropita, Pantespani, Kataifi, Kourabiedes, Rice Pudding, Galatoboureko, Diples, Spanakopita, Finikia, Flogheres. Costumed matrons, who had spent the preceding week baking, explained the recipes to the curious. An adjacent anteroom housed a counter filled with Greek curios and another where one purchased tickets for food and drink. (At all such church-related activities tickets were called "donations.") A large bar beckoned in the southeast corner, alongside the entrance to the vast hall where bingo tables had been set up. On one wall a poster announced "Movie shown regularly, *A Boy Named Panagioti,* filmed in Cyprus."

Outside one beheld areas of interest. A large cleared space was reserved for the Greek dance troupe and the audience who usually participated in traditional dances as soon as the costumed performers had completed their acts. On a raised platform alongside, two youthful bands, the Apollos and the Continentals, played continuously and loudly. Actually, a

# A Spectrum of Ethnics

Greek youth informed me, these dancers were Macedonians, because the church, which received all the proceeds from the festival, would not pay the dancers, so the Greek lads refused to perform. Next to the southern end of the hall, shish kebab and other foods were being cooked and served in several large tents. A dark-haired woman behind the shish-kebab stand, whose parents had come from Crete, told me she did not believe in the evil eye—an admission I seldom heard from a Greek—but stated that if someone admired her children, she would spit "ptu-ptu-ptu" to satisfy those who shared the belief. Anyway, the priest countered its effects through baptism, so there was nothing to worry about, she added.

An open-air Taberna, planned and manned by Greek students at Indiana University Northwest, beckoned, and I recognized Lisa Koukaklis from my class preparing saganaki (similar to Welsh rarebit) on a charcoal broiler. The area next to the Taberna contained a traveling carnival, complete with Ferris wheel and shooting galleries. Each day the crowds grew in density and intensity, and I heard on that day the festival took in $24,000. One Greek youth wore a sweater with the emblem "Bouzouki power." This slogan said it well, announcing the new aggressive Greek image.

What the Greeks could do, other ethnic societies could attempt. The week of July 4, 1976, I saw on the door of a pharmacy at Ridge Road and Broadway the following posters:

2nd Annual Italian Festival
July 28 to August 1
American-Italian Benevolent Society
6220 Broadway, Merrillville
Italian food, games, rides

Macedonian Festival
Saturday and Sunday, July 17 & 18
Spanish Society picnic grounds
1500 East 49th Avenue, Gary
St. Clement American Macedonian Orthodox Church
Games – Bake Sale – Moon Walk – BBQ Lamb

Admission $1 per car    Open 12 noon

Just as community festivals encouraged displays and performances by ethnic groups, so individual strains tended to organize their own festivals, all open to the public and following a common model of ethnic foods and entertainments—a new development of ethnicity for sale.

Festivals have in the past decade begun to attract the attention of

American folklorists, who find a challenge in the diversity and abundance of such events in the United States, so at variance with the calendrical feasts in Europe. Scholars define the American festival as a popular event produced by a community and expressing its traditions. They analyze their generic features in terms of art and play forms; their structures, expressed in opening and closing ceremonies, rituals such as the crowning of queens, dramas and contests, music and food, and outside performers; and their symbolic action, in which the egalitarian, male-dominated social order is reversed, through the creation of winners and regal females. A complex research effort is needed to gather data on all these elements and activities.

In terms of our typology of ethnic folk traditions, these festivals belong in the presentational category. They are staged for the public and intended to show ethnic groups in a most favorable light and to display specialties of food, dress, crafts, music, and dance. Elements of Old-Country tradition recede, as newly forming American traditions impose their imprint and convert these affairs from inward-looking communal rituals to outward-facing fundraisers, spectacles, promotional events, and crowd-pleasers.

## STORES

Certain stores catered almost exclusively to ethnic clienteles. They functioned as repositories of artifacts and foods, as foreign ports of call, or as dispensers of magical preparations and potions. From the point of view of material culture, that is, the physical objects associated with ethnic customs and symbolism, such stores provided an inventory of the things in everyday and holiday use among specific nationalities. Only the most sizable ethnic groups—Greeks, Mexicans, Serbs—could support a novelty shop or grocery store devoted to their traditional needs.

The Acropol, a small shop south of the campus, featured dolls, jewelry, iconography, ceramics, and various objects made in Greece. Its owner, three years in the United States, greeted me affably when I explained that I had met his father-in-law in 1968. Tony, once a radio officer in the Greek merchant marine, now sold portable radios. He came from the island of Kalymnos, as did many Gary Greeks, and was president of the local Kalymnian Society.

One afternoon I shopped for traditional items, handmade if possible, inquiring about their associations and functions; under Tony's tutelage the blur of objects under the glass counter and on the shelves took on meaning. My purchases included a *levanester*, a small incense burner; a small icon of Saint Nicholas, patron saint of sailors; a colored card of youthful St. Michael stepping on a demon and prepared to plunge a sword in its back, with a policeman's prayer to St. Michael overleaf; *bom-bonieres,* favors containing candied almonds given to guests at baptisms and weddings; a *martiria* (or *martiyatiki*), a little white doily marked with a gold cross and tied with a pink or blue ribbon, given away at christenings; bewitching dolls, the most characteristic being the evzone, or palace guard, in white pleated skirt, gold-bordered red jacket, white stockings, red shoes with large blue and white pompons, and a knitted swagger cap trailing a long bushy black braid; a finger-size bouzouki and a larger one, about a foot long, with a key which when turned played a popular tune, in this case "Dirlada"; *komboloi,* the worry beads which men finger to allay stress; a tiny *filakto,* a triangular cloth piece edged with little beads worn on the body under the clothing to guard against the evil eye; and the malevolent eye itself, carved on a small round black disk attached to a brown string with four colored beads.

Tony and his wife, Nicki, let me interview them in a back office. When I asked if they objected to my admiring their two-month-old baby, for fear of the evil eye (*matiasma*), both said no, politely. Tony's expression, however, suddenly changed; he now said he did believe, because when he was a boy, his grandmother had cured him of headaches by putting drops of oil in water and saying certain words, whereupon some of the oil would disappear along with some of the headache, until both were gone. She had given him the words, and he could repeat them to cure headaches, but nothing else. He could transfer the words and the power to a woman, but not to me or any man.

One day Richard Vidutis and Richard March, members of our field team, brought the videorecorder into the shop, and we began an inventory of the objects, which Tony held up before the camera and explained in halting but determined English. An unexpected development added drama, when four men in work clothes dropped into the store, apparently their hangout. Once they understood the purpose of our operation, they became all smiles and gestures. A bespattered young house painter explained that the man by his side was his father, recently arrived from Athens, who spoke no English. An older companion, almost fierce in appearance, began waving an armful of newspapers and said they were yesterday's papers just flown in from Athens, one for each political party. I asked which he read and he said he read them all, to get all points of view. The gathering dispersed as quickly as it had materialized.

When I visited the Region in July 1977 a For Rent sign hung in front of an empty Acropol. Tony had left, as he said he would, to take a position as a radio technician in Cleveland.

A few blocks south of the Acropol another small store catered to Serbians and Macedonians, under the deceptive name of The American Trans-Atlantic Travel Corporation. The owners booked passages to Yugoslavia for their customers, to whom they also sold Serbian newspapers and records. This shop carried far fewer imported objects than the Acropol, and these chiefly foodstuffs—coffee beans, chicken soup, and canned sardines—and one treasure flown over from Yugoslavia, Muska Voda, a mineral water said to restore potency, thus the butt of many jokes.

In spite of its limited supplies, the store-cum-travel-agency attracted a steady stream of persons, who conversed in Serbian and Macedonian with Stella, a blonde Macedonian, brimming with friendliness, who had been born in Prespa. Macedonia, southernmost province of Yugoslavia, prided itself on its independent language and traditions, and Macedonians in Gary maintained a separate church from that of the Serbians—or churches, because, like the Serbs, they had split into breakaway and mother-church factions, Clement of Ohrid the breakaway and Saints Peter and Paul the mother church. Stella belonged to the latter, along with those who wished to make trips back to Yugoslavia. Stella herself returned to Macedonia three times a year. Her eyes dancing, she declared that her heart was still there; people knew how to enjoy life, and went out every evening for visits and parties and promenades.

Christopher Thompson's Religious Candle Shop caught my eye when I first wandered down Main Street in the Indiana Harbor section of East Chicago, an intimate street by comparison with Gary's spacious Broadway, almost a folk street, with small shops catering to a Latino and blue-collar clientele. In such a neighborhood one would certainly encounter *botánicas*, Latino specialty stores selling votive candles, magical preparations, fortune-telling books, good-luck charms, and assorted paraphernalia intended to avert evil forces and ensure health and happiness. This shop differed from other botánicas in one respect: its owner was black.

On my first visit in December I inspected the shelves on the left where a variety of candles, incenses, and powders were displayed, and the counters on the right containing statuettes of saints and angels, occult books, and amulets. I purchased two large glass-encased votive candles, one with a colored image of the Virgin of Guadalupe, the other captioned "Lucky Prophet," described as an "All Purpose Novena," and listing seven wishes and seven desires. On one column was inscribed "Incense is the Essence of Religion. *Pray Daily.* Write your desires here." Following a space these admonitions appeared: "Read 23rd psalm. Dress Candle daily with Lucky Prophet concentrated candle dressing incense. The Sweet Smell of Success." Seven darkish colors in successive layers added to the candle's mystique. I also bought an aerosol spray can shaped like a candle, with captions in Spanish and English reading "Money House Blessing Offering Spray." A heading above this inscription stated "Contains Genuine 9 Indian Fruit Oil." The directions, after starting with pragmatic instructions, abruptly shifted gears to "Let us pray, Make the sign of the cross. Air freshener and deodorizer. Does not have supernatural powers." My new acquisitions also included versions of John the Conqueror, the root of famed magical propensities, in a box of "Dr. Pryor's Alleged John the Conqueror Brand Incense" as well as in a bar of "High John the Conqueror Brand Oil." As samples of the occult literature I purchased a booklet professing to be a "modern grimoire" of charms, amulets, symbols, and talismans, and another billed as a policy-players' dream book. Talismans beckoned. One joined male and female figures hermaphroditically; its label, in English and Spanish, read: "Wear this One Lover Talisman to declare love for your mate. One Lover Talisman proves we are in love till the end of time . . . May God Bless us both, Amen! Note: Must be worn or carried by either male or female."

Christopher Thompson waited on me himself, subdued and ill at ease. But after my purchases, he began responding to my questions. He had come north from Jackson, Mississippi, to East Chicago and opened this store eight years ago, after God had instructed him to do so in a dream. He explained that God regularly communicated to man through dreams. Over the years he had picked up Spanish, so he could converse with his clientele. Becoming confidential, he led me into an adjoining inner room, fitted out with incense-burners, candles, and religious pictures, which he called a prayer room. "People come in all the time and pray; there's a woman out there now waiting to come in. They can leave a donation or not; it doesn't matter." And he showed me his certificate of ordination in the Miracle Temple Ministerial Fellowship and his Indiana license of ordination for Christopher's Spiritual Temple, a project he had not yet realized. Meanwhile he attended a Pentecostal Church in Hammond, where he lived.

The following spring I drove to East Chicago with Gil Cooley and Richard March to see if Reverend Thompson would let us videotape the Religious Candle Shop. He consented, after some hesitation, and talked freely for the video, explaining again how God had revealed to him in a dream the idea for the store. When asked what he knew about hoodoo, Christopher responded that he did not believe in it but that others did. He told of a Puerto Rican woman down the street who had tried to fix him, but in the end she had to sell out and he bought up her stock. The reason for his paranoia became evident when he confided that the Mexicans, Puerto Ricans, and Italians were all trying to ruin him and take over his store, because a black was running a botánica: "People trying to run me out of business right here in the Harbor."

The Supermercado, specializing in Mexican foods, dominated the corner of Main Street and Columbus Boulevard in East Chicago. Well-lighted and spacious, it created the atmosphere of a Mexican carnival, with bright piñatas dangling from the ceiling, great vases and paintings lining the walls, recorded Mexican rhythms beating on one's ears, and shelf upon shelf of canned goods and fresh vegetables flown in from Mexico or trucked in from Chicago, catering to Latin tastes, a long meat counter, a bakery, and a newspaper and magazine stand filled with Hispanic publications. On June 5, 1976, I asked its two young Mexican co-owners if we could do a videotaping. They requested my identification as the Indiana University professor I claimed to be, but all I could produce was an American Express card. Baffled, I said, "Ask me a question about American history." They stared for a moment, then burst out laughing, and one motioned toward his partner and remarked, "He knows a lot too; he has three encyclopedias." They consented to the videotaping and co-operated readily with Phil George and Richard Vidutis. When interviewed on camera, they explained their produce and meats; some of the vegetables and peppers were Puerto Rican, others strictly Mexican.

A Mexican restaurant connected to the Supermercado featured an open steam table and grill. The restaurant had recently expanded from a small snack bar in a corner of the Supermercado. As a meeting and socializing place for the Latino community, the Supermercado and its restaurant bathed its customers with sensory stimuli to delight their eyes, ears, and mouths and heighten the sense of ethnic fellowship.

What did I learn about urban folklore from the ethnic shops? For one thing, they provided rallying points and social centers in the metropolis where members of one national group could meet and gossip in their mother tongue, surrounded by the accouterments of traditional culture. In this respect they served the communal tradition in our fourfold typology of ethnic folk behavior. Also, they made available to their shoppers the magical resources of the homeland. The botánica specialized in such products, while the Acropol featured iconic talismans and baptismal gifts promising good fortune and amulets to fend off the evil eye, and the Macedonian-Serbian travel agency proudly displayed the revitalizing Muska Voda. The stores supported the esoteric traditions held in private by ethnic individuals and, at the same time, provided channels between the industrial city and the parent culture to purvey the folk and popular music, newspapers and magazines, dolls and china, and prized foods that nourished the folk roots of ethnic families.

## CHURCHES

An urban folklorist could without an invitation attend church services or church socials, and in the Region many churches retained a strong ethnic flavor. They might be national churches, such as those attended by Serbs and Macedonians, or Catholic and Protestant congregations organized around ethnic neighborhoods. Some churches in the Region enjoyed the status of institutional landmarks, for example, the Saint Sava Serbian Eastern Orthodox Church in Gary, the Mexican Virgin of Guadalupe Roman Catholic Church in the Harbor, the predominantly southern white First Baptist Church of Hammond, and the resplendent new Saints Constantine and Helen Greek Orthodox Church in Merrillville. These, the oldest or largest of their kind, had historic and symbolic associations and commanded the loyalty of major constituencies. The Saint Sava congregation spoke out stridently in favor of a North American church separate from the Yugoslav Communist-dominated mother church; its various Chetnik organizations continued to rage at the bloody specter of Communism. A sizable portion of Gary's Serbian population, however, opted for the mother church, and built a new edifice, in Merrillville, in 1976. At the ceremonies dedicating Saint Elias Church the president of Serb National Federation, up from Pittsburgh for the occasion, passionately begged for peace among the brethren. Not so with the Greek community in Gary, all happily conjoined in the umbrella national church. Separate clusters coexisted among Greek families, depending on their places of origin; contingents from Chios and Kalymnos would spar companionably, and individual organizations rented the great hall for their own dances and band performances. But regional variations melted before the authority of the church hierarchy, and young and old, Athenians, Peloponnesians, and Aegean Islanders, joined forces to ensure the success of the annual Grecian Festival.

*Saint Sava Serbian Eastern Orthodox Church*

In the middle of Gary's black inner city, an imposing structure stood like an island—albeit an island that would have liked to move. When Saint Sava Serbian Eastern Orthodox Church was erected in 1913, homes of Serbian millworkers surrounded the building. In 1975 the Serbs drove in on Sundays from the suburbs and immediately after the service returned to their great hall in Hobart to banquet and dance kolos. Report, or folklore, had it that Mayor Hatcher was preventing the church's sale to keep white property-owners downtown.*

On my first visit to Gary I had learned most about the church and its history from Jelena Branimirović, cousin of the Gary-born bishop Varnava

---

* The church burned down in 1978. In 1968 I tape-interviewed the priest, Father Peter Bankerovich, in the parish house adjoining the church; within the year he had been brutally assaulted while walking in the courtyard in his priestly vestments by a black gang who beat him senseless with a baseball bat and robbed him of two dollars and a watch. Hundreds of Gary blacks joined the Serbs at a pray-in at Saint Sava's to pray for his recovery. Father Peter survived but had to wear a plate in his head and curtail his activities.

Nastić. In 1975 I called again on this serious, dark-haired widow, devoted to a country she had never seen. Her father had come to Gary from Serbia in 1906 as a foreman on the railroad being built from Gary to Crown Point. He later found employment in the steel mills and in 1921 opened a grocery store in which Jelena worked, in the Kirkyard section of Gary, "a ghetto now." Her husband, a Chetnik fighter captured and imprisoned in Italy, had died two years before.

When I arrived at her home in Glen Park, Jelena had already spread out on the dining-room table many books, pamphlets, letters, journals, clippings—her own private archives and historical collection of the Saint Sava community. She called it the largest Serbian church in the United States, even though it had split and Saint Elias, composed of mother-church adherents, would shortly dedicate its new building. We talked from 11 A.M. to 4:30 P.M. without a break, as she poured out her knowledge of Gary and its Serbs.

In 1968 Jelena had furnished a great deal of information about Bishop Varnava Nastić. Now she added further details about Nastić, who had become a symbolic figure in the bitter fight between the two factions. The Saint Sava people had tried unceasingly to obtain his release from Yugoslavia so he could attend the church's fiftieth anniversary. Jelena showed me a letter from a State Department official alleging that Varnava had forfeited his American citizenship through his residence in Yugoslavia, but the Gary Serbs had hired a lawyer to lobby in his behalf, and they confidently believed that the Bishop would make his appearance at their jubilee ceremony. They hoped he would remain in Gary to promote Serbian culture and inspire the young people, who were leaving the church, with Serbian ideals. The church had invited dignitaries, clergymen, and the press to attend the jubilee and enjoy the presence of Varnava. But Jelena had a premonition that the event would be marred:

✦ On the night of November 11, 1964 [Friday, two days before the jubilee], while lying and looking at the stars that evening, I noticed a comet that came in from the southeast and seemed to dip into the northwest and disappear. At that moment I realized that something drastic would happen. I realized that it must be something as far as Bishop Varnava was concerned, something that was there, that was tying me to him in some way. I didn't give the information to anybody, or tell how I felt, but on Saturday, on returning from the store and entering the home, I heard my husband talking to someone on the phone. Immediately I demanded to know if he had heard what had happened to the Bishop. He wanted to know how I knew, why I thought it was about him. I said, "It can't be about anything else." So I explained what I had seen the night before.

And as things turned up, the St. Elijah Church [in East Chicago] that is aligned with the Patriarch's church in Belgrade had heard from the Patriarch's Bishop Firmilian there that Bishop Varnava had died. I tried to make contacts later with our church, our priest, but he had already gone in to pick up different visitors at the airport for the great ceremony. I finally got in touch with the monastery-keeper at Libertyville, Illinois, and informed him of the message that I had gotten about the Bishop's death.

We didn't know the full details of his death. [Jelena later became convinced he had been poisoned.] It was announced on the morning of the Great Jubilee ceremony; about three-quarters of the service had gone through when a telegram was brought to Bishop Irinej, who read it to the public. And after the announcement was made, immediately they proceeded with the memorial ceremony, a requiem more or less for the memory of Bishop Varnava. It was more like coming to a funeral than to an affair of jubilation.

What determined the decision of an individual or a church to break away (this faction was known as the Raskolniks, or Raskos) or stay with the Patriarch (these were the Federalists, or Feds), during and following the formal split in 1963? Jelena felt that the issue depended on organizations and their leaders in each Serbian community around the country. For example, several military groups of the Chetniks or freedom fighters were strong in Gary and Saint Sava and dominated the Federalists, who left Saint Sava after 1963 to form their own church. The reverse situation existed in East Chicago, where the Raskos supported Bishop Dionisije at Libertyville, who had renounced the authority of the Patriarch in Belgrade and established an American diocese. Controversy and litigation over church properties, reaching the Supreme Court, swirled around his status: should he be regarded as a defrocked priest or a legitimate ecclesiastical official? The Supreme Court is supposedly judging, explained Jelena, "whether the Serbian Church in American is to be free, to be with no connections with the Pariarch and the church in Yugoslavia" (see Epilogue).

While in the Region I formed acquaintances with members of the mother-church groups as well and found identical culture patterns. Both groups followed the American practice of placing the great hall off in a spacious field, separate from the church; both enjoyed kolo dancing, accordion concerts, and chivapchichi snacks and listened to exhortations from their priests. And they displayed equal amounts of ire in their fratricidal struggle over the physical ownership and legal status of their churches. Litigation exacerbated the schism, and atrocity tales of the other side's actions—the lewdness of Bishop Dionisije, the tortures inflicted on Bishop Nastić—fanned the flames.

123

# Land of the Millrats

## *The First Baptist Church of Hammond*

For this to be considered an ethnic church, one must accept southern whites, who compose a major part of its membership, as an ethnic group. Most of them possess common cultural traits, such as a rural background, marginal economic and educational level, strict moral code, and an affinity for guns, trailers, and junk cars. The enterprising and controversial minister of Hammond's First Baptist Church catered to these transplanted southerners as a primary constituency. When he first came to Hammond in 1959 from the largest church in Texas, I was told, a much smaller, upper-class group of parishioners attended First Baptist, but some of the congregation objected to his methods, and the local white aristocracy pulled out. No matter, for single-handedly Jack Hyles had reversed the flow from the inner city; on Sundays close to twenty thousand persons filled the block-long fortresslike building in the heart of Hammond. Few blacks or East Europeans seemed to attend, but a whole section of pews was reserved for Spanish-speaking parishioners—as I discovered when I sat there and was asked to move.

The phenomenal growth of the church and its colorful minister engendered emotional reactions, which cast Hyles in the role of both saint and devil. One mother denounced him, saying that he was turning downtown Hammond into Baptist City; that his youthful recruits, known as "soul-savers" or "soul-winners," had intimidated and seduced her daughter with gifts; and that Hyles used emotional and sexual techniques and appealed to losers: the retarded, the handicapped, the defeated. Others praised him just as warmly. A mature fifteen-year-old told me she had come to Jesus in the fifth grade, thanks to "Brother Jack," and now knew she would go to heaven. Saturday afternoons she scouted the streets with other teenagers on "soul-winning" expeditions, offering candy and gifts to youngsters her own age if they would come to church—the practice so bitterly criticized by Hammond mothers. To the charge that First Baptist was anti-black, Judy cited the Scriptural passage, alluded to by Brother Jack, stating that God had decreed three races—Caucasian, African, Oriental—which should not intermarry. When hospitalized with a sore back, Judy attributed her cure not to her doctor and the efficacy of medicine but to her minister and the power of prayer.

One Sunday I attended the service. It started promptly at 10:45 A.M., with the vast auditorium filled. The choir filed in on schedule and the service began. It was a one-man show, leavened only by a few hymns sung by the choir, soloists, and congregation. Forty-eight-year-old Hyles looked quite ordinary, with a solid build, close-cropped black hair, dark-rimmed glasses, squarish features, a gravelly voice. But the reasons for his fame and notoriety soon became evident: he wore many hats—stand-up comic, impresario, master of ceremonies, southern hell-fire preacher, promoter, organizer, administrator, salesman, businessman, taskmaster.

He began in low key, making a few jokes, but the easy manner was deceptive, for he skillfully orchestrated the whole proceeding, calculated to the moment, from 10:45 to 12:30, when another service was scheduled for young people. Hyles called up to the altar—the stage—all those in the audience wearing old-fashioned costumes in keeping with the theme of "Old-Time Religion"; meanwhile, the congregation sang with great fervor the hymn of that title. People in a great variety of Colonial costumes paraded up the steps across the stage, while the minister stood by with mike in hand making little jokes and digs—such as "George Washington in a crew-cut"—in a running patter. At one point he asked a large woman in ample skirts what she had on underneath; when she raised the skirt to reveal her petticoat, he shrieked in mock consternation and averted his gaze saying, "I asked what you were wearing; I didn't ask to see it."

Billy Renstrom, spare and shaky, was brought forward. Blinded for thirty-one years as a result of a land mine explosion in World War II, he expressed his gratitude to the Lord for the partial restoration of his sight, thanks to eye surgery, and said how beautiful Brother Hyles looked, when he saw him for the first time. Billy thanked the Sunday School for taking up a donation, to which the minister had contributed one hundred dollars, to send him and his wife on a vacation. With great emotion he sang "What Price Salvation?" a hymn written by his wife, who sat by his side.

Hyles opened the sermon by alluding with quivering voice to a news item about a young Baptist minister in Upstate New York who had been kidnaped five days earlier. He dreaded that this might become a fad, like streaking, panty raids, or highjacking, and endanger God's men. After that preamble he launched into his sermon topic: "Shoot All the Arrows," referring to the biblical story of King Josephus' failure to heed Prophet Elijah's command to shoot all the arrows at the Syrians. Hyles drew an analogy with Presidents Nixon, Ford, and Johnson, who should have listened to God's men instead of wining and dining with Communists. The last president to shoot all the arrows—give all you've got to the best of your abilities—was Teddy Roosevelt. And the present President's wife should keep her mouth shut and not give approval to her daughter's illicit affairs. His voice rising, Brother Jack declared that he would always give his best, shoot all his arrows, every time he preached, as if it might be his last sermon. Hyles whipped out his billfold, pulled from it a snapshot of his "daddy," and held it up to the audience. He cried out that every Saturday night before he went to bed he looked at that picture and thought how as a little boy of seven in east Texas he went to church— one of only two times—with his poor drunken daddy, where the minister, instead of giving his best, played a Bach cantata. Little Jack was crying and imploring him not to play that garbage, but to pray for his daddy.

Suddenly Hyles interrupted his sermon to shout at unruly youths, commanding the long-haired heathens to be quiet. (At a later service he shouted at a boy in a front row, "Son, keep your feet down there" and "Don't smile at me when I'm scolding you," and finally had an usher eject the recalcitrant youth.)

The service reached its climax when new church members who wished to receive Christ came forward and knelt at the altar steps while deacons talked to them softly. Many were children, and one little boy about four or five lay head on arms, gradually edging up the steps until a deacon lifted him down. The deacons led the converts to an inner sanctum. A few members of the congregation remained to witness the baptisms that followed in a sizable pool in the wall above the pulpit, on which a spotlight now played through the large glass frame that looked like a giant television screen. Women converts in plastic suits with bathing caps were led in from the left entrance, men and boys from the right; deacons held a cloth over their faces and dipped them backward, submerging them. Hyles sat below alone on the pulpit stage counting the cards signed by the new members and given to the deacons. He had read off the names when they came forward: all Latino or Anglo-Saxon.

During the service-performance I noticed that Hyles seemed very conscious of sound, lighting, staging. He had the sound man turn up the microphone; when not in the pulpit, he instructed his aides by walkie-talkie. Thirty loudspeakers in the church picked up his sermon, which was taped and distributed for $3.75, plus postage.

After the service I joined a guided tour. We were shown a nursery where worshipers could leave infants and young children, a room where the bride composed herself before the ceremony, and a number of chapels where special services could be and were being held. Our greeter reeled off impressive numbers: Sunday attendance ran to seventeen or eighteen thousand out of twenty-two thousand active members, with thirty-six thousand on the books. A fleet of two hundred buses brought children from a radius of sixty miles to the "Largest Sunday School in the World." The church owned nine parish buildings worth half a million dollars, operated on an annual budget of five million dollars, employed six associate pastors, and sponsored thirteen concurrent Sunday services. At the moment the church was engaged in a fundraising drive to collect two and a half million dollars for Hyles-Anderson College in Schererville, which the minister had founded with a local millionaire. Brother Jack

## A Spectrum of Ethnics

Hyles traveled 150,000 miles a year, going on the road every Monday and Tuesday, and often Wednesdays and Thursdays, addressing Baptist preachers on how to organize their churches; he was booked up a year in advance. But he never missed his Wednesday prayer service or Sunday morning and evening services in Hammond. He had a daily half-hour radio program, and his radio ministry extended to over seventy radio stations. He had written over twenty books.

A woman in the tour group asked, "When does he see his family?"

A sense of solidarity unites First Baptist in a way that may be compared with the bonds of ethnic churches. Wearing costumes and singing about "Old-Time Religion" conveyed an attachment to American roots. Brother Jack exalted the dignity of mill labor: "You want to see a great Christian; let me take you over to the steel mills in East Chicago, those steel mills and blast furnaces, where the mill laborer has worked to put you to school." He drew a sharp line between hippies, gays, lesbians, and adulterers—and his membership: "The First Baptist is one place where teenagers don't run the show." He treated the church fathers with familiarity: "I love that little runt, Paul; I'm sure he was bald-headed, because all good men are bald-headed" and "God bless that loud-mouthed, cussing guy, Peter; he's like me. God should have given him two tongues and one ear because he talks more than he listens." As he reduced the disciples and prophets to the common-man level, he upgraded the humble folk of his congregation: "Move over, Peter, Paul, Moses, Elijah—the Hankins family will have to come first."

Like Gary's black Baptist preachers (discussed in the next chapter), Hyles exerted a hypnotic influence over his congregation. But he employed a different style and content and, unlike them, he did not utilize the voice as instrument in chanting, singing, intoning, declaiming. Although he used words effectively, the voice was harsh, raspy, punctuated with coughs. Where the black preachers encouraged the congregation to make a "joyful noise" unto the Lord, to respond, shout, be happy, Brother Jack, once he had completed his delivery as stand-up comic, assumed the role of schoolmaster and cowed his followers. He stressed hard work, racial purity, sexual continence, parental authority, filial obedience, and trust in an avenging God.

### The First Spanish Christian Church of Gary

Some ethnic churches, caught between conflicting cultural-religious traditions, strive to establish a historical identity. I interviewed the pastor of the First Spanish Christian Church in a substantial building in downtown Gary purchased from a fleeing white Anglo church by the small

Puerto Rican Disciples of Christ congregation. Only about forty people attended the service, which was conducted in Spanish. The black ghetto surrounded the church, whose members had been shot at, beaten, and stabbed. The young, dapper minister, born in Puerto Rico but educated in Gary, explained his quest and that of his church for roots and a sense of tradition. "How are we going to worship? Do the candles mean anything? Does the processional mean anything? The organ music? Do we feel more at home with the rhythm instruments and the guitars?" At present, the service combined Anglo and Latin ways. The Puerto Rican church had always emphasized lively choral singing, finding choruses more adaptable than the hymns, so this element was kept. But, because some young people objected to an exclusively Spanish service, English was being introduced, along with a more relaxed atmosphere and increased lay leadership.

At the same time Reverend Luis Ferrer sought to instill knowledge about and pride in the Puerto Rican heritage. He had arranged to bring to the Region dramatic Puerto Rican musical performers, such as the gifted Instarte troupe, and artisans who made sombreros and vases and santeros (wooden figures of saints), "to give our people a contact with something of their own history and culture that's beautiful and that they can identify with. When I was growing up I liked the rice and beans, but I didn't eat it. I was trying to get Anglicized by eating the mashed potatoes and the meat and gravy. That is what I wanted my mom to learn to make, meat loaf and ham. That's changed now. People like Dr. Kanellos at the university and myself have been pounding it back into the people: 'You have something beautiful. Let's celebrate it.' "

Lacking firm historical and communal traditions, the First Spanish Christian Church of Gary was endeavoring to create them. So, too, the minister of Hammond's First Baptist Church reached back to Revolutionary personalities to associate his rootless flock with hallowed American traditions. Jelena Branimirović was creating a new martyr-hero from the Region in Bishop Nastić, while her fellow-Raskos apotheosized Draha Mihailovitch, whose picture hung in the Serbian great hall, along with Saint Sava, former King Peter, and President Ford. All ethnic churches needed the cementing force of historical legends.

In our spectrum of ethnic typology the churches fit within the historical and the communal traditions. Their services often reflect cherished rites and personalities, particularly in the cases of the national churches of the Serbs and Greeks consecrated to patron saints. On special occasions, such as the sixty-first anniversary of the Romanian Saint Demetrius Roman Catholic Church in East Chicago, held in a vast Masonic Hall, the church may sponsor a civic event; this one was replete with civil and clerical dignitaries, elaborate ethnic feasting, and a ceremonial program of speeches, songs, even comic folktales—all to celebrate the historical record of its thrifty, industrious ethnic membership. In rites de passage blessed by the churches—baptisms, confirmations, weddings, memorial services—ethnic communal traditions maintain themselves against the disruptive forces of intermarriage, the mass culture, and mobility.

## CONVERSATIONS

Much ethnic folklore circulates in ordinary conversations. These may take place in homes, cars, offices, or restaurants, with individuals, couples, families, peer groups, or mixed-age groups. The speakers may be teenagers born in the Old Country or oldsters who have never left the United States. In these discussions of diverse matters, from feast-days to haunted homes, city dwellers express strong loyalties and attachments to the country where they or their parents were born. They act on these traditional sentiments in ways surprising to the dominant culture.

### Jelena Branimirović, Serbian Widow

A lifelong Gary resident and devoted member of the Saint Sava Church and the Rasko Serbian community in the Region, Jelena Branimirović lived and breathed Serbian lore. She recited a series of ceremonial customs that maintained the essence of Serbianism in Gary and the United States. One such custom was *kumstvo,* godfathering.

✦ The kumstvo is something very dear to the Serbian people. When a couple marry, they ask a close friend if he will be the *kum.* To a Serb a kum is a title that is far greater than that of a relative, because it's connected through God. Relatives are connected through blood, but the kumstvo is very holy. Then, as children are born into the family, the kum becomes the godfather for the parents, and that's carried on from generation to generation. As the youngster grows up, if the old kum dies, and there are young men in the family, they take over the kumstvo and continue the baptism. And as the young children grow, they become the best men or the kumovi at the wedding. In the church the kum ties the knot; he takes part in the communion with the bridal couple; from the same cup that they drunk, he drinks; and he carries their candles; and he places the ring on their fingers. It's a beautiful service. And at the christening he's the main person; he holds the child. He is more or less a symbol of John the Baptist.

Jelena had just returned from her kumovi in Lafayette, where her son had acted as kum at a wedding to a godchild of his father's, who, since his father's death, had become his godchild. Her statement clarified the behavior of younger Serbs and Greeks I met who introduced their godfathers with a special pride.

A second ritual continued by American Serbs is the *slava*. Jelena stated categorically:

✦ You're not a Serb unless you have a slava. That is the stamp of Serbianism. The slava is what the Americans would call Thanksgiving. It is a beautiful ceremony which the family prepares for a year ahead. In Europe the peasant would save and prepare for a year from one slava to another to have enough. And there was much baked in the way of fancy strudels and cakes and *kolači* or cookies.

It is carried from father to son. The son inherits that particular holiday. Ours in particular is Saint Matt, Michael the archangel, which falls on November twenty-first. Each family takes that particular holiday, or the day nearest to it that they became Christians; they accept it as their slava. And on the slava you have the candle, the *koljivo,* which is wheat, cooked wheat, and it's in sugar, and it's placed on the table with spoons and water. And there is the wine and the *kolač,* which is the holy bread. And the priest comes to bless the kolač and the koljivo, and he sings a *tropan,* that is the song for the day.

Each family has its slava. If people do not know the particular slava that you celebrate, you would tell them: "Oh, my slava is coming on such and such a day; if you like you're invited." It's no written invitation; it's open house. And as far as I'm concerned it was something that my folks had brought us up with, and we accepted it and we loved it and we waited for it. My father and mother celebrated Saint Nicholas, December nineteenth, and to us it was just like having another Christmas during the year. And many of us celebrate Saint George or Saint John or Saint Nicholas or whatever holiday it is; during the year they celebrate it, it's all Lenten dishes. For Saint Michael, which is the one holiday of the year they do not have to have Lenten dishes, you have barbecued lamb, stuffed cabbage—*sarma* as we call it—strudels, the cakes. But it's important that, above all, there's a candle on the table which is lit at noon, at the time the family and the guests sit down to dinner. But the head of the house, during the whole day he makes it a point never to sit in the presence of his guests. He's supposed to see that they're taken care of and respect is paid to each guest that comes into the house.

A third Serbian occasion firmly transplanted in the Region was the *zabava,* which Jelena described as a get-together of people.

## A Spectrum of Ethnics

✦ It's a dance that we have, where plays are given by the members of the different organizations or by the church board or by the Kolo, which is the Circle of Serbian Sisters. There isn't a Sunday that a picnic isn't given or a zabava isn't given. There's ever so many organizations, and they have a certain day that's assigned to them to have their doings, their gatherings. They hold this at the church hall. We have our tamburitzas, the national instrument that is played. Of course they have some of the newer orchestras, but mainly the tamburitzas. And they dance the kolos—I don't think any dance is faster and happier than the kolo dance. It's broadcast on the different Serbian radio programs that particular day they're having these dances or plays. And sometimes they have lectures, where speakers come from different parts. And then they have their conventions in Gary and throughout the United States, the Serbs do.

The kumstvo in the Serbian church, the slava in a Serbian home, and the zabava in the Serbian great hall all contributed to the sense of a powerful ongoing Serbian presence in the Region. These rituals provided a series of widening networks that knit the increasingly scattered urban and suburban community. The immediate family and closest friend joined in the kumstvo, the extended circle of friends in the slava, the social club in the zabava. Feasts, dances, and church ceremonies welded the Serbian-Americans, save for their bitter church split, into a solid ethnic phalanx.

Outside pressures and alien peoples in the Region have strengthened Serbian solidarity. With other East Europeans, even their Old-Country rivals, the Croats, the Serbs interacted in friendly fashion, but a wholly unfamiliar group disturbed them: the blacks. The Serbs had once dominated Gary; now they had yielded the city to the blacks and fled to Glen Park, and were contemplating further moves. Jelena revealed deep bitterness as she contrasted the work ethics of the Slavs and the blacks. Even when the Slavs first immigrated to Gary, they kept their tarpaper shacks clean, worked hard, saved every penny, and made good. Jelena worked for the township trustee and had seen the welfare applications: the fewest came from the Serbs, Croatians, Polish, and Slovaks; the most from blacks and southern drifters. The Slavs were the ones who had suffered, yet the blacks and the Jews received the attention and pity. What was the black's heritage? (Jelena posed this as a rhetorical question.) But the Serbs owned a proud heritage; her son could trace his father's back six hundred years.

Jelena's conversational themes match the typology of ethnic folk categories outlined. The Serbian customs she observes at home and the festive and ceremonial occasions she attends in the great hall represent the communal traditions of her people. The dream omen presaging the death of Bishop Nastić stems from her store of esoteric traditions. The black menace that is driving the Serbs from Gary joins a long sequence of historical traditions involving an insidious foe: in Europe the Turks, Communists, Croatians, Ustashi (Nazi puppets in Yugoslavia), and now in the United States the blacks—shiftless, welfare-abusing, traditionless, in contrast to the industrious, thrifty, tradition-proud Serbs.

### Greek-American Students

They fit no immigrant stereotype I had ever heard of, these poised young students. They possessed the political instinct, and several held positions in the student senate. The women's poetic names matched their appearances: Jasmine Antonakis, Effie Emmanuelidis, Lisa Koukaklis. A newcomer to America, Jim Hasapis, alone lacked fluency in English. These students promoted the Greek cause through social organizations, the university, and the church, the resplendent new Saints Constantine and Helen, with its adjacent hall, in Merrillville. Unlike other national groups, the youthful generation of American Greeks took the initiative in maintaining ethnic tradition. Born in Greece, they had come to the United States to complete their schooling, were at home in both cultures, and fit into an existing Greek blue-collar population in the Region where they could assume leadership because of their advanced education. Lisa, born in Piraeus in 1957, had come to Gary in 1971; her father ran a gas station. Jasmine, born in Athens in 1956, left for Gary in 1968; her father worked for U.S. Steel. Jim had left Athens only twenty months before. Effie, born on the island of Samos, the home of Pythagoras, came to Gary the same time as Jasmine. All four had blood ties in the Aegean Islands, the Peloponnesus, and Asia Minor.

At the outset Lisa affirmed her commitment to upholding her heritage.

✦ I didn't want to let down my Greek tradition. I wanted to continue it. And I wanted to show, really, the Greek people around here how our tradition is. So that's why I started a Greek radio program: Hellenic Discotheque. It's on Saturdays at 3:30. We announce Greek advertisements for the Greek companies around here; they can be American too. But we also have Greek music, latest songs from Greece that we put on. And I have a Greek band: bouzouki player, guitars, accordion, drummer player, seven altogether. [She admitted that in Gary she had learned Greek traditions, such as folk dances, which she had not known before.] To tell you the truth, I didn't know my culture back there really. The only thing I knew was language. I didn't know how to dance the *hasapiko*.

Dorson: What is the hasapiko?

Lisa: Usually they have three guys, and they wear red belts, black pants, white shirts. So they get in line and then perform their own steps. But they do the same step together.

Jasmine: Actually, it was only for guys. I mean, about four years ago you wouldn't see a girl dance the hasapiko. That's a no-no, you know. But now, women's lib, I guess, everybody is doing it.

Jasmine went on to say that its translated name was "The Butcher's Dance," indicating its rowdy aspect, and that "guys who think they are rough and tough would dance the hasapiko," to impress the girls with their virility.

*Evil Eye.* Greek traditions brought to mind *mati,* the evil eye. Every Greek-American with whom I raised the matter spoke knowledgeably, usually from personal experience, about this tenacious Greek belief, and so did these young students.

✦ Jasmine: It's a superstition, if you want to call it that. But as long as religion, our Orthodox faith, goes along with it, says that it's true, I guess it is. And there's a person who knows, how would you say, to exorcise the evil eye away from the person that thinks they got it. And the symptoms actually are, you feel tired, that kind of thing.

Lisa: Headache.

Jasmine: Yes, headache. They say people with blue eyes or green eyes are the ones that put that on a person.

Lisa: Watch it. I got green eyes.

Jasmine: Well, that's what they say. I don't know if that's true. But it happened to me a couple of times. I didn't know I had it, but my mother, who knows how to exorcise—how to get this out of you or away from you—she knew. There is a little saying that you're supposed to say. It was written by a saint, I believe Saint Spyridon. And that's supposed to get this evil eye away from you.

Lisa: Right. I had an experience with that. I guess somebody looked at me, I guess they looked at me a lot. So when I went home I had a big headache. My aunt didn't know what was wrong with me; it wasn't a cold I had or anything. So when she said that saying to me from Saint Spyridon, right away I started laughing and the headache was gone.

Jasmine: Actually it's something mystical almost.

Lisa: It's something inside of me that got out. I was only nine years old. So right away I started laughing and I started playing around with my little cousin. The headache was gone and everything was right.

Jasmine: Yes, it happened to me a lot of times. Over there and over here.

Lisa: It can happen anywhere.

Jasmine: My mother, really she believes very strongly in this thing. And one thing, though, is she can't reveal the saying to me. It has to go from a guy, from a male to a female. It has to alternate. Because if she comes up to me and she says: "OK, I'll tell you the saying," it's like losing power. It has to go from a man to a woman, from male to female, you know. So maybe I could have my dad learn it and he teach me, you know. Because I believe it. I'm not a superstitious person, but when it comes to that I believe it, because like I said, it happened to me a lot of times.

Lisa: You can actually see it working.

Jasmine: Yes, or feel it maybe.

Lisa: Feel it more, okay.

Jasmine: You feel like something is going away from you.

Dorson: Well, the person who does it, does he mean to do it?

Jasmine: No, you don't have to hate the person's guts, you must understand. It can be done just by "Oh jeez, he's cute," or something like that.

Lisa: Somebody that admires you can do it too.

Jasmine: If it's not a physical sickness, then that has to be it. I think it's more of a psychological thing, but I believe it, I just do.

Lisa: I do too.

Jim: I believe it because many times it happened to me. I got the headache, and I tell my mother or sister. They help me. I feel something come out of me, you know.

Effie [who had just joined the group]: Well, it's a superstition. Like you have here, when you go under a ladder, you have a superstition that something bad is going to happen. The same thing. When somebody looks at you, says "Oh boy, she's beautiful," you know. Or, "She's got nice legs" or nice something. Usually something happens to you—you can trip and break a leg.

Lisa: Don't you feel moody and you have a headache?

Effie: That too.

Jasmine: But you know what, the only person who could have that effect on you is a person who is bad at heart. Who means harm to you. A good person who is going to say "Boy, she's nice, good-looking," stuff like that, with good feelings in his heart, does not mean you any harm, and usually nothing happens to you. But if it's a person with bad feelings who hates you, who can't stand you for one reason or another, he has a bad effect on you. He will say something admiringly while inside of him he feels something different from what he says.

This exchange illustrates the passage of the mati belief down to the younger generation. Recognized by the national church, mati bridges formal religion and folk belief, and incidents of daily life confirm the reality of the phenomenon.

## A Spectrum of Ethnics

*The Turks.* Family trees and island ways supplied a pleasurable topic among Greek Americans in Gary. They bantered about the merits of one island people versus another and agreed on the superiority of islanders over mainlanders. But this mood changed when the name of the island that aroused their deepest passion entered the conversation—Cyprus— and its invasion by their ancient enemy, the Turks. The group of students shared bitter personal recollections and horror tales of the invasion, which they saw as a prelude to Turkish conquest of all Greek islands.

✦ Effie: The Turks invaded Cyprus because from the beginning Cyprus has both Greeks and Turks on it, and three-fourths were Greeks. So the Turks claim that they were discriminated against by the Greeks, and that they were, you know, misused. So, with this American aid that President Ford and Kissinger are giving them now, what they are actually doing is giving them more ammunition to kill, rape children, mothers, grandparents, people from every age. The Americans are telling the Turks, "There's more ammunition, go ahead and kill."

Lisa: Turks have tried to get our islands.

Effie: Yes, they've been trying to get our islands. I am from Samos. If you look at the Greek map, Samos, Chios, and Rhodes—not Ikaria—are the islands closest to Turkey. From my town to go across to Turkey, it's five minutes. You can see the lights at night.

Jasmine: Clear. Same as my grandmother's island, Chios. Her village is one of the megalopolises of the island; it's like the second capital, a very big village, and when you go to the coast swimming and the weather's clear, you can see across what's going on, and you can hear the roosters in the morning. I mean it's so close.

Lisa: So now the Turks want to take over our islands. They say they belong to them.

Effie: What they did, one beautiful morning, July 20, 1974, they decided to have a war. So they invaded Cyprus, they invaded the Greek towns.

The students went on to recall their situations and emotions on the day of the attack. When the news "Turks invaded Cyprus" flashed in Gary, residents began calling relatives in Athens, who knew nothing of the invasion because the Greek government, not wishing to alarm the people, had withheld the news. Lisa, who learned of the war while in a village in Crete, rode to town on a truck with men from eighteen to sixty who were turning in their names for an immediate draft; they drove through streets filled with weeping women.

Jasmine declared that the American public knew nothing about the realities of the conflict. She cited a professor who asked why Greeks hate

Turks. Jasmine replied, "Well, it's history. We were brought up not to hate them, but they were our enemies, you know." When the professor said he sympathized with the Turks because they were better warriors, she blew up.

+ Jasmine: And I said, "How'd you figure that out? Why are they better warriors? Because they had the American ammunition and they went in, they raped mothers in front of their children's eyes: fifteen-sixteen-year-old girls in front of their mothers and fathers!" They will rape the daughter, and they had the father and the brothers' hands tied on trees so they couldn't do anything. And they raped their sisters and their mothers in front of them. In Cyprus the Turks went into villages and they got all the young girls and they raped them in front of their parents.
   Jim: The Turkish is a barbarian race.
   Effie: They are barbarians.
   Jim: They are uncivilized people, you know, without education.
   [The students criticized the American army and navy for not assisting the Cypriot Greeks, after Papadopoulos had given the Sixth Fleet access to almost all the harbors in Greece. When the United States cut off aid to the Turks, they charged, it was only because of the efforts of Greek Americans.]
   Jasmine: That's because we had put pressure on them. The Greek Americans put pressure on President Ford and the Congress and we cut the aid. But now we've [she switches the "we" from Greeks to Americans] started again. And during the Second World War, Turkey had never taken part in any of the war. First World War, Korean War, Second World War, nothing; they were neutral. But we [Greeks] have been invaded by everybody. I mean our whole country is in ruins. Turks have never been invaded. And Ford or Kissinger, I don't know which one, he says: "Well, Turks have always been good allies to us." How have they been allies to them? You tell me. They have not participated in any war. Nothing. And some people can't understand why we feel so much, why we were so emotional about the whole thing.
   Like I was saying, this prof of mine, he told me the Turks were good warriors. How do you figure that? And I was emotional; I was actually shaking. He said: "Well, you're not rational now because you're emotional. You're very involved in this thing and you can't say things like that." And I say: "I know what I'm saying. I know what I've lived through and I know what's going on. And you don't. The Turks are trying to get in Greece. They want to get our islands. Look what they did in England in the Turkish Embassy; they had made a map and they had put the Greek islands that I mentioned earlier—Chios, Samos, and Rhodes—on their map. And they were stating that it was Turkish territory!"

## A Spectrum of Ethnics

Well, the same prof again, he says: "How can you say your heritage is from Germany or Italy, or wherever? You're American now." Well, I am American. But I'm Greek too. That's how I came to the world, from Greece. Because I was born there I can't say "I'm American." I came here when I was thirteen years old, and I went to school here. They're both part of me. I love both countries.

The picture of ethnicity that emerges from this conversation shows another facet of America's cultural pluralism. These young people, nineteen and twenty, are completely bicultural. Their Greek traditions belong not to memory culture but to continuing experience, for they return regularly to their homeland. Education is their immediate goal, unlike that of all the waves of newcomers conscripted for the mills and other Region industries, and education gives them a conscious motive to assert their ethnic inheritance. They display a surprising concern about lineage and origin. They thoroughly accept the mati, the evil eye. Their animated dialogue about the Cyprus question, a critical pressure point in their Greek consciousness, substantiates the idea that crises give rise to folklore: the Cyprus issue has produced horror stories of Turkish atrocities, in a pattern recurrent throughout the ages, that attributes to the enemy the most diabolical deeds. Already the personal recollections of the call to arms against the Turkish bully are jelling into an ethnic legend, meaningless to outsiders. Jasmine's professor cannot begin to understand the intensity of her feelings about the Turks, and she must endeavor from her own experience and knowledge to convey to him the savagery of these marauding, raping "barbarians"—harking back twenty-five hundred years to the time when the world was divided into Greeks and barbarians.

In this transcript we can identify the several forms of ethnic folk tradition previously typed. In the mati belief we see the esoteric tradition; in the island folkways, the communal tradition; in the antagonism to the Turks, the historical tradition. All three traditions play an active role. Youths succumb to the evil eye and resort to knowledgeable mothers and sisters and aunts for ritual remedies. Island loyalties continue in Gary as clubs and concerts and networks based on the Aegean homeland and are reflected in sayings such as "I'm from Kalymnos, don't talk to me." Turkophobia finds an outlet in political pressures to sway public opinion and compel the federal government to side with the Greeks against the Turks in the Cyprus conflict. Although not a part of this conversation, the presentational tradition also appealed to the Greek students who managed the open-air taberna at the Grecian Festival. Despite their years, these young Greeks participated actively in all four forms of ethnic folk behavior.

# Land of the Millrats

*Nicolás Kanellos, Puerto Rican Playmaker*

A young teacher of Spanish at Indiana University Northwest told me about the Latino theatrical group he organized. Nick Kanellos, just turned thirty, round-faced and curly-haired, spends much of his time managing, directing, and acting in El Teatro Desengaño del Pueblo, roughly translatable as the People's Enlightenment Theater. I saw performances of this troupe in Gary in the college auditorium and on an open-air stage in an East Chicago park. Once I watched them march into the college cafeteria singing *corridos* and *decimas* with infectious rhythms and with foot-stamping good spirits. Save for a few cavorting youngsters, the company seemed like a casual group of Latin-American students; on stage they resembled, on an amateur level, an improvisational group such as The Committee in San Francisco or Second City in Chicago.

Nick, born in New York City of a Greek father and Puerto Rican mother, had identified with his mother's culture, spending every summer in Puerto Rico. While doing graduate work at the University of Texas he became involved with Teatro Chicano, one of sixty such groups around the United States. On coming to Gary, he founded a like company. "We are a bilingual theater group, made up of students, community people, children, engaged in discussing issues of interest, mostly to the Latino community but also to the general community, in a dramatic format and, too, in a cultural format. As we develop ideas, we look at things from our own experiences, from our own background, and we use some of the traditional media that have always been used. There has been a long tradition of theater in Latino communities, but this specific socially engaged and politically engaged theater mostly developed after Luis Valdez used his Teatro Campesino [Farm Workers' Theater] to promote the lettuce boycott in 1965."

How did one theatrical group relate to another? Nick explained that five or six regions of the United States with heavy Latin populations held an annual festival, and the promoters kept in touch with each other via a communications network, a publication, and many vehicles through which they worked jointly on arts and politics. Theater had always been used by Latin troupes to convey messages and represent commitments to their community, Nick stated. In earlier times theater had presented religious messages; now this people's theater had shifted to political concerns. In some of his research Nick himself had traced the development of this type of political theater from more traditional forms.

"We do use a lot of folklore. We don't go and study folklore, but what we do, we get songs from people and we use or adapt them. And we have

9. *Escuela* (School) performed by the Teatro Desengaño del Pueblo.

10. Milan and Mel of the Drina Band fill a request at Jennie's.

11. Greek dolls and worry beads for sale at the Acropol.

12. Teatro Desengaño actors as Mr. Big Business and Mr. Inflation.

13. Piñatas decorate the Supermercado in East Chicago.

children in the groups, and we use children's culture as part of our message. And they do tongue-twisters and all that kind of stuff within a dramatic format. We use folktales that we hear from different people who are members of the community. And it's really not separate from the university here. Just because I am on the faculty and some of the members are students, we are not, as in many other universities, cut off. It's an overflowing, overlapping. There's a oneness that's going on. That's how come you can have such an activity here at the university, and, on the other hand, various activities that students have are held in the community. So we know parents and we engage with parents and people who have this kind of knowledge in our daily lives."

Nick named some individuals in the group with gifted parents who could recite tales and *bombas* (witty rhymes uttered at parties) which the Teatro incorporated into its skits. Mexicans and Puerto Ricans contributed to the theatricals, whose primary intent was to give these two ethnic groups, and other Spanish-speaking minorities, a sense of unity.

Who writes the scripts? I wanted to know. Nick responded: "We don't really write any scripts. Oh, once in a while we write 'em down. The way we work on things is that we improvise our material together collectively most of the time. Of course there are leaders in creating the stuff, but once we work it out—these skits can last up to half an hour and take many, many lines—once we work it out it stays pretty much the same and we remember our lines.

What proportion of Spanish and English did a given skit contain? "It depends completely on the audience. Do they speak English, Spanish, or both? Another factor is: What is the situation that's being shown? Is it a domestic scene? If it is, it will be most likely in Spanish. Is it a scene in some kind of institution—in a hospital or school or something like that? If it's in one of these institutions, it's going to be in English 'cause that's the language that's spoken in institutions. Unless the persons, the character, doesn't know any English. Everything else is the same as it usually is, and then the skit'll be bilingual, which'll make it appeal to everyone. Some skits are always performed in Spanish and others are always in English, but two or three of a general nature can be in either, and we have to carry both the English and the Spanish scripts in our heads."

Reflecting, Nick corrected his statement that the actors memorized their lines rigidly, noting that audiences sometimes contributed impromptu lines or bits of business that the troupe liked and incorporated into the skit. "Oh, I'll tell you one, an interesting case like that where the audience participated. We do this tale called 'La Avispas.' It's a tale about a wasp—the insect, you know, not white Anglo-Saxon Protestants. This is one I brought from Texas, from our old group that had developed it down there. César Chávez told the tale, so we decided to dramatize it."

## Land of the Millrats

✦ *La Avispas.* What the tale is about is, these two compadres were walking along together, and one says to the other one: "I don't believe in organization. I don't believe in the union. People who go around organizing, they're just doing it out of selfishness or something like that." The other says: "No, you're wrong, because, you see, organization's the only way the poor people can get together." And the guy who believes in organization, he's been messing around with this whip, and he says "Crack." And so, "Hey! What's that?" He tells him it's a whip and he's been cracking the whip ever since he was a kid. And that around these parts no one can be in the way. The other says, "Oh yeah, well let's see about it."

And so they start taking target practice with the whip. And the guy, first he hits a branch off a tree, and then he hits a rock, a stone in the distance, etcetera, etcetera. And then out comes a series of animals. Out comes, say, a rattlesnake, and he whips the chi-chi-chi, the rattle, off of the rattlesnake. And in comes a dog, and he whips the dog's tail. Out comes a fly, and he whips one of the wings off the fly. He's really good, you know. And finally, out comes a wasp buzzing around, "bzzzzzz." And one compadre says to the other one: "Well, here comes another one. How 'bout the wasp? Let's get the wasp." And the guy says: "Oh, no, no, no. I don't mess around with wasps." And the other guy says: "Well, why not?" "Well, because the wasps are organized, and I'm not going to have anything to do with them."

They argue about, and finally the guy calls him a chicken, and the other guy says: "Okay, okay, I'll do it. Just so you don't call me chicken or yellow, anything like that." And he cracks the whip and he gets the wasp. The wasp collapses. And all of a sudden out comes a swarm of wasps and they attack the two men. And they pick up the hurt wasp and they take him out.

So the two compadres get up, all wounded. They say: "They're right. In unity there is strength." The other guy goes off the stage hitting him for having gotten him in such a predicament. And of course the message is: In unity there is strength. Okay, what happened with the audience was that we used to make an announcement in between one of the times when he cracks the whip, saying that if anyone in the audience is hurt it's not our fault, we're not responsible. And we said: "Be careful to put your head down when we crack in every direction." We were using an imaginary whip, you know. So one time we were doing this and all of a sudden somebody in the audience yelled out "ayyy!" as if they had gotten hit. We incorporated that into the skit. We'd plant someone in the audience. Things like that happen all the time.

*Juan Bobo.* Folklore themes provided the basis for several playlets and served to unite Puerto Ricans, Mexicans, and other Latinos, who shared the same stock of trickster and animal tales and supernatural legends.

## A Spectrum of Ethnics

✦ For instance, we've used in the past a character named Juan Bobo. There's a lot of stories about him in Puerto Rico. He's the kind of guy that many times the people think he's kinda dumb. But often he wins out in the end. So we shaped his story, and we have him approached by a drug pusher, who tries building him up from pills to grass to heroin, and so on. So Juan doesn't know what's actually going on. But in the end he switches the tables on the pusher and actually gets rid of him, pushes him out of the way, and prevails over him.

✦ *La Llorona.* And we've used La Llorona [the well-known Mexican legend of the spectral woman in white weeping for her lost children]. We used to do a thing where she would come onstage by herself; her face would be lit up brightly with candles. Everything else was dark. She'd be dressed in white because most people know her around here as the lady dressed in white. And she comes on crying that she's lost her children.

And we make it relevant saying that she's lost the children because they're being devoured by the steel mills. And the industry is, you know, grinding up her children, with the gears and the wheels and the ovens and all its machinery. The message there is that the reason she is crying is that her children are disappearing, and so therefore her culture is disappearing too.

✦ *Compay Tigre and Compay Conejo.* Then we took this Puerto Rican tale about Compay Tigre and Compay Conejo, the tiger and the rabbit. And this tale tells about how the rabbit always takes advantage of the tiger, see. He always fools him. So Compay Conejo was in the woods by himself and saw that Compay Tigre was coming. So he tied himself to a tree. And the tiger approached and said: "Ah, ha! I've got you at last!" And Compay Conejo says to him: "Oh, no, you don't. 'Cause if you don't watch out you're going to be blown away pretty fast, 'cause a hurricane is coming." And Compay Tigre says: "Well now, you're trying to fool me again." And Compay Conejo says: "Oh, no, it's the truth." And he convinces him. He says: "You're going to be blown away and I'm not, because I'm tied to this tree." And Compay Tigre starts begging Compay Conejo to please help him get tied to a tree, too. So Compay Conejo finally begrudgingly unties himself, and he goes and he ties Compay Tigre to a tree. Wraps him up very tightly, and he picks up a big stick and starts whopping the heck out of him.

So we dramatized this but we changed the characters to make it apropos to when Nixon was in trouble. The hurricane was the winds, and the winds were blowing impeachment, impeachment, impeachment; and we changed the message around so that at the end Nixon got tied to the tree.

141

*Bilingual Ed.* Some of the playlets originated in the minds of the director and his associates as they planned story lines to deliver a social message. Nick explained that this was the case with one drama I had seen. "That was a typical thing that we do. We were dealing with the community issue about bilingual education [English and Spanish], and the Gary and East Chicago schools have cut back on it. So there are community-action groups that are trying to get it reinstated and increased. What we do is, we dramatize community issues and bring the message to the people as much as possible, so that they can become sensitized. We worked up our skit particularly for that issue, to inform the people that bilingual education is a right, that Congress has protected the rights to bilingual education, the right to equal education—all this kind of stuff. So all that was included in the skit, and it was through that kind of means we think that we can get the information out to people who do not get this news through the other media. Bilingual education includes teaching in English and Spanish and other languages which the area demands and necessitates."

✦ We put it in the form of a little story. We have three people out there: a superintendent of schools, a politician, and a racist. What happens is that out comes Uncle Sam. And then out comes a parent from the community. And so Uncle Sam actually speaks all the languages that are spoken in the United States. And Spanish is one of them. So he speaks to this guy in Spanish, and he tells him there's a problem here, and he gives the parent a few hints—about liberty and justice and freedom and all that. And Uncle Sam gives him examples: "If you're out looking for a job we have plenty of jobs. If you're looking for education . . ." And the parent says: "Ah, education, that's what I've been worrying about. My children have been dumped from the bilingual education program." Uncle Sam says: "Oh, don't you know that bilingual education is a right? That my Congress in 1968 passed a law establishing bilingual programs?" And so that parent is finding out all about this stuff.

Then out comes the superintendent of schools and throws a cloth over Uncle Sam, covers him up, pushes him to the back, and starts giving the parent some other spiel that he should learn English: "You need English. You need English to eat. You need English to sleep. You need English to—everything, everything." And a play on words: "You need English to ssshhh—shout it out." Then Uncle Sam comes back and chases the superintendent away, telling him about the Supreme Court decisions, and so on and so on.

And out comes a woman who is demonstrating against busing. And she doesn't want her children speaking Spanish or learning Spanish, or doesn't want them going to school with Spanish-speaking kids, and doesn't want Spanish to be taught in the schools. And so out comes Uncle Sam, and this time he's speaking with a black dialect, and tells her: "Well, there's one law of the land, and it's good for everyone," and he'll see her in Boston.

"And finally out comes the politician saying, "Vote for me, I'll give you this and this and this." And the citizen has found out enough now. He confronts the politician saying, "Didn't you promise me bilingual ed?" The citizen says: "I don't want to hear from you any more," and "I'm going to stand up for my rights." He has become converted, he's gotten so knowledgeable. And they both go off singing.

The Teatro performed this skit, and would keep performing it as long as the bill to restore bilingual education was pending. They adapted skits to Vietnam, when that was an issue. Mayors provided another target, and one skit illustrated how Mayors Hatcher of Gary and Pastrick of East Chicago coopted the Latino leadership by offering jobs and positions to buy off the leaders so that they no longer were responsible to the community.

*El Frijol and la Habichuela.* One of the most popular playlets deals with differences between the Mexicans and the Puerto Ricans and ways to resolve them. Nick Kanellos himself conceived the basic idea and assigned two players to work on it, each of whom contributed lines. The final product, first staged in 1971, immediately became the favorite piece in the repertoire. "Our theater group is known by that skit, and people ask for it when we perform."

✦ In English it's going to translate as "The Bean and the Bean." See, there are two different words for beans: Puerto Ricans say *habichuela;* Mexicans say *frijol.* One of the commonest things in the community is that Puerto Ricans identify with food and Mexicans identify with food. But one identifies with the habichuela, the other with the frijol. So what we actually said in the introduction was: Once upon a time there was a great plate that was known as the Midwest. For some reason or other come from the south a Mexican bean, although we say frijol. We don't have to say Mexican because everybody knows, because of Spanish. And from the other side of the plate comes the habichuela. And sometimes this makes a delicious meal, and other times there's such a stomachache that comes out, it's horrible.

And so then comes on stage a bean from each direction and they basically interact by calling each other the names that the community has, the ethnic slurs that the Mexicans and Puerto Ricans have developed for each other. Like, *"Qué habichuela más fea tan aplastada y mojada,"* the frijol says to the habichuela, "What an ugly bean you are, all mashed up and all wet." That uses two things, see: Mexicans eat their beans mashed and watered down; and the word watered, *mojada,* means wetback. And the Mexican bean says: "I'm not an habichuela; I'm a frijol and 100 percent pure Mexican." "Mexican, huh!" says the Puerto Rican bean, "That's why there's such a stink here!" The frijol says: "Stink! That's my chili. And that's how I sting." See, chili has three meanings: hot pepper, Mexican hot sauce, and the male sex organ. So the habichuela answers: "Well, I'm a Puerto Rican bean, and I'm even tastier with my sauce." *Salsa,* the word for sauce, also means the Puerto Rican dance music. There are several levels of meaning, and we have a macho Mexican playing the frijol and a beautiful Puerto Rican girl playing the habichuela.

They go on like that. The habichuela says: "Mexican, why you look like an Indian!" And so he counters by saying "You look black," making references to African influence in Puerto Ricans. She says: "Well, that's true, but I carry my heritage with pride." Well, anyway, they keep swapping each other, and finally what brings them together is a fork descending from above. And one says to the other, "Ayyy! *el tenedor*" (Here comes the fork), and they huddle together facing the fork. And the other one says: "That's right, the fork doesn't discriminate, it can't tell us apart." And the first one says, "That's right; we're equal, we're the same." And they go off together, trying to evade the fork's aim. "We're the same, we're the same."

✦ *Identity.* There's one that's called "Identity." It deals with the definition of Chicano and what that is. It's sort of like an allegory. There are allegorical figures in it, but it's not an allegory. A young man is given either a school form that he has to fill in about who he is, or he's given an employment application. And it says: "Are you Black, Native American, Oriental, Anglo-American, other?" And the guy says: "Other? I can't be Other. I don't see myself here." Then he goes through this whole bit where spirits or ghosts appear to him. The spirit of the Aztec past appears to him and tells him that the blood of Chicano ran through his veins, and the indigenous civilization. And she tells him: "You're Indian. Write down Indian." He says: "Indian, huh? Sounds pretty good, but I thought there was something else."

And all of a sudden comes out a Flamenco dancer, Spanish dancer. And she tells him about Cortes and Pizarro and all this kind of stuff. So she convinces him that he's Spanish. And he's going to write down Spanish. Then he says: "But there must be something else."

So out comes the Frito Bandito. That's me. You've seen that character who sells Fritos Corn Chips on TV? It's an insulting character who is a takeoff on the Mexican bandito. He was originally a revolutionary from the Mexican Revolution, and he had to come to this country to find some kind of job. So he got this job on TV. But he was ashamed of what he was doing, and he decided to fight for the ideals. And he goes off singing the corrido "Adelita," which is the corrido that is associated with Pancho Villa's forces. (We show the American background too. We used to have Nixon come out. The guys do a fantastic impersonation of Nixon.)

And, finally, out comes a modern-day Chicano, who gets disgusted with the fellow. "You mean to say you've been sitting here all this time trying to figure out who you are? You don't know who you are? Do you think that César Chávez spends all night trying to figure out who he is? Do you think Jorge Gonzales and Reies Tijerina try to figure out who they are?"* "You mean they don't?" "No, no. If you play it right, you can be the best of all that's down there. You can take something from each one and make it into a fantastic package." And the guy says: "Oh, what's that?" He says: "Chi-ca-no, Chicano." And the fellow says: "Chicano. I knew there was something out there."

So the modern-day Chicano goes off, and in comes the secretary and asks if he's finished filling out the paper. And the guy says: "Yes, I have it. Here it is." And just as he's about to walk out, she says: "Hey, wait a minute. What's this Chicano business?" And he says: "Well, you may not know what it is now, but you're going to be hearing a lot about it." And she turns away and says: "What ever happened to Other?"

Having made his point about the proud multiple heritage to which the Chicano could lay claim, Nick went on to mention other themes playing on the nationalist sentiments of Latino peoples. "We have demonstrated the history of how Mexico lost its five daughters: New Mexico, Arizona, Colorado, California, and Texas. Which is a historical bit where Papa Mexico comes out, and he had these five lovely daughters, and they all had different charms. One has snow-capped mountains, another one has silver mines. And, let's see, we have done things on how Puerto Rico became a colony of the United States. And we do things on the lettuce boycott, spreading the word about not to buy lettuce."

The synopses of these performances raised a number of questions in my mind about their composition and staging. The repertoire included some thirty plays, continuously taught by Nick to newcomers joining the fluid group. Much rehearsal time was spent developing new material based on contemporary issues and events. The group consisted of fifteen

---

* Nick explained later that Jorge Gonzales was an ex-bowling champion from Denver, author of a well-known epic poem, and celebrated as the organizer of the Chicano School and College; and that Reies López Tijerina agitated in New Mexico to recover land grants there that properly belonged to Chicanos.

to twenty people from Gary and East Chicago, between the ages of five and forty, of whom only four were IUN students. Three families who contributed substantially to the Teatro were the Meléndezes, a Puerto Rican husband and Mexican wife, the Puerto Rican Rentas, and the Mexican Gutiérrezes. Occasional non-Latinos, including Nick's wife, joined the company, which was open to all comers, without auditions.

Suppose they did not have dramatic ability? "No one does," responded Nick, laughing. He himself lacked any dramatic training and learned from other members in the Texas Teatro. "I had always played the guitar, ever since I was a kid, and we used to sing at home and do bombas. So that's how I got into the theater group in Texas, playing the guitar and developing into acting and so forth." New recruits picked up the acting and singing techniques through emulation of and instruction by older members. Because family and school duties interfered with rehearsal and performance schedules, the Teatro alternated between two and even three groups that knew the same skit.

Although the organization had no formal relations with the university, as a faculty member Nick could reserve the auditorium, and occasionally the station wagon. Indiana University Northwest supported and encouraged the troupe in other ways, for example, inviting it to perform on Red Carpet Day, when high-school students visited the campus. The Teatro played before Latino societies and teachers' conferences in Gary and East Chicago 80 percent of the time, but the troupe also journeyed to universities in Illinois, Wisconsin, Michigan, and Oklahoma and had participated in festivals in Detroit, Chicago, Texas, and Mexico City. They did not charge for local appearances; fees for long-distance engagements financed trips to festivals. On occasion the troupe sang corridos and decimas in lieu of enacting dramas. Christmas was an especially busy season.

If a genre had been deliberately constructed to suit the urban folklore model, one could not have fit the bill more effectively than the Teatro desengaño del pueblo. This group derived from a city ethnic folk; it concentrated on immediate social concerns and pressure points, in particular the problem of maintaining ethnic identity; and it employed a traditional Hispanic folk form, the informal dramatic sketch. The actors lacked professional training and came directly from the community, often as family units. They carried the scripts in their heads, enacted their roles with a joyous abandon shared by the audience, and drew story lines from familiar folktales and stereotyped characters. The singing of traditional songs accompanied stage plays, which assumed the character of communal festive events with a minimum of distance between actors and audience. In depicting scenes such as the embarrassment of the Latino child in an English-speaking classroom, the Teatro struck at the most sensitive nerve of the Spanish-speaking population, the rejection of their language and culture; and in playing up the threat of Mexican and Puerto Rican nationalism, the Teatro raised the most ominous specter the Latinos could visit on the majority culture. Performing in park bandstands, clubrooms, and school auditoriums, trooping through cafeterias and parks singing their presence, the Teatro blended into the city scene and added a touch of gaiety and high purpose to the folkways of the metropolis.

In the case of the Teatro Desengaño del Pueblo, the public-presentational and civil-historical traditions merge. Singing actors offer amusing fare to their audiences, as do more polished ethnic performers at festivals and in the great halls, but here the mission and the message embrace social action. The troupe seeks to arouse a Latin-American constituency to the possibility of pressuring the state legislature to protect its Hispanic language and culture. Their vehicle that transmits the message itself constitutes an element of Latin culture: the theater of social protest.

### Juan Gomez, Mexican Urban Man

Juan Gomez, the oldest student in my Gary class, had lived a full and varied life. He was born in San Antonio, Texas, on Easter Sunday, April 4, 1931. Two weeks later his father died, from a fall while washing windows on a high-story building; his mother died when he was three. Juan was the youngest of thirteen children, only five of whom survive. He lived with a sister and brother-in-law, who kept him hard at work making wool cinches for horses. "And I used to see all the kids around me playing, but here I was helping him." Summers Juan went north with his brother-in-law to Saginaw, Michigan, to pick sugar beets and tomatoes and berries. Families gathered in churches and were hauled in little pickup trucks to the beet fields.

On one trip north his brother-in-law stopped in Crown Point, Indiana, to pick asparagus and there heard that the railroads were hiring in Gary for eight dollars per day. So he moved his family, Juan with them, to Gary. In 1940, at the age of nine, Juan attended school for the first time. After graduating from Froebel High School, "the melting pot of many people," he began a series of jobs: clean-up boy in a restaurant; part-time clerk in a grocery store; factory worker at Gary Screw and Bolt Works; paint shop employee steaming wallpaper off and painting walls. In 1964 he was appointed Gary's first bailiff of Mexican descent, but eight years later the City Court judge abruptly fired him for having filed to run for councilman-at-large. When I met him he held the position of building inspector for Gary. For several years he wrote a column for the *Latin Times,* published in East Chicago, about Latino affairs.

Juan, who resided in the Brunswick section of west Gary, spoke of the "horrifying change" and "tremendous catastrophe" that had overwhelmed this once-elegant neighborhood, 80 percent white and 20 percent Latin, now nearly 90 percent black. Urban renewal and desegregation of schools were to blame. One could not go to the store at night or leave the house alone, and Juan always carried a gun. The browns were caught in the middle between the blacks and the whites.

Earlier pictures among Juan's clippings showed him as a smiling, oval-faced young man with a slight mustache. Now he had a black bushy beard and sideburns, smiled infrequently, and appeared careworn. Earnest in manner, he proved to be more informant than collector and revealed a fund of anecdotes and traditions.

One personal-experience narrative dealt with an incident that befell Juan in his line of duty as bailiff in 1964.

✦ *A Bailiff's Story.* What happened was that this particular Saturday morning I was given what they call a reference. They asked me if I would go and pick up this refrigerator, this air conditioner, and a stove. I said all right, that I needed the money. (They paid ten dollars.) So the lawyer called the furniture man, and he sends a truck out there for me. I knew Hammond and Whiting and East Chicago. I knew all the bad areas, so to speak, and I noticed this was the southern Hammond area and predominantly Polish. I thought, "Well, I really don't feel worried." I didn't carry a gun; I didn't want to at this time.

When I got there they opened the door, and here's this older couple, about fifty, fifty-five years old. They opened the door and I presented the papers, and I kinda felt sorry as I always have for people. But they told me one thing when I took the job, "Do not feel sorry for people because you'll lose your job the very next day." So I learned to be hard, so to speak. And they asked me, "Would you give us one more chance and talk to the lawyer?" I said, "Sure, sure, why not?"

As I was talking on the phone to the lawyer, the people, who were, I would say, friendly to begin with when they let me in, but as I turned around, here, holy heaven, they come from the kitchen; the man had a shotgun, the wife had a butcher knife! And I says, "Holy cow!" The telephone was in the little corridor they had, so I just backed away, and away I ran, and the truck driver right behind me. I went to the corner drugstore and I called for help, I called the Hammond policemen; two came over and asked what the problem was. I told them, "Hey, those people are trying to kill me in there." I told him that I was a Gary bailiff. He says, "From now on you know better, you better carry something."

So we went in there, all four of us, and we got the refrigerator and the air conditioner and whatnot. But I'll never forget that. This was a very memorable experience.

## A Spectrum of Ethnics

*Ojo.* Juan married Stella, from Hidalgo, Texas, whom he met in Gary and courted for a year without ever going on a date, according to the edict of her mother, who set a *plazo,* or waiting period, of one year. Their wedding day, June 1, 1956, turned out to be the Golden Jubilee of Gary: "The place was a madhouse. They had the biggest parade they ever had." The Gomezes had four children, all of whom fell victim to *ojo,* the evil eye. Juan explained ojo as follows.

+ Juan: This comes about with a tendency in a woman or a man, especially a woman, has a certain temptation for a cute baby, to touch the baby, but for some reason or other she doesn't. Then the baby begins to feel it; she begins to get fever, and she begins to cry—she just begins to get very crabby. This comes from an old belief: we figured "Well, she has ojo," or "he has ojo." So you break your egg. Then you take a little palm leaf and put it underneath the baby, hoping that she will sleep. She generally does. Then you put some oil on her, some type of little baby oil. And then generally by morning, if the baby has what they call ojo, that egg will be baked. Just like a hardboiled egg. The white will be thick and the yolk will be a ball, just a hard ball, as though it had been cooked in boiled water.

Stella: You take an egg out of the refrigerator, leave it sit out until it gets to room temperature. Then you go over the baby in crosses [making the sign of the cross] with the egg, all over his body, and all the time you're praying Our Father and the Holy Ghost, the [Apostles'] Creed. If you're Catholic, you're supposed to pray the Creed. After you go over the baby with the egg, sort of like a sweep—that's what we call it, "sweep the baby with an egg," you get a bowl of water ready, and you crack the egg after you've swept the baby and put the egg in the water. Then you put a little cross of four-leaf palm underneath the baby's bed, or in his crib. By morning the egg is cooked and it's shaped like an eye.

I'm not a strong believer of that, 'cause I think "Wow! You know anybody can get sick over something." But all the kids have had it, and especially my older daughter. She was always coming sick every time we went by my sister—when my sister touched her. And as long as the person's got the power themselves, they say that if the egg doesn't do the trick, the one with the ojo has to go back to that person, so that person can pray over them, touch 'em, and it'll be over. And from there on, whenever my sister used to come over to us or we used to go over to her, we always told her, "Touch the baby or she's gonna get sick."

Juan: I watched my sister-in-law a couple of times and she has a tremendous eye for that. I know she's gotten our babies sick, all five of them, at one time or another. She just has that power. It's nothing really bad; it's just something persons with that power can't help. It's within their temptations, within their feelings, and there's nothing nobody can do about it. Thank goodness, we haven't had that since the baby was about six months, a year and a half ago. The ojo such as my sister-in-law has works mainly on infants. After the child has grown into maybe three or four years old, the ojo so to speak can't do anything any more, I guess simply because the baby or the child is able to wear off that concentration. Whereas the infant has no power, it's subdued by the concentration of that other individual.

Stella: She [her sister] usually does that because she's tempted to touch the baby, and if she doesn't touch him the ojo comes. One time she had a lady friend, and she liked a lamp the lady had. The lady had other people there. And my sister was tempted to tell her she liked the lamp [but didn't because of the other people]. She told her husband: "If I don't touch the lamp, the lamp is going to break." He says: "Oh, you're just kidding." She says: "No, it will." She was ashamed to go across and just say that she liked the lamp, so she just let it go. And that lamp cracked.

They say when a person does that kind of thing to a baby, its head gets to hurting and it gets a fever and it's very crabby and you wonder what has happened. There's nothing wrong, there's no pin that could be hurting him or her. But you remember that there was a certain woman at somebody's house, she must have done the ojo to the baby. So you think about what your mother or father or sisters told you, about sweeping the baby with an egg, and that's what you do.

*Susto.* Stella Gomez also knew how the folk sickness the Mexicans called *susto* should be treated.

✦ Susto is something like when somebody gives you a surprise, touch you by surprise, and you're shocked. They say that you can feel it after three weeks, you can really know if you have the susto. You feel right in the top of your stomach like it was hollow. If you let it go, it can kill you. None of my kids had it except Gilbert, junior. A friend of his got killed by a train. They were real, real close friends, and Gilbert was *asustado* when it killed him. Juan's nephew's mother-in-law was the one who cured him, because I don't believe that strongly in it, and it wouldn't be that good if I was to cure him. Different people do that different ways. So this lady cured him by him laying down—it can be on the floor or on the bed—and she sweeps the person in crosses all over their joints. She prays three "Our Fathers," three "Hail Marys," and one Creed. Over and over again. This lady does it different from others. She asked me for an alumstone jar, and she done it with that. Some other people, they just grab herbs or some kind of weed outside, and then they just sweep them over, and they pray over them, and then the sick person is supposed to drink some tea.

## A Spectrum of Ethnics

And after she finishes sweeping the person, she gives him the tea, and he is supposed to sleep, go to bed, and he'll sweat. Even if he's only got a sheet on him, he'll sweat; if he's got the susto, he'll sweat. And that has to be done on Tuesdays and Thursdays.

When we came over here [from Texas to Gary] we didn't know any Mexican people, and it was hard to cure the ojo and the susto.

*A Cry for Help.* In addition to encounters with ojo and susto, Juan had undergone psychic experiences of his own involving death portents and revenants. These he related with seriousness and in detail.

✦ There was an event about 1960 which I can recall—there's no reason for me to say that I really solved it—and my wife also. We had about the same experience that night. We heard a knock. It must have been about one-thirty, two, in the morning, and of course at that time in our area we used to leave our windows wide open. We had no reason to be in any fear, our community was very peaceful in comparison to now. It was an autumn night. And we heard this terrific knocking on the door, like somebody was trying to come in. My wife and I had the front room. I turned around, looked out the window through the screen, and—nothing. As I turned around again, I heard it in the back, where our two kids had the back bedroom, and I run to the back porch—at that time we had a sunporch; we used to leave the door open—through the kitchen: nothing there. I mean it was loud! Well, I put the light on, every light in the room, and looked around, and—nothing. Jumped back into bed. My wife had gotten up by that time, too. Must have been in bed maybe five minutes when we heard a tremendous knocking again, just like a real hard knocking, by a human being.

By this time I was kinda worried. "Oh what is it, somebody playing a joke?" So we both got up, and we both went in opposite directions, and—nothing. I'd got up for the third time. We sort of tried to get ourselves together, you know: "You go your way and I'll go that way in case it does happen." And it did happen. Just as I got to the door, that knock did come for another time and disappeared. I know there was no chance in the world, as I came to the door, for anybody to disappear. There was just no chance. I mean there was moonlight, clear, and that particular night I could have seen anyone who had come at the front door at that time. There was no way that somebody could get out of my vision if they was there. Up until the time I can't explain it.

Now we sat down and I told my wife, I says: "There's something about to happen." And something did happen. Stella says: "We'll just have to wait and see till tomorrow."

Sure enough, the next morning my sister-in-law came in and told us,

151

she says: "My boy has just got killed." Her husband was with her, Mr. Trini Gonzalez, who was Freddy's stepfather. He says, "He just got killed; he just had an accident out there in Schererville. He got killed there last night." Freddy's cousin Danny Mora, who was not wearing a safety belt, went right through the windshield and had to crawl half a mile to this farmhouse. To this day he's one of the best karate experts that there is. But he says: "I'll never forget that. If I had been wearing a safety belt, or if I had been on either side, I wouldn't be here either, because Jo-Jo [a third boy in the car], his arm was torn completely off, his ears were off, he died instantly, with Freddy who had a broken neck."

Right after the accident there was a cry of help. And at the time these kids were very new to this area, and they really only knew me. Freddy was a very close friend. I was best man for his wedding. As a matter of fact, that same night they invited me to go with them, and I turned it down. I didn't go with them. I was sitting on the porch and they asked me to go with them and I said "No." So after the accident Danny says they were calling for help.

*The House Plagued with Spirits.* At the close of the 1975 fall semester Juan came to my motel to turn in his class collection and report a supernatural phenomenon he had witnessed exactly one week before. It concerned the house of his niece, in which he had once lived, where strange noises and incidents were agitating the family. They had sent for two priests and a woman spiritualist to bless the house and drive out the spirits. Juan believed that enemies had used witchcraft against his niece, who was seeing a married man. The family planned to move.

*The Shrine of the Virgin of Guadalupe.* Although Juan Gomez had been born and raised in the United States, the strength of his Mexican folk heritage can be seen in this account of his visit to the shrine of the Virgin of Guadalupe, the central symbol in Mexican life.

✦ Back in 1969 I took my family to Mexico City. I had never been to Mexico. And I think that one of the greatest experiences that an individual could have is to visit the Cathedral of Guadalupe. It's very ancient, but it really signifies the great beliefs of the Mexican people. When I got to Mexico City I never dreamed that a man could get so sick as I did. I got so sick from diarrhea that I thought that I had not an ounce of energy left. We stayed there three days, and it was our third day and we were ready to move on, but we had to visit the Virgin of Guadalupe. In doing so we hired a chauffeur to take us to the Cathedral, which was not too far from where we were staying.

When we got there, as always there's hundreds of people there. There is an altar that's on the mountain there that's a self-made mountain, where people go up. This is the place where the said soul, the Indian Juan Diego, saw the Virgin [in 1531]. And it's quite high. I would say, in comparison to buildings it's about five stories at least. And as I looked up, I was very, very weak. And I told my wife and kids, I says: "I won't ever make it. There's no way I could make it up there." I says: "You people go on."

I stood at the bottom and I prayed. And it's hard for other individuals to believe this, because you can only feel the weakness yourself. But as I prayed there was something within that gave me strength. And before I knew it, I was more than halfway up the altar. And I just kept praying; and without knowing it, I was up there. And when I got up there, I never dreamed I could make it.

Belief in the power of prayer, the response of the saints, the reality of spirits, the magic of witchcraft, all enter into Juan's universe. Living in the heart of Gary he encounters haunted houses, hears cries of the dying from a distance, and is alert to the machination of witches.

*The Devil and the Drunk.* The foregoing affairs affected Juan and his family. At further remove he narrated a "true" event involving his wife's grandfather and the devil. He had heard about it through the following chain of transmission: his wife's grandfather told the tale as an incident befalling himself to "my wife's grandmother, who relayed it to my mother-in-law, and she relayed it to my wife, and my wife told it to me."

✦ She told about a father that used to drink so much. And he had to come down that certain road every night. So he was very drunk that one night, and he was coming down that one road where he had to cross a little bridge. And as he was approaching the bridge he saw this tall individual all blacked up. And he says: "My God, I gotta pass it." And he notices that when he says "My God," that that one little shadow grew kinda big and would sort of jerk.

He said, "Well, what the heck, I got no choice, I gotta pass it." So, as he kept approaching closer and closer, that so-called individual called him. He says: "Hey, amigo," he says, "come here, come here. Let's have one drink for the road. Come here, come here."

So this grandfather of my wife's says: "No, no, I got enough, I gotta go home." The black individual says: "Oh, come on, just one, just one." So he thinks: "Well, I gotta get by him anyway," and he came close to this individual. He finally got up to him, and he had a real good sniff of sulphur, and he says: "My God!" And when he said "My God," that individual rolls his face and he could see the eyes, and they were like charcoal burners, and he says again: "Oh, my God!"

The other says: "You see, my friend, I told you to have my drink, now don't cuss at me, don't cuss at me!'' So the drunk—we'll call him the drunk—he realized that he was in a little bit of trouble here. He realized that he was talking to the Devil. So he says: "Well, I'll just have one, just have one with you." And the Devil says: "OK." So the drunk had that one with him, and he said: "Thank heaven, I can go now." The Devil says: "Now wait a minute, I told you not to cuss at me."

By this time the drunk wasn't drunk any more; he was pretty sober. So he looked up in the eyes of this charcoal devil, and he says: "Oh my God, I gotta get outta here." And away he went.

Believe me, he got straightened out, and he never, never crossed that bridge again. As a matter of fact, he was sober for many, many a moon. Many, many a moon. And my wife told me, she said: "My grandfather he never drunk any more, so far as we know." She said: "That straightened him out!"

Juan pinpointed the bridge as right across the border between McAllen, Texas, and Reynosa, Mexico. Although he reported this account of his wife's grandfather as a true experience, it is a well-known international tale, Type 817, "Devil Leaves at Mention of God's Name" (Motif G303.16.8), recorded in Europe, Great Britain, and North America.

"These were original Spanish tales told to me, and of course I'm translating them to you. But my belief is that they do have a moral, that I have heard other older people tell them and I had quite a bit of luck in talking to older people. They used to take a liking to me and I would sit down and hear their stories. As a matter of fact I had a couple of girlfriends when I was younger, and I would tell the stories to these kids and my girlfriend would call: 'Hey don't tell my brother that, he can't sleep tonight.' So I was telling them the stories I would hear maybe a week or a month before that, and they were kinda chilly, but I don't remember them all. They were pretty good stories about ghosts and witches and lloronas and whatnot."

*A Cuento: The Gold Dust.* Juan related all the foregoing narratives as true happenings that had befallen him or members of his or his wife's families. Save for that concerned with his role as bailiff, all contained psychic and supernatural elements that formed part of his ethnic folk belief system. On one occasion, however, he recited a *cuento,* a story he had heard thirty-two years before, when he was twelve, told in Spanish by his brother-in-law, who was from Mexico and "had more tales than you can shake a stick at." Though fictional, the cuento contained a belief element that continued to have meaning for Juan.

✦ This pertains to two godfathers. One of them had a little boy, and the three of them were walking through the old ruins of a little village. And they got tired of walking, so one of the godfathers said: "Hey, look, I'm gonna go down here and see what we can find in these old ruins." In the meantime, the little boy kept playing up on the hills. The two godfathers went down into the ruins and this one said: "You know, my wife is so ill. I just can't get her out of mind, I gotta kneel down and pray here." So he kneeled down to a wall which was more than partly knocked down, and he kept praying real hard. He kept praying that he needed money for medication. Every time he prayed he would bow and hit the floor, which was still concrete there, and he just kept going at it. This other godfather said: "Well, why are you babbling so hard?"

And the first godfather turned around and he says: "Well, maybe the good Lord will hear me, maybe the good Lord will hear me." He prays that way at least fifteen to twenty minutes, and then he raised up his arms and he says: "Oh good Lord, please help me." And as he raised up his arms, sure enough the walls just open up and here comes a gash o' gold, just gold dust coming down from the wall. He says: "Look! Look what I got!" He called Manuel. Manuel says: "Well, I'll be darned." The first one says: "The good Lord has helped me, the good Lord has helped me." So he picked up the gold dust in a little bag.

And the other godfather said: "Well, my God, I need some help too." So he brung himself over to the make-believe altar there and he started praying. All the time he was praying he had this particular greedy insights of himself. And he kept praying for about twenty-five minutes or so, and then finally he hit the floor. And he opens his arms and he closes his eyes. He says: "You gotta close your eyes and pray with your heart." So, sure enough, he closes his eyes, opens his arms, and holy hick! here comes a whole dish of manure where the little boy has just been urinating and taking a crap behind the wall there.

And the other godfather says: "Well, you see what happened there? You didn't pray with your heart." So that was the moral, that you gotta pray with your heart. It's very brief but it does have a moral, that people should believe in what they ask.*

Beyond question Juan believed in the tale's moral, the power of sincere prayer, for he had earlier revealed that "the biggest and the greatest decision" he ever had to make in his life hinged on his prayer to Saint Jude whether or not to permit surgery on his little daughter.

✦ *A Prayer to Saint Jude.* Our girl Paula was only five or six years old and she was very sick. She had a tumor. She had no pain, but she was developing a stomach, a little tummy like a pregnant woman. We were supposed to have lost her back ten years ago. So 1965 up till now I pray every

---

* In response to my query about "gash," Juan said it was his translation of *chorro,* which he also translated as "waterfall," of gold and of shit. Another translation is jet or stream.

morning. I went through three years of hell. I mean complete hell with the consciousness that we would lose our baby, our girl. We can really say it was a miracle, because three doctors have said there was no hope. But with the exception of one doctor, who said: "As long as there's life there's hope." We just didn't know what to do, so our family doctor said that we'd better take her in to the hospital, and we had all types of X-rays made. When they did open her up they took this cancerous tumor, about as big as a little watermelon, in one ovary. They said they had got everything there, but they weren't sure about the other ovary. I had six months to either let them open her up and see if it was stable, or leave it as it was.

I believe a lot in Saint Jude. So I prayed to Saint Jude to let me know, and he made up my mind that I was going to let them find out. They opened her up, and took out the other ovary and took her appendix out. [And Juan pointed to a picture of a pretty teenager, and said that was Paula and that she had just gone to a prom in the party dress shown in the picture.]

*A Joke: The Holy Pole.* As so often happens in folk tradition, the occult-supernatural strain coexists comfortably with the comic-obscene. Juan Gomez reeled off some bawdy jokes right after relating the account of the house in Gary haunted by the husband's first wife. He said he had heard them from other kids in Gary when he was about ten, and he obviously still relishes sharing them with boon companions during coffee breaks or over drinks at the bar.

✦ This particular girl, one day she decided to go to confession. And she says: "I'm gonna go make my confession, and I had enough of this." So she says: "I know I done wrong." She was supposed to have been a virgin, you know. She says: "I can't keep it with me any more. I gotta let it out, tell Father."

So she went and she says: "Father," she says, "I committed a great sin." And she happened to be the last parishioner. The priest says: "Well, since you're the last one, why don't you come back? You seem like you're very upset." She says: "I am, Father, I am." So, "Well come back over here into my lobby, and you can tell it to me face to face." So she says "OK."

So they went back there, and he closed the doors. And he says: "What is it, my dear?"

She says: "Well, Father, I—I don't know how to start to tell you this," she says, "but, but this boy did something to me." And then the priest says: "Well, what did he do? What did he do that makes you feel so bad?" She says: "Well, he—ah—he took my dress off." He says: "Oh my goodness! My goodness! How did he do it, like this?"

## A Spectrum of Ethnics

So the Father took the dress off [ha ha], and he says: "Yeah, and what else did he do?" She says: "Well, pretty soon he took my slip off." And he says: "Like this?" She says: "Yes. Oh, Father," she says, "it made me feel so bad."

He says: "What else did he do?" She says: "Well, pretty soon he took my panties off." He says: "Oh, my goodness. Like this?" She says: "Yes." She says: "Father, Father, you know what else he did?" And he says: "No, tell me."

She says: "Well, he got on top of me." He says: "Well, I'll be darned. Like this?" So the Father [ha ha ha] got on top of her. She says: "Oh, Father, Father! What are you doing?" He says: "My dear girl, I want you to do something for all of us." She says: "What is that, Father?"

He says: "Remember this. The holy book's beneath you. The holy pole is in your hole. So wiggle your ass to save your soul!"

Anticlerical jests turning on the licentiousness of the clergy have a long history. Often the devout and pious recite them.

*The San Antonio Enchilada.* Prized above all foods in Juan's Mexican-American heritage was the "San Antonio enchilada," a dish dear to his heart and stomach. He had come to enjoy it because of his brother-in-law, who raised the orphaned Juan, and cooked enchiladas, after the family moved to Gary, the way he had in San Antonio.

✦ We grind the corn in a Mexican *molino* [mill] and make a *masa* [dough] out of it, and out of that masa we make a tortilla, which is very well known to Mexicans and to everybody else now. Then we would take the thick red peppers and boil it and take the juice out of it, and put the juice with the dough, the masa. And then when you boil it into the blending machine, the masa would be already red. When we would make our tortilla, the red would already be an ingredient in it, and then of course the tortilla would be red.

Then when we make the enchilada, we would take and put it in either margarine or oil, and make it just flexible. But, before we did this, we had already made our rich hamburger gravy, we cut our onion to perfection in very small pieces, made lettuce, made what we call enchilada cheese—which is very hard to find, but some Mexican stores have it—and with potatoes. Well, we would take the tortilla out, put it on a plate, put the cheese in the middle with onions, roll it up, put the hamburger gravy on top, with melted cheese, lettuce, and tomatoes. And that's what you call the "San Antonio enchilada," which you will not find nowhere in northern or eastern or possibly even southwest California. You'll find it in Texas—Houston, San Antonio, Austin. Every time I go back, when I get there I'm pretty hungry, I go to a restaurant, order me a long drink,

Texas-style with a cork, and I order me maybe about nine enchiladas. And they come out just the way I want 'em, with the hamburger gravy on top, melted cheese and all the trimmings.

We ordered enchiladas in Mexico City, and it was the worst meal we ever had. Here again they dump the tortilla in the chili bowl and it would come out like—I don't know, no words to express it—just a buncha mess. And then they would put the lettuce and the cheese in it, and when you eat it you would have all that chili dripping all over you. So that was no good.

Juan spoke fondly of other Mexican dishes: tamales, always served during the Christmas holidays; tacos both hard and soft; *fideo,* a noodle served with tomatoes and onions; *raspa,* a snow-cone, which as a boy he sold in Gary; *chicharrón* or bacon chip; *fritos,* the refried tortilla made into chips. But none sent him into euphoria as did the San Antonio enchilada.

Juan's store of Mexican beliefs and narratives reveals the private, esoteric side of ethnic folklore. Although he led a fairly public life, seeking office, writing a column, his energies had not gone into activist or militant ethnicity. He was a true believer in the occult traditions of his inheritance, and they governed his personal outlook and behavior. His intermittent college education had not weakened his credence in ojo and lloronas and spirits of the dead, which provided him with explanations and redress for certain of life's mysteries and threats. Juan also drew psychic support from communal traditions; he relished the San Antonio enchilada and guffawed at the offcolor tales circulating among his Mexican kin and buddies. Yet outwardly he appeared the urban man, far removed from the stereotype of a Mexican farmhand or migratory worker. Solid in build, deliberate of speech, one might take him for a preoccupied office manager.

He contributed little to his class collecting project, save for an interview with a Polish friend of his wife, whose haunted home he visited. Some spirit, perhaps that of the crazed original owner, caused unhappiness and divorces to couples who moved into the house. Juan himself felt cold sitting in the living room conversing with his wife's friend, until her husband's return brought a sudden protective warmth into the room. Juan empathized with the wife, who spoke firmly to the spirit commanding it to leave—"It's you or me"—and thereafter the spirit caused no further disturbances. To Juan, if this was folklore, he did not need other persons to record such matters.

# A Spectrum of Ethnics

*Milan Opacich, Serbian Tamburitza-maker*

In the four-piece Drina band that often played in Jennie's Restaurant on Friday evenings, Milan Opacich manned the cello. There I first watched him plucking its strings, smiling a wide-breaking smile. Stocky and round-featured, resonant of voice, he exuded friendliness. But, as a fireman, he had a serious side; and, for filing a grievance at being passed over for promotion, he had been assigned to a fire station at 19th and Adams in one of the dingiest parts of Gary. Milan enjoyed considerable reputation as a tamburitza-maker. His instruments sold for prices ranging from two to four hundred dollars, not only in the Region but elsewhere.

The graphic story of Milan's hunt to obtain a turtle shell for his first tamburitza—a yarn not only traditional with him but which fits into a genre of personal narratives by folk musicians on how they fashioned their first instrument—follows.

✦   Well, it probably takes us back to about the age of four. We were living in Gary at 10th and Jefferson. My nearest recollection of music is when we used to go to our different friends' homes. We had this one particular friend that had this small preem that they used to keep on top of their wardrobe.

A preem [short for prima, often synonymous with tamburitza] is an instrument about twenty-one inches in length, has five strings, can be tuned to G or D or E. The sound itself is very much like a mandolin, and it's a lead instrument that plays the melody most of the time. I had a fascination for this instrument that was on top of the wardrobe, and I was always trying to get it down. And one time the wife let me play with it, and I guess her husband didn't like the way I handled it, so he went out and purchased a ukulele that he gave me for a present. Well, three or four ukuleles later [laughter], he got tired of buying instruments and me tearing them up. It gets to be quite an expense. So my dad thought that he would make me one that would be very durable. So he got a hold of some three-quarter plywood and he cut one out and put rubber bands on it. And that thing was more precious to me than the doggone ones that they bought in the store. I think that is probably what has instilled the inspiration in me.

So years went by. I got out of high school and I started working in a place called the Gary Screw and Bolt Works. My brother had worked there since he was about fifteen or sixteen years old. And I got into a machinist apprenticeship there, and I worked as a tool- and die-maker. I was still with music at the time; I was playing guitar and had just entered my

159

first tamburitza group. And I decided to try and make an instrument. I started doing one on lunchhour time. They call those "government jobs" when you do something like that for yourself on company time.

I had seen a turtleback prima that I had fell in love with, so naturally it was going to be a turtleback. So for the body of the instrument I needed a turtle shell real bad. And I didn't know where I was going to get a turtle shell. My brother casually mentioned it to a friend of his who had a farm with a swamp on it in Michigan City, and he said there were a lot of turtles there. So my brother and I went out to this swamp in Michigan City. We sat there half an afternoon. And all of a sudden a turtle raises its head. And my brother, who was an expert marksman, through the services, shoots this turtle. And we went in the swamp after the turtle, water up to our necks. I didn't like the swamp because it looked like a real hellhole—water moccasins around, just gave you an eerie feeling! I can't swim, and on top of that I have a deadly fear of snakes. Anyway we did manage to get the turtle out, and brought it back home to Gary about four or five hours later.

This turtle was shot right through the head, and it's still walking around. It lived the whole day. Now my brother is a guy that feels all game should be eaten—rabbits, squirrels—a big game man. OK, now who's gonna cook this doggone thing? My wife didn't want any part of it: "Not in my pots!" [laughter]. And my sister-in-law says: "No, not on your life!" So, in order to preserve peace, Mama says: "I'll cook it" So we got one of my Mom's next-door neighbors to help us get the meaty part out of the shell, and that was quite a job. I held on the forelegs, my brother held on to the other two, and this fellow cutting it, and it's thrashing about. You could hardly hold this turtle, it was just giving such a terrific fight. It was very difficult, but he finally got it cut out and chopped it up into little pieces and got the heart out. The heart was jumping six to eight inches out of his hand.

So Mom finally puts it in the pot, to make a stew. And so help me, it's walking in the pot as she was cooking it. The darn thing's in the pot with its doggone legs churning about. So I see this, and my appetite, my stomach, is not too great on things like that. My brother has talked my nephew into "We're gonna have this fantastic meal, you know." A turtle has seven different kinds of meat in it—beef, chicken, pork—so I thought I had better go on with the program, 'cause after all he was good enough to shoot the turtle. I could barely get that first spoonful down. I kept visualizing this doggone turtle, as ugly as it was. I've got pictures of it somewhere. It was just one of the worst meals I've ever had. Anyway, I made my first tamburitza instrument out of that shell.

It turned out so bad that I gave it to Jack. Jack gave it to a friend, who gave it to another friend. And it winds up now it belongs to Larry Regan, that we're playing in his little restaurant there on 34th and Broadway. I would like to have that back so I could bury it in the back yard.

Larry Regan told us that he "haunted" Milan with the specter of his first home-made tamburitza, which Larry had acquired and kept as a memento. He himself liked to tell the story about Milan's turtle hunt.

After his initial adventure Milan found a place in Florida where he could purchase turtle shells, until the endangered-species movement closed off that outlet. Turtles in the Lake Michigan area had soft shells, and Milan needed the hard shell, such as the Egyptians first used, to make a high rough type of neck with a spindle on it. He now turned to various kinds of wood: "In some cases I use the box made out of mahogany. Other times on the more expensive models I use a rosewood. The rosewood model is a much lighter instrument and rosewood is a beautiful wood, while mahogany is sort of plain unless you decorate it artistically, maybe by shadowing it like a violin." As well as making tamburitzas out of wood, Milan continued to grind turtle shells when he could locate them; he hoped to obtain some from the Caribbean Islands.

The symbolic meaning in this tale became apparent when Richard March and I visited the Opaciches in their new home in Schererville. Milan showed us his garage-workshop, where he had half a dozen tamburitzas in various stages of completion, illustrated newspaper articles about him tacked on the walls, albums of photographs of tamburitza groups he had admired and with whom he had played, and stacks of recordings. One of a handful of tamburitza-makers in the United States, Milan had achieved celebrity among the Serbian and Croatian groups for whom tamburitza orchestras and entertainments furnished much of the joy of life, even more perhaps in the United States than in Yugoslavia. Hence the story of how he made his first instrument memorialized the launching of his career.

In Milan's home I met his eighty-one-year-old mother, born in the town of Boznich, Croatia. Erect, dignified, and somewhat sad-looking, she was twice widowed. Married first to a Croatian and then to a Serb, she had been caught between the Catholic Church, which rejected her for marrying a Serb, and the Serbian Orthodox Church, which rejected her because she was a Croatian. So for thirty-two years she prayed at home. Two years before, when she was in the hospital, a Catholic priest had visited her, telling her things had changed and inviting her back into the church. She replied that she had worshiped by herself all these years and would continue to do so. Milan himself attended the Saint Sava Church, but as an American-born Serb felt little identification with either faction in the church split. Further, with a Croatian mother and Serbian father, he did not share in the rivalry between Serbs and Croats.

161

# Land of the Millrats

As a youth Milan had worked in a variety of capacities, in the "vertical mills, milling machine, lathes, shaper"; but he never liked such work because he never saw the end product. For the past twenty-five years (he was now forty-eight) he had been a fireman, on the now almost wholly black fire-fighting force of Gary. "It's basically a good job. It helped me progress with my instrument-building" (since he had two days off for each day at work). And Milan gained satisfaction through helping people by fighting fires.

One day I went, with several of the Gary Gang, to the fire station on 19th and Adams. The crew, led by a portly black chief, showed us around the station, pointed out the little shop where Milan continued his tamburitza-making even when away from his shop at home, slid down the pole from upstairs for our benefit, clambered aboard their engine and inched it out the narrow driveway, while a spotted Dalmatian cavorted about and jumped aboard. Milan had begun his fire-fighting career at this station, and been returned to it after stints elsewhere. "It's always been a punishment station, a reprimand house. Always, in the history of Gary, this is where the bad firemen went. You may have rubbed the chief wrong. Well, you'd wind up on 19th and Adams. For the last twenty-five years it's been a slum area, and a high-risk area, with older buildings, and deteriorating buildings, and slum landowners. They just collected the rent and never put anything back. Only black people live there now."

At the Opacich home Milan's attractive wife, Rose, of Czech and German background, recalled several frustrating attempts by Milan to save children from fires, only to uncover their bodies the next day as he sifted through the ashes. "And that's happened maybe six times over the years, where they've lost children. One time there was a fire where they had big bars on the windows. And the little one was reaching out with his arms through the bars, and Milan had his arms on the child, but the flames were so intense he couldn't get in to the child, the child couldn't get out, and the fire is engulfing it."

Milan picked up the story. "This fire was only a half a block from the station. It was at midwinter. The snow was up to our waists. Women came running into the fire station screaming—oh, past midnight. Now you'd think that, gosh, half a block down the street we could do some good. When we got there the gas meters had blown off the wall. They were right by the front door. Just one entrance to this building. And at one time or other this must have been a policy station. Now you have to know a little about the area, the community there to know about policy, but it's a game that's played for money—it's a gambling thing. And bars were put on the windows so no undesirables could get in. At any rate, it had changed and it was a living quarters now. And when we got there the whole place was engulfed with flames. So we ran around to the side, and here are these two kids with their arms poked through the bars, crying out, 'Help me, mister, help me!' Well, the best thing we could do at the time was to put the hose in there and try to knock out the flames. Once Nipsco [Northern Indiana Power Station Company] came to turn off the gas and we did get in, the show was over. The kids—one was burned, the other one had died from smoke inhalation. And the grandmother—all that was left was a rib cage. The following week after this one we lost four kids in a room with a flash fire. The kids were living in this tenement building that was condemned, and no one was supposed to be in it. Evidently they were heating it with the stove. It wasn't uncommon to light up the stove and open the oven and let the heat out. Well, something there flashed. And they were in the next room fully clothed, all on one bed, and the smoke got 'em. And that's usually the case, you find where children are in a fire, it's usually because the parents aren't around."

Once when I spoke with Milan in Jennie's he said he had "earned his pay" in a fire reported that day, May 6, 1976, on page one of the *Post Tribune* under the headline "Fire Kills 3 Gary Tots." The children had hidden under the bed instead of hanging out the window. Another time he had found half a dozen children looking as if they were asleep, but they were dead; the oxygen had been all consumed.

Milan's sense of Serbian ethnic allegiance has taken a different course from that of Jelena Branimirović. She, too, is Gary-born, but her energies flow into church affairs and the all-absorbing schism; she actively mourns the fate of her cousin Bishop Varnava Nastić; and she continues to wage all-out war against the Communists. Milan has turned away from the internecine struggles of Chetniks and Partisans, Roskos and Feds, royalists and communists, Serbians and Croatians, and plunged into the life and politics of the Region. His criticisms are directed not at the church abroad but toward the city government at home.

In terms of the ethnic traditions I have outlined, Milan, in his role as performer of Serbian folk music, belongs to the public-presentational track. As an ethnic-instrument-maker, he falls within an esoteric craft tradition. He combines the most public and the most private of the ethnic folklores.


## FOUR ETHNIC TRADITIONS

The original typology of public-presentational, historical-civic, communal-social, and esoteric-private traditions has encompassed the diverse forms of ethnic folk behavior encountered in the Region. Into the public-presentational cetegory we may fit the ethnic festivals and the performances of the Teatro desengaño del pueblo and Milan Opacich with his

Drina band. The historical-civic classification may be applied to the ethnic churches, with their religious and cultural traditions; to the Teatro, which drew upon the Hispanic folk inheritance to create a political lobby; and to the Greek students venting folk passion against the Turks. Within the communal-social area fall the calendrical events and rites de passage described by Jelena Branimirović for Serbs, which can be duplicated for other ethnic stocks; the informal clubbiness of ethnic stores; and the island folkways and networks the Greek students transport to the Region. Finally, to the esoteric-private realm adhere the occult happenings by Greeks, Romanians, Mexicans, and Assyrians, among the groups I interviewed, the amulets and talismans available in the ethnic stores, and the tamburitza-making skill of Milan Opacich.

Ethnic folklore can assert itself through any one of these several outlets; by taking advantage of all, it successfully maintains vitality in the urban milieu. All four types of ethnic traditions spring from an esoteric base, but the circumstances, pressures, and opportunities of a multicultural society lead them to more open positions, as when the tamburitza craftsman from the Region appears at the American Folklife Festival on the mall in the nation's capital.

"The Region blacks are different than any other blacks you ever wanted to meet."—young white ethnic from Gary

# 4

# BLACK OUTLOOKS

College students on the Bloomington campus of Indiana University were speaking about the Region, where they lived. "It's a place you're not proud of, but you get used to it," said one. "Things started to get bad about ten years ago [in 1966]. That's when Gary started getting unsafe." Another interjected, "When Mayor Hatcher was elected." The first speaker nodded: "That guy's a no-good crook. But I mean that anyone that would get into Gary couldn't do anything anyway. The only way to solve the problem in Gary is to put bombs all around it and blow it up."

These comments reflect the stereotypical white attitudes toward Gary repeated a hundred times in my conversations with Regionites and downstaters. They saw the evidence of Gary's degeneration in the rising crime curve ("Mayor Hatcher is lowering the crime rate by cutting down on the reports . . . nothing is ever printed in the paper . . . there was the girl below us who was stabbed and we didn't even know about it"); in the boarded-up downtown business and residential area; in the vandalized and burned-out shops and homes; in the padlocked Holiday Inn; in the pervasive dread of violence, almost as palpable as the gray smog from the Gary Works. Gary was a total failure, a snake pit.

Gary's black residents expressed a wholly different outlook: the sweet taste of success. They had a great deal to tell—not of traditional folklore, but in the form of life histories, personal experiences, and private philosophies—and they spoke with the ease, eloquence, and intensity characterizing the "man (and woman) of words" whom scholars have identified as archetypal figures in Afro-American oral culture. And after I had recorded black steelworkers, firemen, police officers, preachers, politicians, psychics, schoolteachers, civil servants, janitors, and invalids and talked informally with many others, I recognized one basic formula behind many narratives: the success story. These anecdotal autobiographies, some related in full, some in selected episodes, told of struggles in the white world that, despite heavy odds, ended in proud achievements. Like the upward-bound immigrants, these descendants of slaves accepted the American dream of rags to riches and approved middle-class values of status and income as markers of "making it." Unlike the black militants who rejected and fought the system, they met Whitey on his own terms and proved their staying power. The laborer in the mill and the preacher in the pulpit recited comparable success sagas. Success could be construed in terms of holding onto a job in the face of white discrimination and hostility; of developing a creative other life outside the mills as talent scout, writer, filmmaker, athletic coach; of conquering disease and illness through the Lord's and the minister's blessing; of fighting for and winning clout in the labor unions and the political machine by unrelenting effort and endurance. Success was determined by faith in the Lord and His blessings; by industry and the sweat of one's brow; and by guile, in a positive sense, as the preacher perceived the wants of his congregation and catered to them.

## PREACHERS

The greatest figure in American folklore is the black preacher, Alan Lomax has said, and I agree. As the Afro-American folk tradition is the richest in the United States, so is the preacher the central personality in that tradition: the deliverer of chanted sermons, the butt of ribald jokes, the performer of miraculous cures. In Gary I encountered preachers of local celebrity, whose personal histories and observations included homely anecdotes and constituted narratives of spiritual and secular success. Over two hundred black churches were said to exist in the city; they ranged from storefronts to imposing edifices, some purchased from white congregations. To become a minister with one's own devoted flock was a dream of many black laborers who, beginning with their own families, entered the competition to win a following, possess a building, and operate a going concern. The preacher must be showman, Godly man, businessman, public relations man, and wise man. In his symbols of success—the finest of homes, cars, clothes—he mirrored the achievement of his church.

With success came not only admiration and emulation but also envy and backbiting. The preacher-hero, like all folk heroes and culture heroes, has his detractors along with his boosters. I have heard well-known preachers called crooks and con-artists by responsible citizens, and one black minister castigated his fellow-ministers for their corrupt and sycophantic ways. But no one can gainsay the vitality of the black churches in Gary and the triumphant careers of some of their leaders.

### Dr. F. Brannan Jackson

With one black church in Gary I felt a particularly close relationship: Calvary Baptist, a substantial structure at 2400 Virginia Street east of Broadway in the midst of a rundown black quarter, with a success story of its own. I first visited Calvary in February 1968, after reading the announcement of a program for its annual Homecoming Day. (This was the first time, I was later told, that the paper had printed the church's message.) The building had only been completed the previous December, after an arduous effort by its working-class congregation; before that the members had met in the basement. The day-long program, divided at midday by a fried-chicken dinner in the auditorium downstairs, entranced me, the only white person present; and before the day ended I had been twice called upon to speak.

Calvary's service contained a good deal of the folk spirit. A lady pianist, who occasionally burst loudly into song, to the left of the altar and a male organist to the right supplied music; an energetic chorus of two dozen robed women, along with other young men and women in street clothes, filled the church with choruses and solos, without benefit of hymnbooks; and the Reverend F. Brannan Jackson, head poised like a peacock's as he scanned the congregation, governed the proceedings professionally. He babied, spoke with, prodded, and aroused the churchgoers with a versatile performance, asserting, "They never go to sleep on me." As the tempo heightened, he threw back his head, extended his arms, and delivered his sermon in a strong, raspy voice accented with traces of southernisms and punctuated with staccato phrases and formulaic grunts. The congregation responded with interjections and Amens, and two or three became "happy" and were fanned by nearby friends and attended by a nurse stationed in the front row.

167

## Land of the Millrats

I revisited Calvary Baptist seven years later, recorded several services, and interviewed the pastor in his elegant home in the former Jewish Gold Coast section of downtown west Gary on McKinley Street. A picture of the pastor now hung on the church wall, showing him bespectacled and pear-cheeked, with a full-face beard and less hair on top. More than ever he played the role of showman and authority figure. In our recording session he related details of his personal history and his church, which formed the upward graph of a success narrative. Born in Mobile, Alabama, in 1923, he had been supported by his mother on her wages of $2.50 a week. He had never felt the call till the age of thirty-three, at which time he was holding down a job as a forty-five-dollar-a-day auto mechanic. Before that time he had worked as a cook, butcher, baker, yardman, janitor, chauffeur, and truck driver. Then one Sunday he went to church to observe a buddy who had been under the influence the night before. The pastor related his conversion experience:

✦ I was not a church man after I got on my own. I always had great respect for the church, but I never did go. I never did have time to go. I was doing too many other things, and I would be sleepy on Sunday. So I would find an excuse. I always wanted to go to church though on New Year's Night. I was scared to death to be in a club or some place like that on New Year's Night, 'cause you might get shot. I had a superstition [laughs] what you start doing in the New Year, that's what you're gonna be doing all year. And that was some kind of superstitious thing I had from the south; it was a carryover, I guess, from my parents.

So I went to visit some friends one night at a party, and there was a fellow there just kept singing and singing, and he had had a little alcohol, you know. They told me he was the lead singer in the church. Well I said: "When he gonna sing?" They said: "He gonna sing tomorrow." "Well if this guy's gonna sing in the church, I'll be there tomorrow to see him." I wasn't going to church for the good of church, I was going there as a mockery to that guy who I saw take a little shot of alcohol. And the minute I got to the church, the fellow did sing. But I got so engrossed in the service going on there, I forgot all about the man. And when I left that day I was in the Spirit. But I thought maybe I better not go back again 'cause I might find myself doing like them folks and joining the church. I liked the church all right and I respected it, but I didn't want to be a part of it. My problem was I was somewhat embarrassed as old as I was—I was thirty-two; it was 1955—that I hadn't joined the church.

So finally one morning I stopped outside of the church again. The only available parking place was sitting right there in front of the church waiting for me. I didn't have an excuse to say I couldn't find a place. So I went in and I wanted to sit in the rear of the church, but there was no seat back there, so the usher escorted me to the front of the church and I had the second seat. And while I was sitting there, the preacher began to preach, and an involvement came between that minister, the Spirit, and myself, where I lost all knowledge of all the people in the church and I could see only myself. I could see the perdicament I were in and the life I was leading, and I was sorry for my sins and I wanted to rectify my mistakes. And my desire was for a conversion, for the Spirit of God to come in me and lead me out of the destructive atmosphere that I was living in. Not that I was killing anyone or destroying anyone. I was working daily and gainfully employed. But I didn't have the Spirit of God in me. I couldn't help nobody. I didn't have no advice for anyone that was of any essence. And I was converted that day there in that church. And all my religious life and atmosphere since has been promoting and perpetuating the Christian cause.

Brannan Jackson's new career took off like a rocket. He attended a seminary in Chicago, began pastoring a small church of nine members, which he built up, and then was called to Calvary Baptist in 1966. He had much to say about the charisma of the black preacher, and how his own knowledge of the street and street language enabled him to communicate on all levels with his congregation. The pastor maintained outside activities: he and his wife operated a clothing store on downtown Broadway; he managed a senior-citizens apartment complex in connection with the church; he ran for state representative.

Calvary Baptist attained a highwater mark with its fiftieth anniversary, celebrated on November 30, 1975. The Executive Secretary of the Foreign Mission Board, National Baptist Convention, U.S.A., Dr. William J. Harvey III, delivered a guest sermon. On arriving at the church that morning I paid ten dollars for a 104-page commemorative volume with gold-leaf covers and, on the front, a likeness of F. Brannan Jackson, Pastor, above a relief of the church. The work contained old photographs of personalities and events in the church's history, a brief history of the church, advertisements placed by other Gary churches, and a list of patrons. The church was packed for this gala occasion, and Dr. Harvey, slight of build, almost professorial in manner, made it memorable with his sermon-addresses in the morning and afternoon.

The morning sermon combined a historical overview of the African slaves' experience in America, the emergence of Baptist Christianity among the Negro people, and the prosperity of the Afro-American Baptist churches, by contrast with the wretchedness of black Africans. His story of black America followed in a straight ascent the rags-to-riches theme.

He began with the warring African tribes, their sale of slaves to Arab traders, the Gold Coast (Ghana) Atlantic slave trade, the confinement and horrors on shipboard, and the deliberate detribalizing of the slaves torn from their cultures, religions, languages, so that they could only speak a pidgin in America. After these generalities the preacher turned to a particularized case of a slave man and a slave woman, who were allowed to live together in a cabin for three months, in lieu of a proper family life; the masters used the women as breeders and the men as studs. Dr. Harvey launched into an imaginary conversation between a slave man and slave woman in their cabin. The man is talking. "You know, I heard something today. I took the master and the missus down the road apiece to the chu'ch." "What's that?" He described the church. "They listened to some man called a preacher. He talked about someone called God who made the world and everything in it. He made folks." She expressed incredulity. "You funning me, man." "Oh yes, He made all of us, blacks as well as whites," "Well, what does He have to do with us?" "Well you see, He's a shepherd and we're the other sheep." During this dialogue the speaker shifted back and forth between two microphones on the pulpit simulating the voices of the excited man and the incredulous woman. The male slave continued his explanation. "The preacher-man said his God had made a sacrifice for His flock." His consort thought she understood: "You mean like we used to do in Africa, with chickens and animals?" "No, He sacrificed His son."

After this playlet, performed with antic movements, Dr. Harvey speculated that slaves might have learned about Christianity in some such way. His great-grandfather had lived as a slave until the age of seven, and some race-memory handed down within the family might have contributed to this skit. Black people had learned about Christianity in a way different from any other ethnic group in America, was the minister's point, without preconceived theology, through adversity. In the church, the house of God, the Negro could be free to respond, to express his emotions, to sing and shout. Harvey disliked black radicals who called Christianity a white man's religion, and black college students who looked down on responding and emotionalism in the Baptist service. (This statement drew a chorus of enthusiastic responses.)

Now Dr. Harvey moved toward his climax: the progress and prosperity that the Negro Baptists had achieved.* Fortune had smiled on the Negroes in the United States. When freedom came they buckled down to work, made it through World War I, the Depression, the civil-rights movement, Korea, Vietnam—and now they had proved themselves, they were no longer "the other sheep." Their closets were so full of clothes they couldn't close them; they had so many cars they couldn't get near the church to park. And if luck ran against them, agencies looked after

---

* He expressed puzzlement at what term to call his people: on campuses he had to say "black"; older persons liked "colored"; he preferred "Negro."

them. If they were naked, the Salvation Army would give them clothes; if they were hungry they could get welfare and food stamps from the government; if they fell down in the street the police would take them to the hospital. Contrast this favorable situation with Africa, especially South Africa, where no aid of any sort existed. The Africans were now the other sheep.

From his recent missionary trip to South Africa, Dr. Harvey recounted an episode he had witnessed of childbirth in the bush. He had been called at night to drive in a jeep with a Stillson light ("you camping fellows will know what that is") to a hut where a witch-doctor was trying to help a woman in labor. Blood was oozing out the door; some neighbor women were beating tomtoms while others pressed down on her stomach to force the baby out, causing her to hemorrhage, and she expired. That was Africa. "The poorest Negro in America is better off than the wealthiest African." So now it was time to help the other sheep. In South Africa blacks received 20 percent and coloreds 40 percent of what the white man got for the same job; blacks had to live a certain number of miles from town, in rooms of a specified size.

At the end of the afternoon service the Reverend F. Brannan Jackson announced that Calvary Baptist would give one thousand dollars to the Foreign Mission Board.

Dr. Harvey's sermon stunned me. It turned upside down all stereotypes and clichés of the whites about the Gary blacks. The blacks in the United States, in Gary, in the Calvary Baptist Church had risen from the wretchedness of slavery to the affluence of middle America. What looked like a ghetto neighborhood to a supercilious white turned into a proud landmark of the Gary community, where well-to-do blacks with bulging closets and expensive cars gathered confidently and donated to help hapless black Africans, who lay at the bottom of the ladder the Afro-Americans had climbed so energetically.

The imposing structure of Calvary Baptist, so in contrast with the deteriorating dwellings in the neighborhood, had not been raised without strenuous efforts on the part of church members and, perhaps, an assist from the Lord. The story emerged from interviews with the pastor's wife and his deacon.

*Building the Calvary Baptist Church.* Mrs. F. Brannan Jackson, a serene woman, born in Mississippi but raised in Indiana, spoke with the accent of an elocution teacher. She told me how Calvary was built.

✦ Well, he [her husband] was at the church less than a year, and he got the membership together to build a new church. The amount of money that the church had was way below the amount needed to build a new church. When we went there the church was going on its fortieth year, yet they were in a basement when he assumed the pastorate.

He said he was riding along the expressway going to the church, and the Lord spoke to him, said he wanted him to build a church. Now the finances, I know, was well below at that time $20,000. And he called the membership together after service one Sunday. He had all the women sit on one side of the church and all the men on the other, and he told them that the Lord had directed him to build a church. At that time he asked for a vote to turn over everything to him, all the construction and the plans of whatever had to be done, to let him be the sole person to handle the business. They had a building fund which would have more or less dictated to him. And so at that time the church voted and let him handle it completely. So he undertook it. And with the money he had he went to various banks, but they wouldn't allow him to have a loan or anything.

So he kept struggling. And there are a large number of men in that church who are skilled in doing various types of building, some plumbing, some—I can't name all the various skills. But he took the men of the church, and he never done any construction work in his life, but he was the head construction man. He contacted various companies with materials and whatnot to start building a church with. It wasn't long before the money they had on hand was consumed, and he went out to Grant Street Lumber (Jim Brown owns the place out there), it's right on the corner of Grant Street and Ridge Road, and told Mr. Brown what he wanted to do and told him that he didn't have money; and he told him that he didn't see how it could be done. Something must have touched Mr. Brown's heart, because he told him that whatever he wanted in the line of lumber and supplies, that he'd furnish them.

The church could not have been built without the lumber. You see the church, the way it is now, it's beautiful. There are several brothers in the church whose father was a carpenter, and the father taught them the trade, and they did all the carpentry work. There was an elderly man who was partially paralyzed from a stroke, and he was an electrician. He came in there, and he had men who had a little knowledge, along with his son, who did all the electrical work. All of the work that they did was donated. There were women in the church would come in and serve on the lunch hour. They did this for thirteen months. They started work on the church in late October or early November, and they completed the building of the church in thirteen months. Many times during the winter weather I would tell Reverend it was too cold, or it has snowed the previous night and it was too bad for him to go to work that morning. He said that he would go to the church, and there were men who had already started the fire, to start making the mortar for the laying of the bricks. So during all of these adversities, they built the church in thirteen months' time. That was in 1967.

## Black Outlooks

So we feel like that was a miracle, because to see the structure as it is now, to think that mere men with no real person to lead them except Reverend were able to do it. Several times the wall of the building fell, the wind blew it down, and no one was ever hurt. And there's not one Sunday during the entire construction of that church that we didn't hold service there, in the basement, not one time. The church that you see now was built around the church that existed before.

Meanwhile Brother Timothy Jones, the minister's "number-one man," had joined us. A millworker in the coke plant of U.S. Steel, soft-spoken, father of five grown children though only forty-four, his "other life" revolved around Calvary Baptist Church. Brother Jones related precise details of his job in the coke mill, then he, too, gave an account of the heroic effort of the church members and their pastor to build Calvary.

✦ We started building the Church. We had a funny thing: the bricklayers, when we were talking about it, they told the pastor when they accepted the job that they would have to have men out there every day they were working. Myself and two more of the men, at that particular time, said that we would be those three if didn't any more come out. Since we all worked shift work, we would leave the mill, like, say, midnight tonight, we'd bring our mill shoes out with us every morning, and go to the church and work all day, go home in the evening about 5 or 6 o'clock, go to bed and get up at 9 A.M. and go to work. We did that until the church was built. I guess the Lord just gave us the spiritual strength, but even our foremen, out there on our job, after they found out what we were doing, they seemed to kind of give us a break out there in the mill. If they'd see us nod, they'd let us nod; and they'd tease us a lot about it, working out there on the church [laughter from both].

But it was so inspiring, after we started working, and a funny thing happened to me during the construction of the church. I was kind of like a foreman of the group, and our pastor goes to Hot Springs to a board meeting every year in January. So this particular January when he went, he left me in charge of the work. At that time we were building a wall. He left that Sunday evening, and we had the wall about half way up. And that Wednesday night the wall fell. Everybody was so excited and everything, they didn't know what to do; they didn't know whether to call the pastor. I told them not to call the pastor, that I would go up and take a look at it. It was −10° Fahrenheit. And I went and looked at the wall and called ten men. They came out there, and before that day was over we had all those blocks cleared away and the wall all set to go again. I thought that was one of the most inspiring things that I'd ever witnessed. When you've got −10° Fahrenheit and you get a group of men who'll

173

come out there and dedicate themselves to doing that work—and they did that.

There are so many incidents that I could relate that happened to us when we were building the church there. Now it just seems incredible how we did it. Another time we had the building inspector, who was on us about tying the wall. When the wall fell for the second time, for some reason the building inspector came out that same morning. He never did come around to where the wall fell. He came around to the back of the church and started that way, and for some reason he didn't come around. We don't know yet why he didn't come around and see all that wall that fell down. We knew he would stop construction. But he didn't come around and look, and he told us to "keep up the good work," turned around, and went back out to his car [laughter from both].

Oh, we had a lot of lucky breaks, just so many lucky breaks. Like I say, a lot of the men tease me because they'd never seen me work hard; they didn't think I worked hard. When we were building the church sometimes we'd get caught, whereas we'd have six or seven men out there in the morning and after lunch somebody had to go to work, somebody had to go home, leaving maybe two or three men. There's been many times during the construction of the church that one man would unload a whole truck of bags of cement, lumber, and never think anything about it. By himself, put that stuff in the basement so it wouldn't get wet. We worked out there the whole winter that way. Nobody got sick, nobody got injured, anything.

Nothing like it has happened in Gary. No church in Gary can say that the men have got up and built it, and we built ours from the ground up. I have to give our pastor the credit for that, because any time a man can inspire a group of men to make a sacrifice like that, he must have something going for him, and I'd say it's a gift from God. Like I say, I'd never dreamed that you'd catch me out there working outdoors in that kind of weather building a church. We did that, and steady worked on our jobs at the mill. Never missed a day.

The story of Calvary Baptist parallels narratives about the miraculous erecting and preservation of Catholic churches through the intervention of the saints or Virgin Mary. Thanks to the faith and fortitude of the believers, and the leadership of the prophet-minister, under the providential direction of the Lord, the church building rose from the ground, surmounted the winds and the biting cold, and stood as a living monument to the race, the congregation, and the preacher. Calvary Baptist exemplified the sense of family and community, inspiration and enthusiasm, engendered by the black Baptist church in America. Legendary annals of the church's construction reinforced this sense and contributed to the mystique of the preacher.

# Black Outlooks

*Elder M. C. Bennett*

In his quest for black gospel music John Hasse visited a number of black churches. He reported that Elder Bennnett had created considerable stir among Gary worshipers, who were flocking to his Church of the Open Door. John videotaped a service at some length; watching it, we observed a series of activities: the marching in of the choir; dancing of the congregation in the aisles; the Elder's laying on of hands and the church members' excited reactions; baptismal immersion of the worshipers. The scene conveyed a sense of continuous motion and action, with Elder Bennett the dominant figure.

In July 1977 I drove downtown on a Saturday afternoon and cruised along 5th and Buchanan looking for the Church of the Open Door. I found Elder Bennett resting on the stone steps of his modest home and recognized him from the videotape: a long sallow face, a large loose frame, and a low-slung paunch.

His life history formed an impressive success story. Born in Louisville, Kentucky, sixty-two years before, Elder Bennett had done military service prior to coming to Gary to work in the mills, and spent his "other life" pastoring. While a laborer at the Gary Works he served as assistant pastor for the Church of God in Christ. Subsequently he moved to a storefront church of his own, then to a one-car garage converted into a church off in the woods—he waved his hand in a southwesterly direction. "Sometimes we only collected fifty cents. Then I became very ill with a number of things. I had five hemorrhoids, an enlarged heart, and cancer of the rectum. For over five years I was in and out of Hines Hospital, the Veterans' Hospital in Illinois. The doctors gave up on me. But I had faith in the Lord and prayed to him, and the Lord cured me. Now the hospital has crossed me off their list."

Word of these cures through the Lord's blessing, which Bennett helped spread himself, contributed to the growth of his church, as the sick and diseased sought similar healings through his ministrations. Some two thousand members now belonged to his church, and about seven hundred and fifty attended an average service, which began at noon and lasted till two-thirty or three. The church owned a fleet of six buses and a camper, and we walked over to see them, parked in a yard beside the old church building, which he now used as a nursing home for indigent parishioners. He preached in a former Jewish synagogue, several blocks west, purchased in 1974.

Did Elder Bennett do anything different or special in his church? "The Church of the Open Door is independent; anybody can come. I conduct service every day—night workers or out-of-work people can come—and also three evenings a week, and on Saturdays in the old church. You want to try to arouse people's curiosity, so they will want to come and see what is going on. Also my people go out into neighborhoods with tracts about my preaching to get them to come to church. I try to look after the down-and-out, like drug addicts. Everybody has a hard name for them, but they are people, and I try to help them. I get some, I lose some, but even if I get only one, that's one off the streets." The membership, through donations and tithes, met all expenses for the church and the clean, orderly nursing home. Anyone could Dial a Prayer at any time of the day or night.

On Sunday I drove to the new church, a two-story structure, nearly a block long, looking something like the broadside view of an oceangoing liner below decks. Over the entrance was a Hebrew inscription and a picture of a man blessing a boy. Rows of plate-glass windows with shades drawn stretched along the block. A prayer line had formed down the center aisle, with a long string of people moving up to Elder Bennett; he clapped each forcefully on the head, whereupon some went into a catatonic state, dancing, whirling, and shouting, while nurses in attendance would give them a hand—if they weren't dancing (that is, imbued by the Spirit) themselves. The lone white woman in the congregation gyrated ecstatically when she came out of the prayer line.

After the prayer line dissolved Elder Bennett called for testimonials from two women who had earlier testified privately to him. This business seemed very impromptu, and he had to look around to see where they were seated. One woman, who had become bald from some affliction, had regained her hair through the minister's assistance. He grabbed a handful of locks and held them up for the congregation to see, while she skipped and danced with joy. The other woman testified that she had been cured of a disease with the help of the Lord—as had Elder Bennett, a point he affirmed—and she said sweetly to him, "I love you." The entryway was filled with the crutches and wheelchairs of those cured.

In the lull that followed the prayer line Elder Bennett commenced a kind of exhorting. He walked down the center aisle, holding a microphone and "ministering" (his word). He asked if anyone wanted to come to Jesus, and a lanky young fellow with sad eyes walked up front and stood behind Elder Bennett, shaking his head and swaying; a nurse gave him a napkin to wipe his forehead. He was joined by a second young man, short and dapper, with a trim mustache. The two stood behind Elder Bennett for quite a time, facing the congregation, while he waited for others to come forward. None did, so he turned to the shorter man, held the mike to him, and asked if he wanted to come to Jesus and repent his sins. He said yes, showed some emotion, and was blessed by Elder Bennett.

14. Elder Bennett at the Church of the Open Door.

15. A rehearsal on Broadway of the Greater Gary Community Choir.

16. The New Spirit of Love Baptist Church.

# Black Outlooks

The grand climax came with the tall man, who began sobbing and shaking, stated he was a sinner, asked the Lord to forgive him, got down on his knees, clasped his arms, moaned, and at length lay on his back prostrate on the carpeted steps with his long arms outstretched, in the posture of the cross. Had the moment been choreographed, it could not have been staged more effectively. Elder Bennett looked triumphant at this denouement and asked the congregation to bless the two, which they did by raising their two hands high in the air, arms fully extended—a forest of limbs.

Now came the collection, and the pastor belligerently told the ushers to lock the doors and not let anyone out, as this was an insult to the Lord. I went up front and shook hands with Elder Bennett, thanking him for the service; he cordially invited me to return. In the vestibule the tall fellow who had lain on the altar steps, looking quite composed, was chatting with friends.

Although the Church of the Open Door had achieved considerable success, its minister displayed a lower-keyed and less flamboyant style than that of his fellow-preachers. He exemplified the wish-fulfillment of many a black millworker: to pastor a storefront church and grow to become a full-time leader of a substantial congregation housed in an imposing edifice. His deeds, rather than his appearance or his dramatics, spoke for this servant of God. Before the eyes of the church members he brought a soul to Christ, ministering skillfully to the tormented young man, easing him through his spiritual agony, and leaving him supine, serene, and saved. What Elder Bennett had done for one, he could surely do for all.

## Prophet E. N. Williams

Word reached our Gary Gang of a highly successful black church in downtown Gary: the Prayer House of Faith, presided over by Prophet E. N. Williams. Adrienne Seward had recorded his conversion experience. When working in the mill Williams saw a crane operator, a nonbeliever, enveloped in flames as a result of an industrial accident and heard him call, "Lord, please save me," with salutary results. Beholding a skeptic call on the Lord had a powerful effect on Williams; the incident led him to the ministry.

One Sunday morning Adrienne, Gil Cooley, Richard March, and I trooped to the church at 300 East 15th Avenue with two videorecorders and a Uher tape recorder. A radio technician was already ensconced behind the organist preparing to broadcast the service, so our equipment made little stir. Soon the smallish room filled up with churchgoers. A portrait of Prophet Williams on the north wall showed him clad in a white robe tied with a blue sash, gazing upward, full of face, but in the flesh his features looked smaller. His clothes gave his limber physique its distinction: a tailor-made tan suit, flowered tie to match, platform shoes.

The service began in low key, with a woman reading from a script into one of the microphones for the radio program spiritual hour. Two women offered testimonials to the Prophet for curing them of heart disease and cancer. After the radio program the Prophet began to open up the stops. He made up in energy for any lack of charisma or eloquence, and as he started chanting "The wages of sin is death," the congregation responded with increasing fervor. Women closed their eyes, raised their hands, and moaned; several got happy. The enthusiasm continued for about an hour.

As the congregation was dispersing, a woman with large glasses began talking to me at a rapid clip. Mabel McKelvey, a millworker, fifty-six, with a forty-one-year-old daughter, gave her own testimonial, telling how she had been cured of a cyst on her ovary by the Lord, who spoke to her in a dream. This event, coming after a visit to the Prophet's church, had caused her to change to his congregation. Williams had helped her get her job back in the mill when she had lost it because two white foremen had "done her dirt" and harassed and persecuted her. She told how she had driven to the state agency in Indianapolis, complained about them, and got her job reinstated. But the foremen kept giving her dirty work, and she vowed they would suffer for it. And one had to have open-heart surgery, and she donated blood for him; the other had just fallen ill with a collapsed lung. She was explaining the use and power of votive candles to bring about one's wishes, when the Prophet approached and invited me to lunch.

I accompanied him in his car, a custom-made red Rolls Royce on the lawn by the church. (Later I was told that this was one of only ten such cars in existence and cost forty-five thousand dollars.) Over lunch Prophet Williams revealed something of his life and philosophy. He had begun his career as a conventional minister, then for some years went on the road as an evangelist, and eight years ago had founded his own church: the Prayer House of Faith. He recognized different kinds of worshipers—those who just wished to sit still, and those who "wanted to make a joyful noise"—and this latter element chiefly made up his congregation. The Prophet said he had discovered his psychic powers through a dream, while living in Cincinnati with his uncle, who had designs on his wife. When the Prophet confronted him with the charge, the uncle admitted its truth, confessed his shame, and departed. But though acknowledging his psychic abilities, the Prophet did not take special credit for the cures of the diseased and afflicted who came to him for help. Seventy-five percent of them, the white as well as the black, believed in hoodoo. Their parents and grandparents from the south had believed in it, so it was natural for them to continue the belief. In his sermon Prophet Williams had declared that great things were done in Gary, just as they had been done in Tennessee, Alabama, Louisiana; the same miraculous cures and deliverances which the evangelists from the south were always talking about could be duplicated up north. But he now told me that his recipe was simply to give his clients some dirt and tell them to wrap it in a piece of paper and flush it down the commode; assign them a prayer from Scripture to read; and admonish them that if they had faith the affliction would go away. And most of the time it did. "People want to believe. If you stood outside and looked up at the sky, soon a lot of people would gather around you, and they would see what you wanted them to see, or what you said you saw."

That evening, when the Prophet presided over another service in the Prayer House of Faith, our group returned with equipment which refused to function. The Prophet had the recalcitrant hand-held video camera placed on the piano by the altar and blessed it; the bugs vanished, and the team recorded the proceedings without further problems.

In every way Prophet Williams typified success: in his packed congregation, his luxury car, his sartorial splendor, his cures and succour of the distressed. Members of his church reflected his winning ways. Mabel McKelvey, with the help of the Prophet and the Lord, had triumphed over the white foremen in the mill—and not only wreaked vengeance upon them, but then practiced Christian charity by donating blood to one of the ogres. Problems with jobs, alcoholism, and disease melted away before the ministrations of the Prophet, who utilized people's occult beliefs to help them find success through faith in themselves.

### Reverend L. K. Jackson

One afternoon Adrienne and I had an appointment with the Reverend Lester Kendall ("L.K.") Jackson. We drove to the west side of Gary, to an area of substantial homes but bare of landscaping. A sign in front of one house announced "The Old Prophet." At eighty-one the aged militant had survived two strokes and two heart attacks, and was living alone. He met us in his dressing gown, a strongly built figure with flashing eyes. He talked two hours, filling up one ninety-minute cassette and spilling over into another, in protracted response to a few questions about where he came from and what brought him to Gary. The Old Prophet gave as his reasons for coming north the racial injustice in the south and a cruel whipping of a Negro by a white. He described how in Gary he had fought to elevate Negroes from labor jobs into offices and city work and businesses: "I killed myself trying to save this town." He delivered his first sermon in Gary in May 1943. He was contemptuous of other ministers, black and white, for playing to the power structure. Periodically his eyes filled and his voice quavered, but he came back strongly each time. He showed us a full-page story about him, in the *Post Tribune,* December 21, 1975, headlined "Church service in '43 greeted activist 'Old Prophet'," which detailed a number of civil-rights accomplishments of the self-proclaimed "Hell-raiser from the east." In his view he had succeeded in saving Gary from perpetuating the racist social structure he had known in the south.

*Five Classes of Negroes.* The Old Prophet's recollections fell into two halves: his tribulations and difficulties in the south, and his trials and struggles in the north. But unlike most such sagas, he castigated blacks as well as whites. Twice he referred to his "Daddy" as an "Uncle Tom, easygoing, 'yes sir, boss' type of Negro" and wondered: "I don't know why that blood didn't drip down in me, but it didn't." He distinguished "five distinct classes of Negroes"; he refused to use the term "black."

✦ The first-class Negro of sixty to seventy-five years ago wished to send his children to Harvard, Yale, and Princeton and see them educated to be doctors and lawyers. In the south they owned big plantations and sawmills and textile mills and had folks working for them. The second-class Negro wasn't born with anything, but he had something inside of him that made him work himself to death or get something that he could call his own. He would come of age when he became twenty-one, and they would turn him loose, free. He'd save every cent he made to be able to buy him a mule at the end of the year. He going to rent next year. Now that's what you call the second-class Negro. The third-class Negro said: "If you furnish me a house and furnish me something to eat and furnish me this and furnish me everything, I'll work for you." That's what we call a sharecropper; man who worked on the halves. He furnished the labor, and my Daddy [obviously a second-class Negro] furnished the equipment to make the farm. My Daddy got half, and the sharecropper got half of what was made. Now the fourth-class Negro, you couldn't get him to be a sharecropper. He said: "I don't want no mule, because it may get the cholera and die. I don't want no farm, because I ain't working myself to death all the years for a farm and right at the time I ought to be at the other end of getting something we may have a famine or may have a flood. If you want me to work for you I'll work for you as a wage hand." That's by the month, you have to pay him by the month, if you got sense enough to keep it. If you ain't close, he borrow it all; he go out and gamble it up at night and be right back on a pinch farm. See, he get himself in debt, he stayed there. That's what's the matter with the Negro, this man who beats his wives to death.

## Black Outlooks

[The Old Prophet never did get to the fifth class, which was clearly composed of men who would not work at all—the winos, the junkies, the deadbeats.]

I haven't read it in any book, I haven't see it anywhere, but I classified them myself. Now what I'm trying to say is that 90 percent of these people who came here to Chicago, to Hartford, to New York, to Philadelphia, to Boston, to Baltimore, 90 percent of them at United States Steel, Royal Tires, Firestone Tires, were either the third- or fourth-class Negro who never had nothing, never wanted nothing but a pistol. That's why the people who came from down south had such a hard time getting started, getting it to turn over. Why, people who come right from there don't know anything about getting anywhere. When I come here, not a Negro in this town knows what working in a bank is. He couldn't wash a cuspidor nor empty a wastebasket. There wasn't a Negro in this town working in a store behind anybody's counter. There wasn't a Negro in this town who knew what a conductor on a streetcar was. I said, "That [white] man learned it and he came from the bottom of Mississippi. He came up here, he's driving a streetcar, why can't you drive one?" That kind of person he doesn't have any get up and go. He don't see any need for to make it better for his children and his children's children.

All the leading folks in Chicago, in New York, in Philadelphia, they are from the south. The northern-born Negro, he never done anything but had a job as a janitor. And when, back out sixty years ago, when I went north, you say you were from anywhere below Virginia, they looked at you, they just kept on looking at you, trying to find the bag that you carried your tail in [laughs]. Swore you were a monkey.

*Getting an Education.* The Old Prophet grew up in Clay County in southwest Georgia, where his father owned an 1,850-acre farm. Racial incidents drove him to depart hastily at Christmastime 1915 for Hartford, Connecticut, where his sister lived. The following year a representative from Tuskegee University spoke at the First Baptist Church in Hartford and fired up young Jackson with the desire to get an education. He ran home and woke his sister up.

+ I said: "Sister, get up please now and get my clothes together. I'm going to leave here. I don't know where I'm going. I'm going to school somewhere." Just like that.

I went to Georgia State College. I had gotten a catalogue for Tuskegee, Morehouse, and all those schools around there, and that was the cheapest-rate one that I had any knowledge of. Bought me a ticket for Savannah, Georgia, and I believe the ticket was that long. I went there. I hadn't any principal writing a letter for me. I hadn't made any preparation what-

181

soever to go to Georgia State College. I just got up Monday morning and took my little handful of rags and put them in a bag and took off. They sent me over to get registered. Went through the desk and I didn't have any application. I didn't know what he was talking about, talking about "app." I said: "Application, what is that?" He said: "You've got to have an application; we don't take anything in this school here." And, oh my God, that hurt my head. I went to crying like a baby and I laid him out: "I'm not into anything. I'm after a first-class education, and I don't think it's right for you to be depriving me to anything. Will you please tell me (I had sense enough, more sense than he did, way back there then), will you tell me where the president is, how to get in touch with the president?" I never met the president, didn't know a thing about the president. Old Major R. R. Wright was the president of Georgia State College. It's not that now; they changed the name. Major R. R. Wright, he was a major in the Spanish-American War. He came back from the war and they made him president of Georgia State College.

So that man [the registrar] got a boy to take me to the president's office. Happened weren't nobody in the office but him, and I just went on in and I told him what I was doing there, see. "Oh," I said to him, "just give me a chance. Give me thirty days' chance, and if I don't make it send me home." The president said: "Jackson, I'm going to try you. There's something in you, the Lord is helping you. You take this note right over to this same man (who just got through telling me they don't take any trash off the street). You got to have an application signed by the principal of the last school you attended. Your pastor got to sign this." I didn't know you had to pass your civil-service examination to get in there [sarcastically]. That registrar made me so mad I was crying like a baby.

Well, at the end of the month President Wright said to me: "I want to take care of you. You have passed the test in glowing colors to the satisfaction of everybody concerned. I want you to go over there now and register as a student. First class student in Georgia State College." I went over to register. I paid the registrar. I gave him enough money in advance to keep for me to pay him for next year. And I got me a job cutting wood. I'd get up at three-thirty and four o'clock in the morning; I'd go out and cut this old, twisted, short-leaved Georgia pine, one-half or a quarter of it, and roll it in by seven o'clock. They give me four dollars for that.

Faith in himself, coupled with zeal to better his lot through education, in spite of the odds and risks, provides the thread for this episode. The talk by the Tuskegee spokesman induced a kind of conversion experience: "it meant more to me than any speech I ever heard in my life." In this personal success story, the hero (the Old Prophet) wins the treasure (the college degree), in spite of the ogre (the registrar), with the aid of a magic helper (the president), and performs impossible tasks (cutting the wood, passing the test).

*Fighting for Civil Rights in Gary.* The climax of the Old Prophet's history dealt with his militant efforts in Gary to uplift the black community, as he lashed out at black and white ministers and leaders alike for pussyfooting and selling out to the powers that be. As a Republican he could criticize freely the manipulation of blacks by the Democratic machine.

"I took charge of the St. Paul Baptist Church on the first Sunday in May 1943. I been here thirty-three years and one month this coming Sunday." As soon as he arrived in Gary, the Reverend Jackson set about his main mission, which he construed in political rather than religious terms: to give his people "a better political life." According to his recollection, he castigated the chairman of his trustee board for his sycophantic ways. "He was a crook. He was ambitious as he could be, politically. I used to give him hell by the half acre. I said: 'You are pitiful, Ben, you are worse than pitiful. For the privilege to call one of these Polacks by his first name—to call Joe Finnerty "Joe"—you'd burn your grandma's house down and choke your sister's baby to death.' " The Old Prophet discovered that Negro pastors sold the votes of their churches to the political bosses, that one "guy called himself a bishop; he took money from the underworld, and bought himself into the bishopry." Shortly after he came to Gary, L.K. addressed a "big city-wide meeting" and set forth his mission to render the black community independent of corrupt politicians.

✦ I said: "I'm informed that Judge Murray, his honor the judge of the Circuit Court of Lake County, is here." And I demonstrated my preaching; I was as super as a cat. I said: "I want to urge you, I want to pray you, I want to beseech you to line up with me in helping me to accomplish my mission by coming here to give my people a better political life. But we can't get a political life if you politicians are going to sit down on us. I'm asking this Judge Murray, who stayed at Crown Point for some forty years, do you know what would happen, what you judges would do to poor me and my little tribe that I'm trying to get out of here, to lift them up out of this muck and mire and injustice and cruelty and unfair play?"

A Negro down in Mississippi had a wife and ten children and no job. The train came along loaded with coal, and the coal from bumping the railroad shakes down, and lumps of coal would fall out. Man got him a sack and got behind the train and stayed behind it till he got him a sack full of coal to go home and warm his wife and children. Police saw him behind the train, picking up this coal. They arrested him, put him in jail, did fifteen years. How you gonna make it? So now this white man don't steal a sack of coal, he steals the coal mine, he steals the train that's hauling the coal! They give him ten years, and he gonna stay six weeks and he get a pardon and come home, and the campaign starts, and he runs the campaign, is elected governor. Can you see the fear of God looking down on anything like that? What I said to the judge, looking right in his eye: "Now that's going on everywhere. That's not confined to Mississippi."

Now the thing that tore it up, somebody here named Johnson had been sent to the penitentiary and come back and they made him major.* Everybody just died because they thought I was after this man, when I didn't know anything about it.

Throughout his career in Gary, ably summarized by James B. Lane in *"City of the Century": A History of Gary, Indiana* (1978), the Old Prophet fought boldly for civil rights. "My interpretation of the ministry is that he [the minister] ought not to hold his hands out here, begging folks for this and begging for that. You've got to stand up if you want to be helpful to your people and to the world in which you live." The Reverend Jackson stood up and fought—to permit Paul Robeson to speak in Gary (at his own church); to keep Froebel High School integrated; to allow blacks to use Miller Beach; to get black reporters on the *Post Tribune*. Though a Republican, in 1967 he supported Hatcher for mayor. The liberation of Gary, from blacks as well as whites, the Old Prophet regarded as his personal triumph.

The role of the Old Prophet contrasts with those of the other preachers described in this chapter. For him the church was not an extended family, a flock to shepherd, but a platform from which to launch jeremiads against the city. He counted as triumphs not the souls he saved but the bodies of fellow-blacks whom he elevated to previously closed positions on newspapers, in banks, in schools. He fought not to overthrow the system but to make democracy live up to its ideals.

While the Prophet contended against a white man's Gary, the younger generation of Afro-American preachers built their churches from a Gary gone black, and hence felt little need to talk of civil rights or better economic opportunities. They had largely won that battle. The Executive Secretary of the Foreign Mission Board could tell Calvary Baptist how well-to-do they were with their big cars and closets full of clothes and request donations for their hapless brethren in Africa. Calvary stood midway between the decorous First Baptist Church and the revivalist Pentecostal-type congregation of Prophet Williams and Elder Bennett. Wor-

---

* Roswell O. Johnson was removed from the mayoralty of Gary on March 28, 1925, and jailed for conspiring to violate the prohibition laws, but was pardoned by President Coolidge and reelected in 1929.

shipers at Calvary responded and got happy, but in moderation. Their pastor brought them into the Baptist framework, led them to a Baptist convention in Saint Louis, traveled on a Baptist foreign mission touring African countries. The Reverend F. Brannan Jackson was a businessman and politician as well as a churchman, riding the crest of the new Gary and bringing speakers from the outside world into his church.

Prophet Williams and Elder Bennett gave their independent congregations free rein to make a joyful noise unto the Lord. They encouraged possession by the Spirit, dancing in the aisles, and testimonials of faith healing. The Prophet wore a shiny suit and indulged in psychic tricks; the Elder wore rumpled trousers, laid his hands on worshipers and plunged them into the baptismal pool. Each attracted a wide following with his reputed ability to cure the afflicted. The Prophet candidly revealed that his prescriptions were placebos for his people, who had grown up believing in hoodoo. The Elder sincerely believed in the power of faith in the Lord, which had cured his own serious ailments. Both had won the confidence and admiration of large numbers of Gary's blacks. Where the Old Prophet had used the goad, the younger pastors offered carrots. In their several ways, all had tasted success.

## MILLWORKERS

*Wilbert Harlan*

The longest interview I recorded in the Region took place on a rainy Saturday in May 1976 at Jennie's Restaurant, where owner Larry Regan had set up an appointment for me with Wilbert Harlan, a black laborer he knew in the mill. Larry described him as a short fellow who had literally fought for his job at a time when any workers caught fighting were fired on the spot; he had been the first black to gain rights of promotion in the mill. Crippled by arthritis from bending over to shovel slag, Harlan was reduced to janitorial work; but, unlike other janitors, he kept the washroom so clean you could eat off the surface, Larry said. Five days a week after work he voluntarily coached a girls' track team. On this evening the restaurant was closed, and we had to wait for Jennie to open it. But Wilbert began talking while we were still in the car; once inside he talked steadily for three hours, refusing to take a bite of food or a sip of water. Adrienne Seward and Inta Carpenter, who were also there, went to the restroom, my stomach growled, we fidgeted, but Harlan continued until I had used up two ninety-minute cassettes. Larry later told me that Wilbert talked this way in the washroom, and that he had to back away to end a conversation. Poker-faced, sturdily built, forty-nine-year-old Wilbert Harlan seemed in good enough shape to go on forever.

His was heroic talk, a triumphant autobiographical saga, really a series of interlocking victory tales of a black man's struggle to gain a footing in the white man's world. The initial success episode of his life history dealt with his first job, at the age of thirteen.

✦ *The First Job.* I was born in Chicago, went to Clement, Tennessee, when my father passed, to stay with my aunt. She passed too, then I moved to Green Oak, Kentucky, and stayed with another aunt, who seemed to didn't care whether I lived or died. So I solved the problem myself by leaving, caught a freight train and went to Louisville, Kentucky, with about thirty-five cents in my pocket. I was thirteen. And from that day on what I put in my mouth and on my back, I earned it. And I had an experience that I repeat to a lot of kids I work with all the time. It came from my aunt down in Tennessee that reared me. She would always state the thing about Booker T. Washington: it was a point to "make sure you do a good job of whatever you do."

So with my thirty-five cents in Louisville I was walking around trying to find a place for something to eat, and I went in the back of the Walgreen drugstore downtown and asked a guy about food, said: "I want to work. Have you got anything for me to do?" He said to the people in the kitchen: "Give this boy something to eat." They fed me and told me that the guy that cleaned up didn't show up and he wanted me to clean up the place for him. He showed me what he wanted me to do, so he locked the place and left me there.

All the Walgreen drugstores had a big kind of a cafeteria place where they eat and a bar where they serve pop and cokes and things, a fountain. And so the floor was real dirty. It was a white and green tile floor. The guy that worked there he had got drunk, didn't show up. I put all the chairs on the counter and got the soap, and I scrubbed the floor, and all the dirt came up. Got it completely white, and I waxed it. And I cleaned the bar; it had glass which didn't shine through 'cause it was dirty, so I cleaned it till it shined. And it looked like altogether a new room really.

So when I got through I set back and kind of nodded and went to sleep with my feet up. The guy come in and he said: "Boy, what did you do with the floor?" I thought I had done something wrong, you know [laughter]. And he went next door and called the guy there and said: "Come on here and look at this place. I can't believe it, what the kid did." And he asked me did I have any place to stay. I told him the situation I was in, and so he made a place out of the storeroom. I stayed there.

Thus the opening chapter in the life story: a neat, clearly framed moralistic tale embodying the American maxim, channeled through Booker T. Washington: Work hard and you shall be rewarded. Throughout his life Wilbert applied himself to menial work others despised; as he had once cleaned the floors of Walgreen's cafeteria at thirteen, so now thirty-six years later he still took pride in polishing the washroom in the mill. Passing the test of his first job, he found a patron and established his independence. His new boss played the role of a surrogate father to Wilbert, who entered Central High School, played halfback on the football team and set records in the 100- and 220-yard dashes. "Matter of fact at age fourteen I was about the only black guy had a car and riding to school. My boss he got me a driver's license at that age." When Wilbert left for college in Ohio on a football and track scholarship, he carried with him a thousand dollars and a suitcase full of clothes. In Harlan's sophomore year his patron died suddenly of a heart attack, and the boy lost the urge to continue his education. A new path opened up, one that meant hard work but brought in the money, the job of a steelworker. Now commenced the central saga in Harlan's history.

✦ *The Fight to Get to the Floor.* This friend of mine that was living in Gary, he told me: "Hey, come on, go back to Gary and get a job in the mill." That's the first time I been here and I came and got a job in the mill, and as the old story goes, I never got back [laughter]. I started making big money, more money than I ever had in my life. And I started going to Chicago and seeing the big, the tall buildings and night life, and had a lot of fun. That was in '48 I went to the mill, and I worked there for about a year. I got hired at Number 1 Open-Hearth; I was labor. During that time that was the black man's job in the open-hearth: labor. And a matter of fact, all over the mill very rarely you see a black person get achieved anything higher than labor.

When I went there, I stayed there about five years working labor, and I saw guys hired in younger than I was. Younger in seniority, and age, too, that got on the Floor right away. On the Floor you was a success story. You got to the Floor, that's where the money was.

The Floor was the open-hearth floor where they make the steel. The first, second, and third helpers put the ore and stuff in the furnace and make the steel there on the floor. On the other side is the pit side where they pour the molten metal into the mold. We was working down on the ground level, and the open-hearth was up kind of high. We was fixing the big ladles, where they put the steel in with the mud and brick and stuff in there. That was a labor job.

So one day I went to the superintendent, said I had five years' seniority. It had been stated to me that no blacks would never go on the Floor because they didn't want them on the Floor. Some of the guys I heard them say at the washhouse: "They don't allow no niggers on the Floor because we'll walk off; not going to have them on the Floor." Some black

187

guys before me had tried to go on the Floor, and I think when one guy got on there one day they walked off and they had a stink about it and they got rid of him. So I talked to the superintendent one day. I said: "Mr. McDonald, I'd like to go on the Floor." He said: "Oh, you fellows want to go all over the place. Stay on the labor." He told me stay down that way: "You're all right, stay down there." I told him I had a family; my daughter was just born, you know, I wanted support. But he told me to stay where I was.

So I went to the union. I didn't know anybody in the union, see; I didn't never go to the union hall. It was my fault. I just didn't have time; I was running around. So the griever told me, he said: "OK, I'll file a grievance for you." Oh, he raised hell, but I found out later he was going along with the company, with management. That I shouldn't be on the Floor because the guys going to walk off. I just told him: "I don't need you no more, and the heck with it."

So one day, I was supposed to be working days, I decided that day, I said: "I won't go. I'm not going to work. I'm going to the Division Superintendent's office and get my money. I'm going to quit if I can't advance on this job." Because I was just really hurt, wasn't angry. I was just hurt really. You know, a defeated kind of situation, and I was taught not to be defeated.

So, I went to the superintendent's office. I was supposed to have been to work. And I was saying to myself: I going to get my money today because of my race; I can't get a job and I got a little daughter. I had no other idea about a job; that's for the principle of it. I was going to quit. I was definitely going to quit. And I went in and the first time I went in the lady at the desk said the superintendent was busy. So I went back to canteen. The next time when I went back in there, some guy was coming out, and I just rushed right on in the office. And the lady at the desk: "Wait, hold it a minute." But he says: "How ya doing? What you want?" He turned around, told me to sit down. So I sit down. I wanted to explain that I had five years' seniority in the mill and I wanted to get on the Floor; and the superintendent over there [at Number 2 Open-Hearth] says I couldn't get on the Floor, and they hired twenty other guys younger than I was; and I wanted my money because I don't want to work any more. I mean I done my job. I come to work. My work record's better than a lot of guys working on the Floor, 'cause a lot of them laying off and drunk, they was. The Floor was a heck of a situation, had some terrible characters on it, fighting and drunk on the job.

So I went and talked to the division superintendent, his name was Wood. I told him I said: "I'd like to have my money now," because I wanted to quit; because of my race I couldn't get to the Floor. "I want to work; I don't want to steal. I've been taught to work." And he said: "Oh sit down here a minute, let me call." He called down the basement and he got my record. I had a good record, and so he called over to Number 2 Open-Hearth and asked McDonald: "Here's Harlan here; he got five years' seniority and got a good record, come to work all the time—I think he missed about two days work out of five years—and he want to go on the Floor." McDonald says: "Oh, we just hired eight guys last week." Wood said: "He approached you four months ago about going on the Floor. He's a good man, his work is OK, and he's a heck of a lot better than some of these other sowheads like we got now. We got problems with them coming to work, you know. Try to get a man up there that's going to work."

So Wood told me, he say: "How you working?" I said: "I'm working days." He says: "Well, you come up to the Floor four-thirty tomorrow; you the third helper." I told him, I said: "Now the guys, some of the white guys on the Floor said, they're going to quit if a black guy comes on the Floor." He said: "You come on up there. I'll take care of that."

Next day at four o'clock I went up. I got me a shovel and I went upstairs. The third helper needs a shovel; they shovel that stuff in. So I had my shovel; I was standing by the door. McDonald says: "What are you doing up here?" And I said: "I'm the third helper. I'm going to work, trying to get the metal foreman to assign me to a furnace." And at that time they were tapping the heat in the 55 furnace. They were tapping chrome heat; it was expensive heat. And the guys come up to me, and Sanderson—they called him the hillbilly, he was from down south, Tennessee somewhere, W. H. Sanderson—he came and said: "What are you doing up here?" I said: "I'm third helper."

So he told the other guys who was tapping the heat, and they walked off the job. And the metal foreman, Sylvester, is back there trying to throw the stuff in the furnace, try by himself to keep the heat from being destroyed. By that time Wood walked up. He asked Sylvester, said: "Hey, we got a five-hundred-thousand-dollar heat going here, and they're going to destroy it. What's happening? Where's the men at?" Sylvester said: "The guys walked off; they're the bunch down there 'bout in the middle of the shop."

So the division superintendent called: "Come here." So Sanderson knew Wood; he came up. Wood says: "You got to tap this heat or you going to destroy a whole heat like this. What you guys doing?" Sanderson says: "You got a nigger up here working on the Floor; we going to quit." He [Wood] said: "What did you say?" He [Sanderson] said: "Well you got a colored fellow up here." So he [Wood] told him, says: "Now, you guys don't want to work, just give me your name. Got some guys down on Broadway ready to take your jobs. Just get your money tomorrow. Give me your name." So when they saw he was going to fire them, they started to go in behind the furnace, go back to work, went to the job.

[But the transfer of Harlan after pressure from the division superintendent proved only the beginning of a series of harassments by white fellow-laborers.]

Now Sylvester, he's a metal foreman, but he was one of them drunkards too. He stayed drunk on the job, but he was just barely hanging on. So the plant superintendent put the pressure on him to get rid of me. The word got around all over pit side and everywhere. Don't want Harlan to stay up there. So I made up my mind I was going to stay. They tried a little bit of everything. One of the first things Sylvester done was, he told me: "Now your job as third helper, you clean up all these furnaces, three furnaces." But it wasn't that way. I was third helper on this 55 furnace, but I knew I wasn't supposed to clean it up. He told me: "Clean up the whole thing." But I said: "I'm going to do it." I went on and done it; I cleaned, I really cleaned. I moved some stuff out from behind the dolomite machine, and I just cleaned. I worked eight hours. I was so tired when I got home at night, couldn't hardly get in the house. But I felt good. I was determined I was going to stay. Two weeks I was there; the third week we got a blue ribbon, when the safety people came by and saw what I had done.

We would tap a heat, and the third helper got a little shovel. The second helpers got big shovels, to throw the stuff into the furnace, the third helper doesn't go too close, he has the smaller shovel. The guys in the crew would take my shovel and throw it away or hide it, so I got to get a big shovel. It was a joke to some, and a racial problem to some, but later on I found that it wasn't necessarily racial, I don't believe. I think it was self-survival. 'Cause what was happening was, see, a lot of those older guys was bringing their sons and their relations in. So they was looking out for their own, you know. They didn't want me up there because I was taking away a job that maybe some of their relatives could have. The big shovel would make me tired; it was harder, I had to do the same thing the others did with the little shovel. But I decided I'm going to keep up with this big shovel.

And there was another thing they would do. When you walked up to the furnace, normally the door's like this right here [indicating a median height]; you go up and throw the stuff in the door. But when I go up there they raise the door all the way up. Make it hotter, oh! And so I bought a sweatshirt, a long-sleeved sweatshirt, and they started calling me "Smokey" after that. That's my nickname, lot of guys they call me "Smoke." Well, I'd go up there and I'd be smoking and I'd throw the stuff in there and I stuck it out.

And I had a couple of incidents where the guy on the pit side said I was hitting the stopper. They got on me about that. They put me right next to the furnace where the heat was. The ladle's down here, and we up here on the platform throwing it [the manganese] down in the thing [the furnace]. So the pit-side guys, they all got together, they was saying I was incompetent, I couldn't throw it in there right, I was hitting the stopper. To hit the stopper, there's a thing down there in the hole that if you hit that, it make it break and the hot metal would start coming out before you get a chance to pour it in the molds. So they come back accusing me of doing that. And just that time I blew up, I told them that's a lie, and I showed them where ain't no way in the world I could hit the stopper—couldn't even see the stopper, you know.

One day Sylvester, the metal foreman, he told me—I was filling the dolomite machine up, the machine where they spray the back wall in the furnace—he said: "Sambo, you get that dolomite machine full, Sambo. That's your name, Sambo, isn't it?" I said: "No, that's not initially my name, but you call me Sambo, and nigger, anything you want to call me. You call me names and I'll call you names. So we'll just call each other names." And he said: "Oh, your name Willie, I'll call you Willie; my brother's named Willie, you know." Got talking like that.

So we got along. Things went along all right until one day we had a first helper working on the furnace I was on, and he didn't really want me up there. We had a lot of trouble on the furnace; everybody was working hard, sweating, I was wringing wet with sweat, just working like mad. And that day he started calling me, from the time I got to work: "Here nigger, here Sambo, here black boy, come on nigger, come on let's go." So I took it, I said: "Look it here for Christ's sake, why don't you grow up like the other men?" So the rest of the guys began to kind of halfway treat me pretty good. Well, this one time I went to the water fountain. I wouldn't never bother him, but I went to the fountain, bent over to get some water. He put his foot on my behind. I turned around with the shovel and went up side his head with it. See, I hit him on the side of the head with the shovel two or three times. He threw his arm up, I hit him on the arm. That was all. I didn't want to hurt him, so I hit him with the flat part of the shovel, not all that hard you know, because I didn't really want to kill or hurt him. When McDonald found out that Louie was hurt, that he was horrible bleeding and I was hitting him, he called us to the office. He said to me: "Now you're fired."

So, while I was in there a guy named Johnny Hatcher—he was a German from Winnimeg, that's quite a ways from here; he used to come from there to work in the mill—he walked in the office. He said: "Hi, Willie. What's going on, Willie?" I said: "I'm leaving; they're going to fire me." And so Johnny told McDonald, said: "Now, you got a good man here. If you fire this good man, if you call up the plant [to fire him], you got about eight more good men going with him." And he says: "If I'd been him, I'd a done kill that Polack a long time ago, because he's been messing that boy, and all this time he's been taking it. Louie's been riding him for the last three months. I would have busted his head a long time ago." So McDonald says to me: "You go out." And when I went out, Johnny was in there about ten minutes. He come out, says: "Come on, Willie, let's go back to work." It was all over.

About four or five months after that the first helper, Marv Addison, the first helper on the 66 for the middle furnace, he said: "Willie, you're taking everything that they give you; you're a good man, Willie, you're really a good man. Really appreciate working with you." And he said: "Whatever you want to know, let me know and I'll help you." So in front of everybody he gave me a little shovel, and he said: "Take that damn thing [the big shovel] and open the furnace and throw it up in the furnace"— burn it up, you know. And he started shoving me food and stuff. "Come on, come on, get some of this," drinking out of the coffee pot. "Take a cup and get your coffee." Everybody putting money in the coffee pot. I said: "No, I don't care." "No, you drink, take a cup," and he insisted I take a cup of coffee. So I drank it, though I didn't particularly like coffee. After that everybody started coming around, pretty soon it was one happy family. I was part of the gang, and some of them are my best friends now, Johnny Hatcher and some of the guys on the Floor. We finally learned to know each other, and they accepted me for a man instead of a black man, and it turned out all right.

This personal narrative of a black steelworker's rise from the Pit to the Floor corresponds in its structural pattern to the märchen, or fairy tale, that once entertained rural households. It embodies certain American mythic themes. The core of the recital consists of a series of trials through which the underdog hero advances in the face of hostile ogres who torment and seek to destroy him. Some of the ogres are personalized in the guise of the plant superintendent McDonald, the hillbilly Sanderson, the drunken metal foreman Sylvester, Louie the first helper, who devise various schemes to bait, insult, and break Willie—all of which he circumvents. As in the fairy tales, the hero overcomes his enemy with the support of friendly magic-makers; to his aid come the division superintendent Wood, the German millworker Johnny Hatcher, the first helper Marv Addison. The forces of evil are arrayed against the forces of good, and the hero ultimately achieves status and acceptance among the inner fraternity of steelmakers. Meanwhile he maintains his dignity and composure and moral sense. He does not kill his enemy when he has the chance, but he will not shake hands with the defeated ogre. The series of tests that the hero must undergo forms a recurrent element in märchen adventures.

American mythological traits also enter into the saga. The work ethic pays dividend to an indefatigable worker, who labors in an inferno—the open-hearth Floor. Human and civil rights win recognition in the continuous crusade for democratic justice that Vernon Louis Parrington conceived as the American cause. Wilbert is accepted as a man in his own right. The rags-to-riches-ascent finds its metaphor in Harlan's climb from the Pit to the Floor. America's favorite hero-type, a physical superman, is embodied in Smokey, the black third helper who shovels manganese with a shovel that would have crippled an ordinary mortal, and defies, even revels in, the hellish conditions that surround him.

*Coaching a Girls' Track Team.* Like many millworkers, Wilbert Harlan devoted his main creative energies to an "other life" outside the mill. His other life involved community activities and coaching young people, and in particular the training of a girls' high-school track team whom he coached to a magnificent victory. This success story pertains to his other life.

In 1965 Harlan went to Mayor Hatcher to obtain support from the Youth Service Bureau for a girls' track team representing the city of Gary. In 1973 they qualified to go to the nationals, and trained arduously.

✦ We got on the plane and went to California. I didn't sleep that night or I didn't sleep the whole time. We had two days for the meet. I had a nervous stomach. I eat about twenty-five things of Tums. And the uniforms were there—those nylon long pants, some of the mothers cut them off, and we had some kind of T-shirts. We went out in those uniforms and we look the greatest thing in the world. So we had a coaching meeting, and the big coaches there that flown to the nationals, from Tennessee State you know, and I'm sitting up in there, everybody talking about track: "Hey, Sam, how ya doing? What your girls doing? Oh, you're going to win this thing dead, man." And I'm sitting there looking scared, trembling, but not necessarily trembling. I really believed in my heart I worked those girls so they was going to win. It all depends on Latanda moving out and Robin getting that baton, I told the girls. They said with tears in their eyes: "Mr. Harlan, you stood by us; we going to win it for you," and they was crying. I said: "Okay, now you do the best you can. I'm going to stand by the finish line."

They call the one-hundred-yard dash. Deborah Clay got the second. She and the other girl got photo finish, and right now I believe that Deborah won. I know she qualified for the Olympic team [the first two qualified]. The only one that didn't do what I said to do was Robin Williams. She got third in the 220, and the girl did beat her 'cause she leaned and Robin didn't do it; they was tied at the finish, but Robin didn't lean though I'd been teaching her.

So the relay was coming. The girl that beat Deborah was anchor for the last leg. So Robin got the lead from the second-best girl there; she got the baton okay from Latanda. And she gave it to Sherry, and the other girl passed her, about that far [spreading his hands]. When Deborah got the baton they was in front of us, and Deborah's running against the girl that beat her in the one hundred. Now Deborah's the kind of person that nobody never beat her twice. Now the coach supposed not to be on the track, but knowing Deb, I know that was going to happen. I looked in the bag I had and I got that smelling salts. I put that in my pocket and jumped over the fence out there on the finishing line. When Deborah got that baton she started coming, and there was about six thousand people there and everybody was standing. That was the hell of a race I ever seen in my life. She passed that girl and beat her about that far, and when she went through the tape, she done collapsed, and I caught her, and she and I both fell off the track.

In certain ways the account of the relay victory parallels the account of the fight for the Floor. The underdog laborer is matched by the underdog female runners. Obstacles must be overcome to get to the goal: the open-hearth or the track meet in California. Once the goal is reached the heroic struggle commences to win recognition in that arena. In the mill, Harlan ends up encircled by newfound buddies who ritually drink coffee with him; at the meet, he ends up with Debbie prostrate in his arms after the momentous triumph of "the youngest girls . . . that ever won in the history of America." Again the effort of will, the hard work and single-minded determination, pays off.

A new element enters the track meet story in the figure of Mayor Hatcher, who symbolizes black pride in Gary. When Harlan began working in the mill, the city was still under white political domination; by 1973 a black mayor and a black influx have transformed Gary. In the first case Harlan was fighting for the black cause in general, as he sought equal treatment with white millworkers; in the second he is representing the black city of Gary in a national competition.

The role of Mayor Richard Gordon Hatcher as hero-savior of black Gary comes to the fore in another segment of Harlan's annals: the successful transformation of Gary from a white city marked by corruption and prostitution to a reborn and revitalized black metropolis under the leadership of Hatcher.

*Gary Redeemed.* As Harlan perceived his own life as a sequence of episodic success stories, so did he visualize the regeneration of Gary as a generalized success chronicle. Before Hatcher's advent, Gary deserved its reputation of Sin City, and Harlan himself had succumbed to its vices.

✦ At that time Gary was wide open. People walking the streets more at night than during the day. You leave 25th and go up to 15th and you would have about ten, fifteen gambling joints wide open. Every poolroom had a gambling joint in the back. Wide open just like Las Vegas. It was illegal, but the administration at that time was having people collecting money off of it. See, they got their 40 percent. As long as the guy running the joint could pay off he could run it. And they collected off of the prostitutes, the pimps down in the Border [as the area was called]—a hell of a situation.

But along came a guy, Richard Gordon Hatcher. He done more for the black people, I think, than any human being ever. Like everybody else, I was saying what could I do; nothing I could do, I didn't get involved. Hatcher came to Gary, he got involved in the council, and he was talking to us openly. He's the first black man ever went out to the city council and tell us about the plights of the black people in Gary. And the first speech that he made when he was trying to run for mayor, he was saying that he wanted to teach the black people that they can survive without illegitimate or near illegitimate operations. When Hatcher became mayor, he closed down most of the places on the Border. He came as a big savior.

I was a gambler. I called myself a gambler at one time. I made a lot of dough but, I'll never forget it, I went to 15th and Broadway, I lost five hundred dollars in about thirty minutes; I was broke. I came out, thought about my family. I had a little daughter at home, hadn't paid no rent. I ain't got no food in the house, nothing. I said, should I commit suicide here, walk in front of a car or bus? I just want to die. But I knew a friend of mine at that time, Mac, a policy operator, I had taken pictures of his family. I went to him and I told him I needed one hundred dollars; I had to pay my rent. And I got the one hundred dollars and paid my rent and got the groceries, and that was my last gambling episode.

The whole era's gone. Prostitutes they gone. Some moved downtown on 5th, but nowhere near like it was; it was so open. You never take your family in your car down Adams Street. Women be out there shaking their breasts at you, pulling their dress up, and panting; they're so bold. I was able to mingle with and know some people that was going through horror down there. The pimps were beating the hell out of the women and putting them on dope. I seen a lot of little young dope addicts—fifteen- and sixteen-year-old dope addicts in the black community—at the State Hotel, down on 17th and Washington. You get all the dope you wanted to. And the administration collected money off of that too. Everything was going on. Till the mayor came in. And a lot of people said he's no good and he didn't done this and didn't done that, but I sincerely believe God sent him, for he sure enough deliver the black people.

There's nobody, nobody in the world, can beat Hatcher in Gary. And he got a lot of people jobs. You go down 9th and Madison, City Hall, 5th and Broadway, lot of black women working there now, in different agencies, in banks. Used to be the only thing that a black woman could do in Gary was catch that train to Chicago. Now there's more money in the black community in Gary, I think, than any other city I know of in America.

This is a heartfelt testimonial of deliverance and resurrection, with Hatcher as the Christ-figure. Harlan offers himself as an example of the sinner, depraved and redeemed by providence, who now strives for the betterment of his people as a disciple of his savior-mayor. And the mayor has indeed succeeded in saving the city, spiritually and materially.

Yet the cause must be sustained, and the black population of Gary should not slacken their efforts to dignify their city, Harlan warned in a related cautionary tale. Hatcher was victorious over the corrupt machine politicians and showed his people the way. But after his election they had relapsed into inertia and complaining. In the following episode Harlan assumes an unpopular role, counseling his black constituents that they cannot simply blame Whitey for their problems, but must, literally, clean their own house.

✦ I got to be committeeman. I had a building [in my precinct] down on Madison, and some guy in Glen Park owned it. And they were telling me to come look at it. When I went to the building I saw the garbage in the corner and rats and roaches. I said: "Like to have a meeting at Roosevelt Park?" We met over there, and they called me Uncle Tom and everything else. I told them, I said: "Now there's no way in the hell I'm going down there and tell that man till you do your job. Did that man put that damn garbage in the corner of that building? Did he have that garbage all over the place? You been living in all that stuff and you don't clean it up." I said: "I'm not going to tell that man he's responsible for rats and roaches. Now the plumbing down there, he may be responsible for that, I'll see. But I'm not going down there and condemn that man and charge him about rats and roaches when you not doing your job. You clean that thing up, then I can see about the rest. And that little boy (I knew him 'cause he played on Little League), he had a hammer and he'd go and knock the plaster off the wall; now that's somebody's responsibility. The man can't take care of all that." I said: "Now you do your part, then you can complain about something else."

They said: "You no good, you Uncle Tom." You know, they called me everything, and "I'm not going to vote for you no more." I said: "I would like for your vote, but I don't give a damn if you don't vote for me, if you that kind of person. I'm here not as a politician; I'm trying to do something for the community where I live. I live here; I'm not going to Glen

Park or nowhere. I love this place. I love my neighbors on both sides. Got beautiful neighbors; they got a key to my house, I got a key to their house. I won't leave there. Right by Roosevelt School. I love the area. One time, you know, I got a little money, I'd be saying we going to leave. Almost got right to the point of buying it; my wife she want to go in the swimming pool over Gary Heights somewhere. I say: "Nope, I'm not going. I work with the kids here, I wouldn't leave. I get a million dollars I wouldn't leave, because I love and I'm a part of the community, and I'm doing something for 'em." We helped clean it up; we got a clean precinct. And I talked with people; I gave them some citation for not getting a garbage can. They're mad at me, but they love me and they know I care about their children and them. It's a thankless job, no money. The precinct men used to make some money, but since Hatcher been mayor they ain't making no money. Damn thing, I went in my pocket thirty dollars this time. I was madder than hell. Every damn body got no money. I mean I go in my pocket and spend money.

All the civic virtues come to the fore in this narrative: loyalty to the mayor; fairness to the white landlords; appeal to the tenants' pride and parental responsibility. Harlan exhorts his constituents to maintain cleanliness and order; he describes his love of neighborhood, his willingness to take abuse for civil principles and to make financial sacrifice, his scorn for the old corrupt politics and allegiance to the new savior. He contrasts the father-figure who is leading his people out of the wilderness with the slack and indolent followers. Modeling himself on the mayor-savior, he admonishes the ghetto blacks to pitch in, to beautify their Gary, to share his love for their city. The people respond, and clean up the precinct.

*Robert Jackson*

He typified Gary's new, aspiring, black go-getters. One Sunday in May 1976 Adrienne Seward and I called on him in the new home he had just purchased in Glen Park. The house was furnished with water-dripping lamps, elaborate standing ashtrays, plastic-covered sofas. He admitted that he loved to talk, and we recorded ninety minutes of his thoughts and ideas about Gary, the business ethic, black-white relations, and his own career—a mixture of homespun philosophy, couched in street talk and delivered at galloping speed.

Robert Jackson's life centered on Gary, to which his family moved from Kalamazoo, Michigan, in 1937, when he was two years old. He considered the 'Velt (Roosevelt) the greatest high school in the world. Kids from every ethnic group attended the 'Velt, and he had starred in three sports: as a halfback in football; as a sprinter, running the hundred-yard dash in 9.7 seconds; and as a Golden Gloves boxer, fighting above his 145 pounds because he couldn't find anyone his own weight to take him on. "Sports are the black man's salvation." He still looked fit and capable of holding down two full-time laboring jobs. In addition, he was sales representative for a consumer company, which eliminated the middleman. Jackson exuded energy; he was positive in movements and speech, unsmiling save for one moment when he suddenly broke into a laugh. He had written three to four hundred songs, none of which had been published; but he had sung them to himself until his lip had been cut in an auto accident in which his car had rolled over nine times. He still performed as an instrumentalist. He had no time for sports now, and his muscles complained for lack of exercise. Religion played no part in his life; he attended no church, and said he could tell good from evil on his own. At school he had been an indifferent student, but now he read up on everything he wanted to know. If his daughter asked a question about her schoolwork that he could not answer, he went to the library and got out all the books on the subject. He could, he said, remember everything he heard and warned us that he could repeat everything we talked about.

The practical rather than the occult obsessed Robert, although his mundane affairs sometimes bordered on the folkloric. Of his sex life, he mentioned that at one time thirty-five women had sought his favor, but he curtailed this activity when he realized that his body required six days to rejuvenate after an "ejaculation." He saved all his energies for money-making, for the betterment of his family and his standard of living, and to him Gary offered the best of all possible worlds.

✦ The only place I know is Gary. I've been other places, but my life-style centers around Gary. I love Gary; as far as I'm concerned, there's no other place in the world. There's nothing that you can find any other place in the world that you can't find here. Gary is the seaport to the world.

Gary has a bad reputation for vice, corruption, low living standards. They say you can't walk the streets at night because everybody's always afraid of the junkie. This is political. The same things happen in Chicago and New York, but because we are a smaller city, people pay more attention to us. We also have a bad reputation because we are 57 percent black and have a black administration.

Gary isn't even a hundred years old. It was founded as a streetcar cobblestone town. Twenty-five years ago this was a dirt road. I used to hunt rabbits out here. Gary wasn't designed as a metropolis. Chicago was designed as a metropolis, so they had time to tear things down. Gary's so small that they can't tear down one section of the town, so they just let it all go to pot and then will rebuild the whole city. Gary's going to be the best place to live in Indiana. Because of evolution. This changing over is a ten- to twenty-year process, so it's going to take time to change. Downtown, for every store that closes, another one opens up. In Chicago they close up a big store and it's in the paper one day. But in Gary they close one little store and it's national goddamn news.

The problems of the Gary blacks stemmed, in Robert's eyes, from pernicious influences of the white man. He declared that blacks had only begun committing suicide within the last ten years, as they learned lifestyle and values from Whitey, and with them, frustration and dependency.

✦ The honkey is trying to kill the nigger—divide and conquer, in other words: the light-skinned from the dark-skinned, middle-class from the poor. It's all political.

All the Jews came into Gary about forty years ago, built these stores, made money, and then went back to the Old Country. They just said: "Fuck the nigger!" They had the money in their pockets and they hit that highway. Anyone who lives here will have to rebuild the town. The money is still here, but the white man has it locked up so he can come back here and live when they rebuild a new Gary, and he wants you and I [black folks] to leave.

The whole negativism of the blacks came with the influx of heroin. If you take out the dope you take out the problem. Blacks drafted into the white man's army were taken overseas—1939, 1940—and sold some dope and got turned on to something they didn't know nothing about. Came back and said: "Hey, man, I've got something that's way out. It'll make your whole body light up." So he thought he was getting into something hip. (Originally the whole world was centered around slavery and prostitution. That's how Rockefeller got rich, that's how the Kennedys got rich: prostitution, alcohol, and dope.) So as time passed, more blacks go to the army, more blacks become gullible. You never heard of a goddamn perverted black man until the black man went to the army, to Sweden and France. "The dope addict must have sweet and he must have heat." So when they bring this stuff back, we are Oreos. There's no more black man; the black man is in Africa. We have black covers with white images within us because we have been brainwashed to think the way the honkey wants us to think.

But as far as Gary's concerned, we live here because we love this place, because we make more money here than a layman can make anywhere else in the world. You can't go to Detroit and get a job where everybody makes eighteen, nineteen, even a hundred thousand dollars. People in

Gary aren't buying five-thousand-dollar homes; they're buying forty-five-
and fifty-thousand-dollar homes. They buy Mark IVs and Cadillacs, and
they buy books, and they go on vacations and wear funny fur coats, with
a motherfucking rock on their finger. They don't be stealin'; they don't
be peddlin'; they don't be pushin'—they be flat out gettin' it. 'Cause that
U.S. Steel is open. The doors are always open, twenty-four hours a day.

Making money, which he called "smacking doobers," preoccupied
Robert's thoughts and consumed most of his time. He had gone through
a kind of conversion to capitalist values in 1957, when white society
began giving the blacks more of a chance. In his words, he belonged ideo-
logically and historically "to the left of nowism and to the right of slavery," meaning that he had been born after slavery but before the civil-
rights battle had been won. He saw the turn of the tide as dating from the
return of black soldiers from overseas after World War II. The first black
pilot in the Air Force, Cornel McCollum, had graduated from the 'Velt
and won an appointment to Annapolis, he mentioned. Desiring a larger
house so that his wife could entertain, and wishing to send his two sons
to college, Robert drove himself unsparingly in his two blue-collar jobs
and dabbled in a business on the side.

✦ Number one, I work at U.S. Steel. I work physically, at the rail mill to
turn railroad tracks to go to the Amtrak trains. The rails are thirteen
yards long and weigh between 1,800 and 2,100 pounds per rail. I turn the
rails for inspection that they may see any hairline flaws in it that will
cause a line to break or damage. That's my number one job. Number two
job, I work at the BUDD Company [auto bodies]; been at the company
going on six years. I'm a hooker, I hook steel. Steel's transported from
one place to another place by cranes, and the crane can't just pick up the
steel. Must have a man to put the chains around the steel to hold it in
proper places so that it can be set down properly. That's the hooker's job.
The craneman's forty feet up in the air, I'm on the ground, and I direct
him manually with my hands or with my voice or whatever.

Thirdly, I work for the consumer organization. The stores [in downtown Gary] are going out of business seeing how they aren't making any
money, but the reason they're going out of business is because we [con-
sumers] have become educated to the point that we know that I don't
have to pay you three hundred dollars for this lamp. 'Cause I got the
same from the wholesale house for eighty-five dollars. See, I sell the
wholesale commodity, saying that if you pay an initiation fee to join this
particular club, we will make it possible for you to go to the factory and
get everything you want. The whole thing's buying and selling with the
elimination of the middleman. That's the third job.

## Black Outlooks

I read fifteen years ago some place that anything you do, or are engaged in doing, you can do ten times as much if you prepared yourself properly mentally. So when I make my mind up, it's a mental situation. It's not physical anguish. 'Cause if I'm not working, I sit around, maybe I drink a highball or look at TV till twelve or one at night. But if I'm working at night, I still get the same five or six hours of sleep. So why not make that energy pay me? Why should I lay around or look at or argue with my wife or argue with the kids or wrestle with the dog or whatever and not get paid for it? They pay me nine dollars an hour to get tired. I can't get nine dollars sitting around here. Sure I get tired. My legs hurt. I get cranky. I get evil. But I feel I'm doing a service to somebody other than myself; and after a man becomes twenty-one years old, he doesn't owe himself every day. Especially if he has a family. After a man has a child, he doesn't owe himself for anything the rest of his life. His whole life is dedicated to his child. 'Cause this child did not ask to come. He should have planned for the child after the child is here; he owes the child everything. He can't look at his child when his child gets to be fifteen and says to him: "Well, I wanna go to school. I wanna be President of the United States. Will you help me be President of the United States? I need education in order to be President of the United States. Will you help me be President of the United States?" He says: "No, I only make $13,000 a year." I can't say that. I brought him here. So I say: "Well, since you have the desire to be President, I'll give you all the mechanics so that you may be President if you desire to do so." That costs me time; it costs me work. So I got another job.

Did he ever consider going into business for himself? Yes, he replied animatedly, he was seeking a franchise for International Pancake House and had been to Chicago to talk about it, needed to put up $55,000, was waiting for an exit to be constructed from I-90 to Broadway to bring shoppers downtown.

His two chief heroes were Mayor Hatcher, who had done wonders for Gary and made it the center of America, and Muhammed Ali, who made millions and told Whitey where to get off.

Robert had proved his point, had bought his middle-class home, was contemplating going into business for himself, was educating his children. He possessed full confidence in the future of Gary. He understood its problems as compared with Chicago and made a shrewd point about their relative size. With U.S. Steel providing good jobs and Mayor Hatcher at the helm, black Gary would prosper, so long as black people worked hard and avoided Whitey's vices. Robert knew street culture and street talk, and he held laborers' jobs, but he was branching out into capitalistic dealings, and he welcomed us in a house filled with brand-new furniture. Gary-bred and Gary-proud, he had nothing in common with the black southerners from whom I had once collected folktales.

## A PSYCHIC

We kept hearing about psychics, seeing psychic and spiritualist shops, and reading newspaper accounts of psychic performers. A *Post Tribune* feature story stated that some two hundred psychics, black and white, practiced in the Region and singled out Kirby Jeffries for a detailed portrait. Jeffries, black and highly educated, had achieved a local reputation with daily radio shows. Gil Cooley of our team had been concentrating on black practitioners of occult arts, for comparison with the hoodoo informants he had collected from in the south, and he set up an appointment for us with Jeffries. My interest in meeting a reputed psychic was particularly piqued as I became aware of the prestige attached to the term. "Psychic" designated not an oddball, crank, or charlatan, but a recognized community figure on a par with a minister, teacher, doctor, or lawyer in his possession of esoteric professional skills with which to serve his clientele.

Kirby had his headquarters on East 5th in a tawdry neighborhood. His meeting room and office matched the surroundings—dingy and drab and lacking any of the bustle described by the reporter. A redheaded woman sat at a card table in one corner, with a husky black fellow lounging alongside her; both looked bored stiff. An impassive black woman, whom we learned was Kirby's sister, stood by the cash register at the west end, prepared to sell the few candles visible in a showcase. At the opposite end of the hall, an altar displaying various sacred objects indicated that religious services as well as fortune-telling were conducted in this chamber. Becoming restless, for nothing seemed to be happening, I told Gil I was leaving, when Kirby's sister approached and said the Psychic would see us now. She led us through a curtain next to the showcase, and we found him seated behind a desk piled with books and a large Bible on which some bills of high denominations were lying loose; he removed them with a laugh and a wisecrack. Jeffries had a long face, buck teeth, and a gurgly laugh; he talked constantly, forcefully, and elegantly. He had studied and taught at Grambling College in Louisiana and had spent some years as a high school German teacher and as a specialist in adult education.

✦ I don't want to teach anymore; I want to be a psychic, so that I can learn and then apply whatever I have. I belong to a Spiritualist Church; I am a reverend and an ordained minister; I have an honorary doctorate's degree. In my ministry I got a call, and I am able to use my psychic ability, my spiritual ability, to enhance my ministry. In fact, when I get in the pulpit, it gets dangerous, if I want it to. I can do things that you don't even know in the world!

Well, I am probably the only minister in all of Indiana who, being an ordained Christian minister, would work side-by-side with a witch—the lady with the red hair out there, sitting at the table. She is an ordained bona-fide witch; she belongs to a Satanic church. I am also a nightclub entertainer, a television entertainer, a radio entertainer, and I entertain at country clubs and social house parties. In fact, this is the way that I make my living. It is a sizable living; I can't complain. I haven't held a job, a bona-fide position, for six or eight years. The radio station pays me thirty-nine dollars per week, and that's all I get for the show. I used to pay my chauffeur that much to take me to the station.

I am a part of the Metropolitan Spiritual Church of Christ, Incorporated, in Chicago. Did you ever hear of the First Church of Deliverance? Well, that is probably the largest Spiritualistic church in Chicago, maybe in the world. I was born and raised in the Baptist church. But the Baptist church goes only so far, and then the Spiritual church goes further. The Baptist church does not have a decision as to whether you can communicate with angels; the Spiritualistic church does.

It [his former church] is a very small storefront type church, and whenever I would have programs, they were so dynamic, until there would be crowds of people so large that traffic could not get by in the streets, trying to get into this little church on 17th and Massachusetts, right on the corner here in Gary. I used my mediumship. In fact, I could stand from the pulpit, pick somebody out, and tell them their home, the things that are on their table, what their husband's name was, what questions they had and problems, and turn right around and keep on having prayer and service. It has turned into quite a thing.

As we were talking the Psychic showed increasing interest in Gil and, turning to him with a penetrating look, said: "I keep picking up the vibration of your being interested in religion. Are you aiming to become a preacher?" We stared in astonishment, and Gil replied: "Oh, why you *must* be a psychic! We were talking about this outside and I told Professor Dorson that I may be a preacher." (Later I speculated on whether the chair area had been bugged or Jeffries' sister had overheard our conversation and passed it on to Kirby.) "I sensed that," declared the Psychic triumphantly and, raising his voice almost to a shout, continued: "Oh, if I were to just start reading you, I could probably tell you a lot of things. I'll amaze you sometimes, even on the telephone. Like my radio show, I stopped and asked people if they had on a dress that was blue with white flowers or white with blue flowers, or pictures on the wall, or yellow roses on the table, and be right, even from talking to them on the phone. I can listen to you think, like you talk to me out loud. *You have no secrets from me if I really wanted to know* [this with great emphasis, boring in on Gil]; none. There are some things that I don't desire to know," he qualified, "and I have a conflict with my consciousness, in terms of my present frame of thought and subconscious thought, which regulates and rules."

When Gil raised the subject of voodoo, the Psychic responded quickly.

✦ Voodoo is a very powerful religious science. It does exist. Any aspect of mental influence which is set forward can change, I believe, a person's frame of consciousness or his frame of physical being. Now that's a heavy statement, but when you play it back and hear it, you will stop and think about what I am saying. It is the mind which does the work. You reach up and do it through spirits, or you can do it through the mind. I believe that such a thing does exist. It is verified in the Scripture and is verified scientifically. Aside from that, I have relatives and friends, and I myself, have been personally involved in it.

People are not ashamed of being what they are. In fact, one of my very good friends, the Reverend Catherine White, is a Voodoo Queen. I had a birthday party at the Merrillville Holiday Inn and I invited many people to come out. Reverend Catherine White came, and she is a Voodoo Queen, ordained into the Queen of Voodoo at Haiti—that's what she went there for, that's what she got ordained for. She came back with it and she is not ashamed of it. We had a big birthday cake, which cost me about one hundred bucks, and we asked all the ministers who were there, regardless of what they were, to come in and put their blessing on the cake. Reverend Catherine White came and gave her voodoo blessing. All the ministers who were there blessed this cake, and that cake got so funny, you were afraid to even eat it. We had witches who were there. We had pagans who were there. We had priests who were there. We had ministers. Some of everybody was there, and everybody put their blessings on the cake.

Several years ago I had a young lady who had a relative who came to me. This was her aunt. I told her aunt that she had a niece whose name was Thorn, so she said yes. And I told her that the niece was having a problem that she didn't want to stay in school. And the aunt said: "Yes." I said: "I know what the problem is: she doesn't have any hair; she has had scarlet fever." I told her that the Spirit (and this is a term you very often hear when you are talking with psychics or spiritual people; we use the term Spirit; we don't say "God said" or "His angels said," we simply say "the Spirit said") that she would take a bath in a particular kind of salts and a particular kind of herbs that would grow hair on her head. The doctor had said that she would never have any hair. She took a bath with the salts and the herbs, and now she has an Afro this wide! And mine isn't even that big!

A few days before a Czech steelworker had told about some of his psychic abilities and experiences, and how he could see auras around a person's head. I now mentioned this conversation to the Psychic, who picked up the thread.

✦ I can do that. In fact, I can even do it over the telephone or radio. You should hear myself! The aura is made up of colors; and the holy pictures—or the masters or the teachers or some of the other great people in the world who have these illuminated lights around their heads—this is a part of the aura. Except that that is not around the head, but that is where it is most intense, because of the mental energy which is there. The aura is around the whole body. If you find someone who doesn't have an aura, in three days they will be dead. It goes out before you pass away. Whether you are going to get hit by a train or otherwise, it goes out. I don't understand why, so don't ask me; I don't know, but it goes out. I have seen it. Usually if I find someone who doesn't have it, I won't read.

Sensing what was in my mind, he turned to me reassuringly: "By the way, yours is brightly shining, you don't have to worry."

When Gil mentioned his interest in the folklore of ghosts, the Psychic responded: "There have been a number of things which have been both public and private with me concerning ghosts. I was just this past Saturday in the home of a young man who had recently gotten married again. His first wife had died of cancer. She had a very bitter passion about passing away, and said that she was going to haunt him, and if he ever got married again, that she would see to it that they would not be happy. So they came to me and asked me to go out to the house and get rid of this spiritual entity. It was an experience, believe me."

*The Cline Avenue Ghost*

The Psychic recalled a well-publicized ghostly adventure in which he had played a prominent role. It concerned the ghost of Cline Avenue, a spectral figure frequently sighted at that busy thoroughfare, whom Mexicans in the neighborhood associated with their legendary La Llorona, the wailing woman in white, searching for her children. The idea occurred to the station manager of deploying his program psychic to contact the Cline Avenue ghost.

✦ On the Indiana tollway, at Cline Avenue, before the tollway was built, there was a Cudahy factory, and the Cudahy girl's ghost was supposed to

205

appear there every Halloween. So on our radio show we did a publicity stunt, and Anne Rose and I went there to do a live radio broadcast. We were going to visit the site of the Cudahy ghost and the whole thing. They had forgotten that I am a real psychic and Annie is an astrologist. She works through the planets. I don't need a planet to do anything. If I want to, I can just tune in. I have enough whatever it is that it takes to get the job done.

They had representatives from the police department, the coroner's department, truck drivers, people with picnic baskets—there must have been about two hundred to three hundred people there. This was a live radio broadcast. We got there late; we were supposed to have gotten there just before sunrise, and we were going to take part in it and broadcast the tail end. And people were there who had been publicizing it for days and days, and there were crowds of people there. We got there late, about 8:30 or 9:00 A.M. The sun was high; it was bright and there was not a cloud in the sky. The river "smokes"—it has steam on it. So, we were talking about all this, and we were picking up little impressions, such as this must have been where such a thing happened. By the way, that used to be the "bump-off place" for the Chicago syndicate, back in the early twenties, and there are lots of unusual things seen and heard in the area. If you ever want to go out there and see if you can rattle up something, that's the place to go. There have been three or four policemen's bodies found in it, a couple of kidnapers found in their cars that had been lying there for three or four months before they were discovered—all kinds of "goodies."

So we went out there, and I started talking about this bride. According to the story, the woman who was the Cudahy ghost was abandoned at the altar. She went to the bridge, jumped off, and killed herself in that river; and this is the ghost that is supposed to come up. On Halloween she has allegedly gotten into cars with people and asked if she could have a ride to some hospital or somewhere, and while the car was going, she faded away. I have never seen her fade away, but this is what the story says. Newspaper accounts tell about a lot of people they had to take to the hospital, because they are so rattled after these experiences. But whatever it was that was in their car talked with them and then just disappeared.

At any rate, we went to the bridge, and about two hundred and fifty to three hundred people, television cameras, radio crews, state police, the coroner's department, and crowds of people were out there. And something happened on the river. Now you can call it a ghost if you want to. I raised it really. This thing came up, about eighteen- to twenty-feet-tall, dressed as a bride with a bouquet of flowers in her hand and her bridal veil, and started for the bridge. We didn't have to ask anybody, do you see it? We didn't have to ask anybody, what are you going to do? Me and everybody else got off that bridge, and you talk about running like hell! The truck drivers, the camera crews, they dropped tape recorders, cameras—we were going to talk to this wonderful ghost and to see if we could have it enlighten us, to tell it that it should go on and make its progress and pass on into the world of the spirits. And people went this way and that and left the bridge. This was a live radio broadcast. That can be proven. That is radio-documented fact.

This was October 21, probably 1974 or 1973—I am not quite sure of the year, but the radio station will know. In fact I started to write an article about it and send it in to *Fate* magazine, but I never did.

In the persona of the fast-talking Psychic we see the transformation of the old rural southern hoodoo doctor into a modern urban occult performer with a city clientele. He uses the media, he has acquired formal education and esoteric learning—at one point he declared: "This is a heavy mysticism; I have taken you through five years of intense study in about fifteen minutes"—and he employs a sophisticated vocabulary. Now the older themes are cloaked with Spiritualistic and Rosicrucian references, but he still professes belief in the reality of ghosts, spirits, malign forces, conjuration, prophecy, and voodoo. He sets these ideas in a rationalistic system that accounts for development of psychic powers as a logical, intellectual progression. Within this framework he relates individual success stories of psychic feats: the exorcising of a vengeful spirit; the raising of the Cudahy ghost, an event that epitomizes the urban legend-making mechanism. The saga of the Cline Avenue ghost blends with the Mexican ethnic legend of La Llorona, the American-wide legend of the Vanishing Hitchhiker, and the underworld legend of Syndicate murders. Local legendary traditions fasten onto a prominent part of the landscape, perhaps a cliff, a pond, a cave, a gnarled oak, a spring. Here we have an urban setting known as the "bump-off place": a spooky spot off a heavily traveled artery by a bridge where steamy vapors ascend and crime-related deaths are frequent. That the Psychic should raise the Cudahy ghost in front of cameras, newsmen, radio broadcasters, and the curious crowd perfectly exemplifies the modernizing process that maintains the archaic tradition.

## A QUILTMAKER

One evening in May 1976 a black schoolteacher delivered an inspirational guest lecture on the art of quiltmaking, a tradition she had absorbed from her mother and grandmother in the rural south and brought to Gary. We know little of the material culture products of Afro-

## Land of the Millrats

Americans, in contrast to our familiarity with their vast wealth of oral expressive culture, hence the special interest of this presentation.

Anna Davenport taught career education in the seventh and eighth grades at Froebel School. Born in Canton, Georgia, the home of her grandmother, she was raised in Alcoa, Tennessee, near Knoxville, where her mother, Beulah B. Brown, lived. She had come to Gary twelve years before, after teaching on Indian reservations in Nebraska and Alaska. Another black teacher in my class had arranged for Anna to come to this session, at which the students were giving reports on folk art. Anna hung patterns from the top of the blackboard and piled quilts across the desk and over the chairs. We took colored photographs of the display, and with Anna's help I marked them: Hills and Valleys, Railroad Tracks, Crazy Quilt, Grandmother's Tulips, Steps to the Statehouse, Log Cabin, Cathedral Window, for the quilts; Laurel Wreath, Wedding Ring, Blazing Star, Tulips, Windmill, Lily Corners, for the patterns.

Studious-looking, with spectacles and birdlike features, Anna spoke with charismatic fervor. Her remarks constituted not simply an informative lecture but also an exhortation for moral and spiritual improvement. In talking about quiltmaking, Anna was embodying her philosophy of life, her productive use of time and materials on the hurried, hectic urban treadmill. Imbued with missionary zeal, she broadcast her message in short, sharp bursts, with hardly a pause, and with a firm sense of the larger values to be learned from quiltmaking.

✦ Good evening. I want to tell you what I've done today. I got up about five and I cleaned house and I went to work; and my son was supposed to clean one of the post offices in Gary, but he didn't do it, so Mama had to clean it. Can you imagine that? Then I ran home and got it together and here I am. *I'm tired* [laughter]. Ah, but it's a good tiredness. And some people have asked me, where do you get all of that energy from? And I say, I got it from my mother. So I will be mentioning some of that because I think, you often wonder, why does a person like me get interested in a hobby like this. Well, this is just a recent hobby that I started in August.

So, energy-plus—that I learned from my mother. She is seventy-five years old and she had raised eleven kids and she only went something like sixth grade, and my father third grade. But they had a belief that you don't throw away anything and you make use of everything you can, and, number one, you don't waste any time ever. Time is too precious to waste. Well, I'm still learning this lesson at fifty and I find that you don't only create something, but a hobby like this is a way—and I have a joke around school—of getting rid of all your frustrations. You come home tired teaching kids at school, probably things didn't go the way you wanted, you are kind of disappointed—oh, I didn't get done what I wanted. Well what can you do? You don't want to kick the car and you don't want to kick the kids, so you get a needle and thread and you sew away your frustration. And every time I stick a needle in the cloth I'm saying: " 'Scuse me, dammit, dammit!" [laughter]. And I get a lot done. So it's a way of getting rid of your frustration and also creating something. I also make a joke, that I never finish anything. None of 'em are finished really, 'cept maybe this one. Because I get a kick out of just seeing how it's going to look. Take a picture out of a pattern, out of a book, and say: "Gee, wonder what that would look like?" And so I do a little bit of it. That's the reason I have all the patterns. I asked my mother once, I said: "Would you make a couple of these for me?" She said: "Do it yourself." "I can't," I said. She said: "Why can't you? You got two hands." So I got busy and I started this and I just can't seem to stop. It's really got to be a good hobby.

[After formal remarks on the history of quilting the speaker resumed her folk wisdom.] Well, it's like that old story. You look, you gotta chop down that forest out there. So you look at all those trees in that forest and you say: "No way I can chop 'em all down." But if you chop one down a day, you eventually get it chopped down. So if you made a couple of squares a night, and then do something else, you eventually finished. I think it's like anything in life. If you look at that far-off goal, you might get discouraged and say: "No way!" But step by step, and I'm still learning, take it day by day, and you be surprised what you can do in just a little bit of time without being too discouraged about the whole project. And that's the way most of these are done. I teach evening school during the regular school year, adult evening school. And I teach consumer education at night. And I was trying to tell the ladies, you must make something out of nothing to be a good consumer. So we sit down, and I say: "Every one in here is going to make a block." And then you can use these blocks, see, to make pillows. So this was about five weeks ago, and I said: "OK, I'll show you how easy it is." So I made one block and I got 'em started. I said: "Well, since I started, I just make the whole thing." So in five weeks, just at night, it can be done. So don't look at the big project and say: "Um, no way." One step at a time and you can get it done.

It doesn't take too much, I would say, aptitude for sewing, if you can hold a needle and thread. If you can cut out a square exactly, well, then you can do it. Some people ask: "How do you get all the little points and things?" Well, can you cut a picture out of a magazine without chopping it all up? Then you can chop this cloth up, like this. And I cut 'em out as neat as I possibly can, being exact. Have you ever tried to put a jigsaw puzzle together? All of the pieces must fit exactly, don't they? Well, it's the same here. If you cut 'em out exact, then they will fit together exactly right, the corners, everything. So I usually sit down, and one or two nights cut out all the little blocks and put each block in the bag. This will be one block like this. Then after I get the whole thing cut out, I start matching 'em and putting 'em together. And I have set a goal of two blocks a night. I only need thirty blocks. In fifteen nights I have another quilt made.

I had thought before coming here tonight: "Maybe I could encourage someone in this class to try one," you know. And then I said: "No, I'm not going to put that strain on you." [laughs]. But when I started this talk I meant to pass out the blocks and see if I couldn't even get the fellas to make one, because I got the fellas to do it in my night class. And if you could have seen the expression of those young men, walking out of there, and they were not a bit ashamed. "Hey look what I did! That old bat made me do it." And they were proud of it. So, don't say it's just for girls there, fellas. It might be interesting for you to know that there's a fireman in Gary who always wins first prize on his quilts at the Lake County Fair. He started this because, sitting around the firehouse, he wanted something to do, so he started making quilts.

All right, and about the cost. I don't think I have spent over five dollars for everything you've seen in this room. Because, where did the stuff come from? I see someone sewing and I say: "Hey, are you gonna throw that in the wastebasket? Give it to me." I'm a pack rat. I take it home. My mother's the same way. One day she's coming down the street. Had to make a shortcut across an alley in Knoxville, Tennessee. And she saw piles and piles of scraps laying out behind this building. So she knocked on the door, asked the man: "May I have those scraps?" And he says: "yes." So every so often she goes to Knoxville, brings back truckloads of scraps [laughter]. And this quilt is what came out of those scraps in the alley. Just I only had to buy the filling.

Most of these quilts came from the garbage can. Someone was going to take it to the dump and burn it. Well, some people will say: "Hey, aren't you shamed to do that?" I'm not shamed to do anything that's honest, OK? Now if I was stealing those scraps I would be ashamed. But I didn't steal 'em. My mother didn't steal 'em. She asked for 'em. They say: "Sure, we're gonna burn 'em up anyway." When people throw their scraps in their wastebasket: "Hey, you throwing away good stuff there. May I have it?" I don't mind doing that. It's honest. So take it. Make something out of it, see. I make something out of most everything. I use a baby food jar to hold my little supplies. Somewhere I have a potato chip box that I keep my scissors and stuff in that I'm going to use. Some of these little bags of socks; things come in plastic bags, and I can fill a bag like this with a spool of thread and a thimble, and I keep a few pins in my purse. Have you ever noticed how much time you spend waiting? Say, waiting in a doctor's office. Waiting for a class to start. Waiting, waiting.

## Black Outlooks

You wait an awful lot of your life away. Well, while I'm waiting, I pull out the little bag and I start quilting. And while I'm doing that, often I make a new friend: "What are you doing?" I show her. And we get started talking. And you meet new people that way. It's a good ice-breaker. I was sitting and doing this one day in my doctor's office, waiting until he could check my ears. And he's the one that offered me five hundred dollars. And I said: "No way. I'm going to keep it for my grandbaby."

Are there any questions? Because I have another thing I could say. My father is one of those self-taught Baptists, son of a line of Baptist ministers, who love to talk; especially if they think they saying something that might help someone, they talk your head off. Well, that's me too. Are there any questions?

["Don't you use a sewing machine?"]

No, I like to do it all by hand. One I made on the machine, that's the Crazy Quilt one. All the rest I do by hand. One reason, to me it's more relaxing to sit there and sew it by hand. And I talk and look at TV and I tell my son: "Get that homework done." I can be more exact if I do this by hand and get all those points, but to try to do that on a sewing machine is more tedious. I don't do it, see, to really make production. It's to relax. And to see what I can make. And then, too, I don't know if any of you do this or not, but I stretch out in bed and prop some pillows behind my back with my feet up, because I very seldom sit down at work. I walk a lot in the classroom. So I want to get my feet so I can relax better; I sit with my feet up, and I do all of this in the bed. And sometimes you can't get in my bedroom. I know one of my students asked me: "Miz Davenport, your bedroom must look awfully junky." Yes, but it's my junk. So it doesn't matter. I had that question before: "Why don't you do that on the machine?" I don't think it would be as much fun even.

Quilting is one of the most traditional of American crafts, associated with colonial and pioneer and farm women. Yet here is a black woman in Gary enamored of quiltmaking and seeking enthusiastically to convert city students to her leisure-time pursuit. The original purposes of making quilts in an agricultural and frontier society—to keep warm at night and to provide social occasions through quilting bees—have undergone radical changes in the urban scene. The end product has become an ornament, a trophy signalizing the victory of city dwellers over urban demands on time and pocketbooks, a conquest of the waiting line and the cost of living.

Out of salvaged time and salvaged scraps Anna pieces together artistic quilts. She turns the impersonality and tedium of the doctor's waiting room into a friendly circle of new acquaintances, with the quilt-in-progress as a conversation opener. Instead of succumbing to the pressure

211

to purchase more and more consumer goods, Anna demonstrates how wasteful Americans can produce their own goods out of other's throw-aways. She rejects the machine for her own needle and thread, symbolically and practically, for she can relax in bed with her spools and thimble. Imaginatively, with her mother as mentor, Anna has demonstrated how a harassed urbanite can meet new people, overcome tension, practice thrift, and "sew away your frustration" through an old folk practice.

An analogy may be drawn between the completion of Anna Davenport's quilts with their six or seven thousand little hand-sewn pieces and the construction of Calvary Baptist Church block by patient block. Take one step at a time, squeeze minutes from the racing days and nights, and the small task faithfully done ends with a grand accomplishment: a five-hundred-dollar quilt or a fifty-thousand-dollar building. The quilts and the church represent a labor of love, with the tiniest capital investment—some old scraps of cloth, or lumber advanced on faith—plus the time and devotion of dedicated souls. Such a spirit lies behind the success stories of Gary.


## A SENSE OF PLACE

The speakers of this chapter live and work in Gary, the blighted city spoken of with such fear and disgust by dwellers in other parts of the Region. These black speakers see a shining metropolis in the inner city, bounded on the north by rows of lakefront mills that sit under an eternal smudge of smog, perforated by six-lane Broadway running north-south, with dingy streets to the east named for states and to the west for presidents, bisected by Fifth Avenue running east-west into East Chicago. This is the heart of black Gary, which teems with its own life. The black churches scattered off the foreboding main arteries of Broadway and 5th take on gay and colorful appearances when filled with preachers and deacons, choirs and congregations.

Gary boosters refer pridefully to downtown locations. You go down "9th and Madison, City Hall, 5th and Broadway," observes Wilbert Harlan, "and you'll see lots of black women working there now in offices and banks." He would not move from his home on Madison even to Glen Park, because "I love this place. I love my neighbors on both sides . . . I love the area." To the members of Calvary Baptist Church, the structure they have erected on 2400 Virginia Street stands as a monument to their determination and their pastor's leadership. The Psychic noted that throngs tied up traffic trying to get into his storefront church.

These Garyites exhibit perhaps the strongest sense of attachment to place of any of the Region's people, for they are staying put.

# 5

# CRIMELORE

Crime in its various forms rivets the attention of city dwellers everywhere
today; in the Region, criminal acts provide one of the chief topics of conversation and apprehension. According to statistics, Gary and East Chicago lead other cities in Indiana in incidence of violent crime. If you drive
through downtown Gary, even in the daytime, you are taking your life in
your hands, goes the warning. Half of the students in my fall 1975 class
had a personal crime experience to relate. Muggings, holdups, robberies,
rapes, murders, assaults, break-ins, vandalism, thefts of cars and car
parts—all breed cycles of tales that enjoy ever-widening distribution.

These tales of crime, I soon realized, bear hallmarks of folkloric narratives. Clever robbers assume the guise of tricksters; sadistic assaulters
correspond to ogres and demons; valiant and "cool" customers who repel
the criminals appear as heroes and heroines. The police often enter—or
fail to enter—the scene as slackers and simpletons. Not only does the
cast of characters conform to the dramatis personae of the folktale, but
the narrative style, too, follows the patterns of traditional storytelling—
with clearcut episodes; internal dialogue; emphases of inflection, intona-

tion, gesticulation; a mood of suspense moving toward a climax. The crime-tale by its very nature possesses dramatic tension: it involves an act of aggression and a response, either submission or retaliation. Urban audiences hang on the words of the storyteller, for these tales of the city carry warnings, lessons, danger signals, precepts. Like ghost stories of an older time, which conveyed a thrill of unease and disquiet and mystery, so crime-tales of today titillate potential victims who—if they have not already undergone the fright—may one day be surprised by an attacker at home, on the street, or in a parking lot.

How crime preoccupies the minds of Regionites can be documented in many conversations. An afternoon's talk with Rose Le Van, historian for the East Chicago Historical Society and editor of the 75th Diamond Jubilee history of East Chicago, yielded a string of such references. Rose, referring to her German, Hungarian, and Czech forebears, called herself an "oleo." A former reporter, she knew the west Region inside out; her father had been a steelworker, blacklisted as a strikebreaker in 1918, who later became township assessor for East Chicago; her husband, who had changed his name from Lebanowski, was a civil engineer.

Rose explained that the historical society met at 4 P.M. because people would no longer go out in the evening.

+ My sister-in-law has been mugged three times. One evening as she was coming out of the Moose Lodge on State Street, across from the Hammond library, a black grabbed her purse, the door banged on her, broke her glasses and injured her arm. Another time they jumped her car at the red light. You are warned: lock your door, never pick up anyone, don't lower your window to talk to anyone—that's what she did. They have black people here who are afraid to go to Gary. Several years ago a girl, a Latin, was raped by a gang in the Sunnyside area and beaten so badly that she died.

It's the rape cases that upset the people most; they seem to be perpetrated by youths from fifteen to twenty-five. You'll get no help from the police in rape cases; the first question the police ask is: "Did you have a good time?" That, besides all the shame and indignity. Some hospitals don't even want to handle them. Then there is the problem of the abortion if it develops that way. A lot of this is due to dope. Neighbors stopped a young colored boy trying to get in my back window. They asked what he was doing. He said: "I want to see the people here." One of the neighbors said: "Why don't you wait till she's home?" He said: "That's a good idea." He must have been crazy, trying to climb in the back window at 9 A.M.

A number of formulaic elements appear here: warnings about driving in Gary; horror tales of gang rape; comic tales of the bumbling thief; apathy and callousness of the police.

# Crimelore

Newspapers have long specialized in crime stories, but the oral versions behind the journalism have not yet caught the attention of folklorists. A front-page report in the Indianapolis *Star*, May 1, 1978, illustrates my points.

## The Heroic Bystander

✦ EX-MARINE DISARMED MUGGER

Subway Hero to Use Reward for "The Kids"

New York (UPI)—A 5-foot-1-inch ex-marine who stood up alone and disarmed a mugger who had passengers aboard a crowded subway train cowering in terror was offered a $200 reward Tuesday. He said he'd use it to buy sneakers for the kids' basketball team he coaches.

"I wish more people would think about the kids of this city and stop blowing me up," said James Harris, a youth-organization worker, as newspapers chronicled his heroism in large type. "If they want to do something, let them do it for the kids."

Harris, 30, was on his way to coach a basketball game in lower Manhattan Monday when a knife-wielding 6-foot black man stepped onto a southbound train and announced he intended to rob all the white women in the car.

Harris, who also is black, looked around and saw other male passengers cowering as the frightened women handed over their money.

It was too much for the unarmed Harris, who said he was "tired of people saying they don't want to get involved."

Although the man was nearly a foot taller than he, the 118-pound Harris jumped up and used the voice he always uses when he talks to his kids on the basketball court. "Throw the money on the floor! Give me that knife."

The startled mugger did what he was told, and other passengers jumped on him, trussing him up with belts and sitting on him until transit police entered the train at the next stop and arrested him. He was identified as Robert Mangham, 32.

Harris' courage made headlines, and on Tuesday, Jerry Preiser, president of the Federation of New York State Rifle and Pistol Clubs, offered him the group's $200 Courageous Citizens Award and a plaque.

Harris declined to accept the money for himself, Preiser said. "He wants to meet at a sporting store ... take all the youngsters and outfit them for sneakers, which I think is a beautiful gesture on his part."

Normally, the gun club gives its award to store and home owners who use weapons to defend themselves against criminals. Preiser said the group decided to honor Harris, because his efforts "caught our imagination."

## Land of the Millrats

Harris said he stepped in, at the risk of being stabbed, because "I'm not going to stand by and see people hurt if I can do something about it.

"I don't want to see this city destroyed. I love this city. What we're going to do is not let the muggers run the city of New York and the only way we can stop them is to be firm."

This narrative contains the classic elements of the modern crime-tale. Its setting is the New York subway, cavernous hunting ground of human predators in crimelore. The hero is undersized, unarmed, dauntless, modest, selfless. His courageous act in subduing the ogre, through sheer force of will, only partly illumines his virtues, for he represents social as well as personal ideals of heroism: he donates his reward to aid under-privileged youth—to help them play basketball and keep from becoming street criminals like the ogre. And as a social critic, the hero shames the inert and fearful members of society who close their ears to Kitty Geno-vese's pathetic cries for help. He sets an example for them and shows how simple it is to subdue the forces of evil. He fills three heroic roles, each with special mana: patriot (ex-marine); youth-organization worker; basketball coach. By contrast, the towering black demon-mugger, armed with his phallic knife, threatens to rob (rape) all the white women in sight. (In the 1970s the hero, too, should be black, a point mentioned unobtrusively.)

We are accustomed to reading such newspaper crime stories written in the third person by reporters, but a folklorist will ponder the first-hand oral versions that must circulate following each event. The attacked per-son or persons and the witnesses disseminate to their families and friends a particular account of the chilling episode, which the listeners may then repeat at second-hand within their own crimelore repertoires. One crime-tale triggers another, in the universal process of storytelling, and the actual events mingle with the embroidered and the apocryphal to form a pool of frightening stories.

A tale heard some years ago in New York, before I had recognized the genre as folkloric, indicates the oral character of crime stories. It is re-constructed from memory, but in the form in which I have retold it my-self. My sister was entertaining in her apartment overlooking the East River, in a neighborhood becoming increasingly apprehensive about se-curity and protection. The talk turned almost inevitably to crime in the streets, and we discussed the instructions in a leaflet that a civic agency was distributing to New Yorkers on precautionary measures to observe while on foot: walk in the middle of the sidewalk; avoid dark and deserted places; avoid walking alone; do not talk to strangers. A recently emigrated Greek colonel, a short, muscular man about forty, related in animated voice his experience with a stranger.

# Crimelore

As part of his personal fitness regimen, he jogged around the block every morning at seven A.M. This particular morning as he completed his circuit and entered his apartment building, a stranger followed him inside, past the doorman. Assuming him to be an occupant of the building, the colonel held the elevator door open for him, pressed the button for his own floor, and asked the other which floor he wanted. The stranger whipped out a knife, pressed the blade against the colonel's stomach, and growled: "I'm going to your apartment." As soon as they entered the apartment, the stranger demanded to know where the colonel kept his ties, then bound and gagged him. The robber helped himself to suits and the stereo, warned his victim not to call the police for thirty minutes, and made his exit. The colonel freed himself after a few minutes, called the police right away, and waited for two hours for them to come, only to hear them say there was nothing they could do.

This personal narrative serves as a cautionary tale. Even the strong, athletic male right on his own premises can be tricked by a bold and wily thief. And of course the police help not at all. The moral: beware of all strangers.

Another cautionary tale presents the police point of view. This I heard in 1968, at the East Chicago home of a Serbian steelworker who had invited a group from his church to explain their side of a church dispute. The conversation moved from their religious position to other topics and, as happens so often in Region discourse, touched on crime. A city police detective present, sharp-featured, with a rough, solemn speech, explained why his department faced such difficulties in apprehending criminals.

## The Unwilling Witness

A gunman had recently held up an East Chicago clothing store owned by an old couple, seized the man's wallet and a rack of clothing, and escaped in a getaway car. The police caught him, with the wallet and stolen clothes, and brought him to headquarters to be identified. As the store owners entered the police station, the husband recognized the thief and was about to bear witness, when his wife kicked him. He choked back his words and denied having seen the accused before. The detective had no recourse but to free the thief. "Why didn't you identify him?" he asked. "Well," replied the wife, "after you leave, we still have to live in the neighborhood, without any protection. Better to lose a few suits than to have the windows broken and get shot."

Unsupported by a frightened citizenry, feeling themselves handcuffed by the courts if they do succeed in bringing a criminal to trial, the police could tell despairing tales of their own in the losing battle against lawbreakers. The preceding two narratives led to my conceiving of the crime-tale as a folkloric genre. Accordingly, during extended field sojourns in 1975 and 1976 I consciously sought, and readily found, stories of lawlessness. I attended criminal trials of youthful gang members at Hammond and Crown Point, as part of my education in the lore of crime. A recurrent motif in this lore was the asseveration that the Gary *Post Tribune* and Mayor Hatcher, independently or in collusion, withheld reports of criminal acts. A steelworker's wife expressed this sentiment: "Mayor Hatcher, he doesn't seem very responsible to the people. His method of solving the crime in Gary was simply to not permit any crimes to be reported. The press cannot get the crime statistics. They cannot find out about anything that happens because he doesn't want to look bad. You hear about a lot of things that have happened, people being robbed or murdered, but it's never in the paper." The distinction pointed up here between orally circulating versions of a crime as a separate vein of communication from printed newspaper accounts particularly intrigues the folklorist, who wishes to capture, clarify, and explain the perspective of these floating reports.

According to the typology I later developed, these three crime-tales fit into clear categories. The newspaper story of the subway holdup is a version of "The Tricky Intended Victim." The intruder-into-the-apartment narration belongs under "The Tricky Thief," with the element of "Passive Policemen." And the thief-let-go tale can be pigeonholed with "Passive Victim" accounts. As my file of crimelore grew, I perceived certain recurring character types that defined criminals, victims, and police.

### Passive Policemen

A constant motif in talk about crime centers on the apathy, indifference, and sloth of the police. A leading member of the Serbian Saint George Church in East Chicago stated bitterly that the church had been vandalized five times during the winter, yet the police took no action. Accordingly, the church membership proposed to set up their own security guards for round-the-clock surveillance. When informed of the plan, the police warned that if the guards injured anyone who broke into the church, the guards would be charged and prosecuted. The fault actually lay, my informant felt, in certain permissive Supreme Court decisions, in consequence of which prisoners were paroled, judges demanded more and more evidence, and counselors (lawyers) and the state bar softened the laws.

The thirty-seven-year-old son of a black pastor in Hammond, in the course of discussing the lack of black representation in the Hammond school system and police and fire departments, said it was useless to call the police. They usually took thirty to forty-five minutes to respond and, once at the scene of the crime, did nothing. On one occasion the police answered a call from the Mount Zion Baptist Church, whose officials pointed out that all the furniture had been stolen from the lounge and named a suspect. The police officers found the furniture at the suspect's home, but declared that, lacking witnesses, they could take no action. It was the church's business, not theirs. So the church people took their furniture back and reinstalled it in the lounge. A few days later the thief stole it again!

A steel executive from Ogden Dunes told me that his black cleaning woman from Gary carried money in her shoe rather than her purse, after having her purse cut away twice. Hatcher would not take measures against the young black hoodlums, my friend said, because he saw them as his power base. Also, many white policemen on the force saw no point in getting hurt in a fight between two blacks.

## The Tricky Thief

Keith Caldwell, professor at Indiana University, Bloomington, during a vivid recital of his experiences and memories growing up in the Region, spoke of John Dillinger.

+ The most colorful outlaw or criminal in The Region—at least he was as-sociated with the Region as well as Chicago—was John Dillinger, who at one time was incarcerated in the county jail at Crown Point.

A friend of mine at that time was sheriff, a woman, Mrs. Lillian Holley. Her husband had been a dentist in Hammond, who had run for sheriff and been elected and then had been killed in an attempt to bring in a mentally deranged citizen who was shooting at people from his cabin. And then Mrs. Holley was elected, as often is the custom in this coun-try—when the governor dies, the governor's wife becomes governor.

But Dillinger was captured at one point and incarcerated and waiting trial in the Lake County jail. While he was there, he engaged in whiling away his idle hours in whittling. Well, what he whittled was a wooden gun [laughs]. And at a strategic moment when some food was brought to him, he pulls out this gun. Somehow he managed to get something to blacken it and was able to capture his jailor and capture the sheriff, Mrs. Holley, and handcuffs them in his own cell, you see. The attendant of his cell was also a woman. He locked them in the cell and he said to them: "Now be good girls," and went on his way, you see.

Now this jail break caused a great scandal. And shortly before that the county prosecutor, Robert Estill, and Sheriff Holley had had the misfor-tune to be photographed—it had been published by some photographer in the Hammond *Times*—in what was called the "happy family picture," you see, with Dillinger in the middle and Mrs. Holley on one side and Estill on the other. It looked like he had his arm around Dillinger's shoulder. So there was a press attack upon them. Then of course the post office at Crown Point was flooded with all kinds of postal cards. The postal service delivered mail addressed to Wooden Gun, Indiana [laughs].

But there's a piece of true folklore, if you will: John Dillinger and his wooden gun. At any event this was one of the more spectacular things that occurred in the Region at the time I was living there.

### The Bumbling Thief

In the course of an informative rundown on the Gary scene, Jennie Regan told a comic story about robbers who broke into a house and carried out a TV set. When a neighbor asked what they were doing, they said they were taking it to be repaired. She said: "Oh, please take mine too; it needs to be fixed." So they carried her TV off as well.

In the big city individuals posing as various kinds of service or delivery men manage to effect entrance into homes; and thereby hangs a slew of yarns. A Miller housewife spoke of the phony rug cleaners who came to a house and asked the tenant if they could take the carpet to be cleaned; the unsuspecting renters even removed the nails with which the carpet was tacked down. But excessive suspicion can backfire, harming the innocent. The wife of a dean at Purdue-Calumet University recalled the time she successfully fended off a would-be intruder. Neighbors in the condominium where she lived had gone on a trip and asked her to watch their apartment, take in the mail, and so on. While they were away, a man came to their door and inserted a key into the lock. "I opened the door and asked him what he was doing. He said he had come to pick up the dry cleaning. There were so many keys floating around the condominium I became suspicious and wouldn't let him in. Then when the owners returned and I told them about it, they said they had made arrangements with the man to pick up their cleaning and had forgotten to tell me."

Many people relate accounts of tricky repairmen. In May 1978 I heard three versions in the space of two days from members of the Smithsonian Council in Washington, D.C. Claudia, the wife of a well-known author, described how a well-dressed stranger had entered the New York brownstone of a wealthy heiress, posing as a friend of guests at her party, and stolen her jewels. Her husband recalled how in 1970 the Chinese servant in their own New York City home had given their television set to a young chap who came to the door and said he was a repairman. The servant ushered him up to the third floor saying, "thank you, thank you,"

and bowed him out the door. The president of a prestigious Academy told me about a thief posing as a TV repairman in Philadelphia, about fifteen years ago, who was caught. He was operating in a section of Philadelphia where the houses, in the English fashion, were identified by names rather than numbers. The thief came to the door and said to the owner, whom he supposed to be the cleaning woman: "Mr. Dale asked to have the TV fixed." "Wait, I'll speak to the madam," said the hard-working mistress of the house, who left the room and called the police. They arrived at the house called "Dale," its own name, not that of its owner, and arrested the impostor. In this case the Tricky Thief became the Bumbling Thief.

A store manager gave an account of a bumbling robber. I was about to show a film about crime in the city to my Gary class one December evening, when Tim Gale stuck his head in the door and asked for his wife, Dorothy. She had not yet arrived, so I invited him in to see the film. He retorted that he had no need to see it, for he had been held up only that morning. Changing the invitation, I asked Tim to relate the happening to the class as a personal experience story, and I taperecorded his account. Tim managed a Thom McAn shoe store prominently located in Hammond, with large plate-glass windows allowing full visibility into the store from the street. The gunman had committed the holdup at 11 A.M. and, according to Tim, appeared naive and unsure in all his actions. A black man about twenty-five, wearing old black boots, he seemed a normal customer when Tim waited on him, talking about current fashions and how shoes looked on his feet. After about ten minutes they decided on a pair of boots. Tim suggested some hosiery to go with them, and the customer said "Fine."

✦ And as I turned to go to the hosiery rack, I felt something in my back, and he was pushing me to move. And I realized what was happening, and dropped the shoes on the floor, and went where he wanted me to go. And he pushed me over to my full-time salesman, and his customer (a businessman about fifty). At which time he grabbed the customer and started saying, "Move it, move it," and pushed us into the back room.

And when he got us into the back room, we saw definitely that he did have a gun; it was a .38 short barrel. And he told us to strip, which we didn't do, just took off our jackets. We all three had jackets on, so we took them off and threw them on the floor. And he said: "Empty your pockets." We emptied all the money we had in our pockets into his hand. He had the gun in one hand, waving it around, and we stuck the money in his hand, and he kept dropping the money. He kept dropping a twenty here, and things like that, but he was over there waving the gun around, so we emptied our wallets. The customer was just completely unaware.

## Land of the Millrats

So unaware, that when the holdup man reached into his pocket to see if he got all the money out, he started to take his car keys, and this customer started complaining violently that he shouldn't take the car keys. And I had to keep reminding the customer to shut his mouth and do whatever the guy wanted, because he seemed to have a better advantage of us.

And after he was satisfied that he'd got all the money from us, he had us go all the way back into the back of the store and lay down on our stomachs and faces. And, with a few side comments about if we moved what was going to happen, he left.

In telling his story to the police, Tim reported that the gunman said: "If you get up, I'm gonna blow your head off." The officer asked: "Were those his exact words?" "Not quite," Tim admitted, "he said, 'I'll blow your mother-fucking head off.' " The police officer nodded knowingly.

In his haste the holdup man overlooked the cash register and the safe. Although Tim had been warned not to call the police for fifteen minutes, he called them immediately. He could give no details on the car, but was able to identify the suspect pretty well, having seen him in the store for a good ten minutes. Thus, the police nabbed him as he was driving out of Hammond, toward Gary and out of their jurisdiction. Tim said belief (folklore?) had it that if the police did not make an arrest within an hour after a holdup, they would probably never catch the gunman. In this case he lauded their promptness and efficiency and was planning to write a letter to the Hammond *Times* praising the police action.

### The Tricky Intended Victim

The counterpart of The Tricky Thief of crime-tales is The Tricky Intended Victim. In these narratives the attempted robbery, break-in, rape, or holdup is averted by fast thinking and cool behavior on the part of the person to be victimized.

Seventy-eight-year-old Reverend Hobson Jackson, a frail black man on crutches, who had lived alone since a speeding auto driven by a dope-crazed youth had killed his wife and left him with a fractured skull and broken legs, interspersed a couple of break-in stories in a wide-ranging conversation. During our taping session he broke into chanted sermon-ettes, prayed over the phone to a lady with an aching stomach, discussed the function of the preacher, and deplored the rising tide of crime in Gary.

✦ Yes, I'se just saying to Brother Malone [who had introduced me to Reverend Jackson in 1968] and you, too, and all of you, be careful who you let in your house, now. Somebody come and ask for water or something, and they don't want water, see. And so this woman, she's dressed nice and went to a kinda elderly lady's house and asked her for a drink of water, and say: "Let me in." She let her in. And when she got inside the door, she said: "Ain't no water I want, but I want some money." The elderly lady (she told me this) says the stranger put a gun in her back and told her to "go on back to where's your room and where the money is." And her boy happened to be in the bedroom, and he didn't say anything; he just stood behind the door. And just as the woman passed the door, he put that club right in her neck and knocked her down, see. And he stepped on her arm and took the gun away from her. And after that they moved away from there. But everybody be knocking on your door ain't knocking for no good.

✦ And that's just like one that did me; come in and said he wants some money. My door was shut there, see. And I said: "George, get that gun and come there and kill out that kitchen window." And when I said that he [the holdup man] called him a airplane. He flew. Halfway near flying. He ain't been back no more, but I been staying ready if he happen to come back.

The invalid preacher explained that he had installed a burglar alarm six months earlier. "Just anytime you raise one of them windows, when you open or break the glass, the switch is turned on and that make the alarm go off. Cost me $499."

A burglar alarm may protect the apprehensive homeowner or apartment dweller, but how does a lone woman fend off assailants in a deserted parking lot? Coolness and quick wits saved the attractive journalist-teacher-wife of a steel executive, who was in my class. She speaks at a rapid-fire clip, breezily and wittily, and could probably talk her way out of any situation.

✦ It happened in 1972, in Sears in downtown Gary. They were wearing miniskirts and cleavage then. I came out of the rear entrance to the parking lot, and a young, nice-looking black called to me. A second black man was with him. As I had parked in a prohibited zone, I thought he was a store detective, especially since he was in a dark car, which I mistook for a police car, and that he was calling in connection with that. So I went over to his car. He said to me: "I've just gotten back from Vietnam, and you're the most beautiful woman I've seen. Would you come with me for a hundred dollars?" At once I thought: two of them and one of me in an empty parking lot, too much odds. That's why I took the tack I did. I'd heard of people being mugged in parking lots and other people in the distance said: "Oh, I heard a little noise."

## Land of the Millrats

I realized I should not show panic or hostility, resentment or indignation. So I said: "That's one of the nicest things anyone ever said to me. My husband was in Vietnam so I know what you must have gone through. I'm proud to know you. My husband flew combat missions in Vietnam and got an Oak Leaf Cluster. What division were you in?" I led the conversation in that direction. So he talked about his experiences, said the American people did not know what was going on. I said: "I'm very flattered. I can see that you and your friend are very nice-looking too." It ended with his saying he would like to meet and talk with my husband. I asked him for his phone number, "so my husband could call you and we could all get together and have a drink and talk about the Vietnam experience." See, I took the aggressive role, so he wouldn't think he had lost me, to give him a chance at a follow-up and let him save face, both for himself and in front of his friend. Also to let him know he might be accosting an officer's wife. He didn't speak to me in a disrespectful way. I thought he might be disoriented from the war experience and that the best chance lay in playing it cool, and meanwhile bringing in the allusion to my husband. So that's the way it ended.

At the time I was teaching at Locke Grammar School, 10th and Gary. The physical education teacher and I were the only two whites in the school. So I felt at ease talking with black persons.

This scene can be interpreted as an enactment of the black man's desire for the white woman, a symbolic expression of his attainment of freedom and act of reprisal on his white oppressor.*

### The Holdup Foiled

Akin to the Tricky Intended Victim, whose guile and quick wits fend off the assailant, is the hero who employs machismo to prevent a holdup. A savvy Romanian, John Miku, had played such a role. John worked as an outside cook on catering jobs for Jennie's Restaurant, and Larry Regan introduced us at the Elks Club in East Chicago, where he was cleaning up after a dinner. A spry old chap, John reeled off a string of anecdotes while he moved briskly about the kitchen; it seemed impossible that he could be seventy-five, but he showed his driver's license as proof. Work, he said, was the secret of his good health. "The fellow who retires from the mill and says he will never do another lick of work, never lift a finger, and sits down in front of TV with a beer, dies within a year."

---

* In the words of a black prison inmate speaking to Eldridge Cleaver: "Every time I'm embracing a black woman I'm embracing slavery; and when I put my arms around a white woman, I'm hugging freedom." (Quoted in Daryl Dance, *Shuckin' and Jivin'* [Bloomington: Indiana University Press, 1978], "The White Woman and the Black Man," p. 101.)

# Crimelore

John had worked in and around restaurants much of his life, and served John Dillinger and his gang in the American Legion Restaurant in Indiana Harbor. Dillinger lived across the street from the restaurant, and Miku told some anecdotes about him.

✦ The Lady in Red who betrayed him was Bulgarian; she ran a whorehouse in Gary. Ann Sage was her name. Dillinger's father brought produce to the 9th Avenue market in Gary, and the son roamed around the streets on his own and met her. She turned him in because the immigration authorities were after her to deport her. I was standing in the hotel looking out the window when they arrested him; he'd had his face lifted and we didn't recognize him. It wasn't the FBI who shot Dillinger, but three East Chicago policemen. They knew him.

On the legend of the wooden, or soap, gun Dillinger used to escape from jail, Miku claimed it was a real gun. One legend he did not repeat concerned the size of Dillinger's sexual organ, which prevented him from satisfying Ann Sage because he could not get an erection—or, in another version, wore her down—hence she made the deal with the police.

Miku had worked as a short-order cook in The Minute Restaurant on downtown Broadway. One day he was behind the counter at 6 A.M. frying sausages when a black fellow entered with a redheaded white woman. His suspicions aroused, John kept watching him out of the corner of his eye and kept one hand free to reach for the gun in his pocket.

✦ I saw the black guy start to get up from his stool and heard her say: "Not yet." There were three four other people there. Then he started to get up and reach for his gun and I whirled around and shot him right through the shoulder. He fell down on the floor, and I stood over him and was going to shoot him right through the head, but she began to scream: "Oh, don't shoot him, don't shoot him!" I said: "Get him out of here." Everybody else had run out. She got him on his feet and they went out the door. There was no blood; the bullet had gone right through him and into the wall. I called the police and they asked: "Where's the body? Is there any blood? Where's the bullet?" I told them he had gone and there was no blood. So they came the next day at noon.

Several stereotypic elements appear in this narrative. The gun John Miku kept in his pocket bears witness to the constant danger of holdups in downtown Gary. A racially mixed couple—particularly a redheaded woman, a folkloric warning signal—signifies trouble. The quick draw on the trigger follows the best tradition of western gunfighters. As befits a

## Land of the Millrats

hero, Miku shows compassion after vanquishing the ogre, in response to the entreaties of the ogre's witch-woman, and spares his life. The police of course fail to show up on time.

Miku's story suggested one to Larry Regan. He told of a black man who came into his restaurant one Friday (the evening when bands played) and sat near the door, laying a purse on the table. He stayed until the end of the music and then left, leaving his purse behind. A waitress found it, looked inside for identification, and saw a loaded gun. Frightened, she called Larry.

✦ I took out the shells and threw them away. The fellow then knocked on the door of the restaurant, which was locked for the night. I opened the door, and he asked for his purse. I gave him the purse and told him I had taken the gun out and removed the shells, and that he could have the gun back but that he would have to buy new shells.

The fellow stammered that that was all right, he was a policeman and that was his gun. He took his purse and empty gun and left again.

Larry theorized that the man might have been planning a holdup, using the forgotten purse as a ploy to get back inside the restaurant after closing time. Or he was just carrying a gun, the way every black and many whites in Gary carried guns. Or he might even have been a policeman.

### The Lucky Narrow Escape

An innocent bystander caught in a holdup recounts this first-person shocker. Juan Gomez (see Chapter 3), who lived in a deteriorating Mexican neighborhood of west Gary, provides precise details. The subgenre into which it fits might be termed the Lucky Narrow Escape or Exceedingly Close Call.

✦ Well, it happened this way. I was coming from school—I'd been carrying fifteen hours—and it was a Friday night. I'll never forget that, because I was very tired, and it had been very tiresome for me for years, working, going to school, looking after my family, and whatnot. On the way home I kept thinking that I'd like to take my wife out for some fish, or—I like dances, I like music, I really go for old Latin soul music. And I got to our community grocery story about 9:15 P.M., and the girl was just putting the money away.

I asked if I could make a personal check, and she said she was sorry, that she had just put the money away. I said: "Oh, holy cow! Well, I'll be right back." I ran to the Embers Club; they were open until twelve midnight. I used to go in there and have a beer once in a while. Not that I was a big drinker; I knew the bartender 'cause I used to stop and pick up a quart of beer and bring it home; but I won't hang around taverns any more; I never have really for the last four years. I went in there to talk to Jim the bartender. I said: "Jim, can you cash me a personal check for ten dollars?" He said: "Sure." I told him I needed some groceries and milk and bread and whatnot. Also I had the idea that I wanted to go to East Chicago that night.

Just then the lady bartender, who was the day bartender, and two of my friends were walking out, and I noticed that Jim was the only one there. And while I was making the check out, he said: "You know what, Juan, I think somebody cased my place." I said: "Do you really think so?" And I said: "Well, hurry up and give me a beer"—you know, I wanted to be sociable—"and I'll go to the phone and call the house." In doing so, I took my gun from my holster and put it in my jacket, figuring I could get to it quicker. I was dialing on the phone, and I know I didn't get to finish, or maybe I did, but here two figures walk in, young punks, must have been about sixteen to eighteen years old. One had a navy peacoat with a bonnet, a little bonnet, and he was about five-foot-one, and the other guy (they were both black) was bareheaded, but he had a long coat, beige, with a fur collar.

I seen these two characters standing no more than five feet away from me, and I seen them mouthing to the bartender, and I said: "Hey, hey, what's going on?" While doing so, I pointed the telephone in their direction, which might have indicated that I was pointing a gun possibly, because I heard a gun shoot, so one of them must have thought that I had a gun. The other fellow pivoted around; I seen him pivot around. There was a little concrete partition there, into which I took a quick dive, through the grace of God and my quick reflexes. This guy took a shot, and the only thing I remember is that I was sitting facing the wall (about like this, like I'm doing now), the telephone was dangling, blue smoke was in my nostrils. I kept feeling my chest and my body to see if I was all in one piece. I thought for sure I was a goner. And then I seen the dangling of the telephone and I kept grabbing at it, and I realized that I was still alive, and I heard the most beautiful sound—the voice of the operator.

She was on the phone; she heard the whole incident. I said: "Please, please send help. There's been a robbery." I couldn't think of where I was, and finally I said: "5th and Clark Roads." I must have struggled pretty bad because she kept telling me, I remember: "Please play it cool, play it cool now." I said: "OK." It was a matter of a minute or so because the next thing I knew the cops were there. And I thought it was a dream, but I looked up and there were these pellets by the telephone, where they would have killed me. The two empty shells of the shotgun were on the floor.

When the cops came in I said: "Did you catch them? Did you see them out there?" They said: "No." They immediately started after them. I wasn't drunk, but I couldn't stop shaking when I realized what I had gone through and I got kinda polluted after that. Then I gave the report to the police. The odd part about it is that they never called me to investigate. They said they'd call some people, they'd call the bartender, but they never called on me.

Familiar motifs here are the alleged indifference of the police, and the accidental sequence of events—need to cash a check, closing of the grocery store, recourse to the tavern—that caught the near-victim in a potentially dangerous situation. The crux of the lucky escape crime narrative turns on a fortuitous factor, in this case the concrete partition that deflected the criminal's bullet. Only a fortunate survivor can live to tell the tale.

To what extent are these crime-tales folklore? By my criteria all of them qualify. Even if they are first-person narratives of holdups and break-ins, they live by word of mouth, they awe and shock listeners, and they display formulaic character types and actions. But tales of unimpeachable folkloric credentials also turn up among the crimelore. Consider the following, which I heard within a fortnight of my arrival in the Region, from Tim Gale.

*The Crime Carried Out (The Castrated Boy)*

✦ I heard a story, I believe about ten years ago, it would be about 1965—I was eighteen then—about a little white boy who had gone shopping with his mother in K-Mart, and he had to urinate. So, for the first time the mother decided to let him go in by himself to use the men's washroom, rather than going into the women's with her. He was in there an exceptionally long amount of time, and she got worried and asked some gentlemen to step in and see what the problem was, if there was a problem.

And they found the little boy laying in a pool of blood with his penis cut off. Subsequently they found three little black boys walking through the store with a bloody penis in their pocket. As it turned out, they had cut the little white boy's penis off as a orientation, a method of getting into a gang that they wanted to belong to. And to get into the gang they had to cut the penis off a white boy, which they did do.

When I mentioned this macabre business to my class I was informed that the episode had recently transpired in the spectacular new Southlake Mall shopping center in Merrillville.

# Crimelore

✦ Juan Gomez: There's a fellow who works for the Sanitarian Department in Gary, he drinks coffee at Bars coffee shop every morning, and he told me that his little eight-year-old boy went to the bathroom in the Southlake Mall, and that his mother was supposed to be waiting outside. And she waited and waited, you know, and consequently these two fellows came out of there, of black extraction. And she kind of worried because the little boy didn't come out. So she sent somebody in there. They found the little boy drowned in the commode.

Shortly afterward I drove to Southlake Mall and peered at the restroom on the upper level where the boy was supposedly mutilated. Someone had told me that a clipping of a similar incident, reported as happening at a mall in Indianapolis and printed in the Indianapolis *Star,* was on the bulletin board in the *Post Tribune*'s advertising office, two doors from the men's room. Affable Roger Kyes, who had clipped out the *Star* article, said he recognized its similarity to the account attached to Southlake Mall, an account he considered groundless, "because it would certainly have been made public by the police, coroner, and parents of the victim." Although Kyes disbelieved the incident, he recognized that a number of area residents definitely gave it credence and stayed away from the mall. Among the shoppers who braved the mall, he observed mothers taking their boys into the women's rather than the men's restroom. He knew the mall's manager and salespeople were reluctant to discuss the rumor for fear of starting it up again and further hurting business. Some of the mall's personnel attributed the grisly tale to downtown merchants, or even Mayor Hatcher, as a means of discouraging shoppers, who were deserting the inner-city stores, from venturing into Southlake.

Many versions of the mutilated boy in the restroom eventually came my way. A black student gave me several texts in which white youths had killed a black boy. Whenever and wherever I gave a talk on folklore and mentioned the restroom murder, one or more members of the audience would counter with a rendering set in their locality. "A Tale Told Too Often," an article by Florence H. Ridley (*Western Folklore,* 1967), gives examples attached to shopping malls in several states, customarily within a year of their opening, and traces the history of the legend back to Chaucer's "The Prioress's Tale" and earlier. A Christian lad walking through the Jewish ghetto is flung into a cesspool. Every century since, the episode has surfaced. Bernard Malamud wove it into his novel *The Fixer,* set in Russia. In the English traditional ballad "Sir Hugh, or the Jew's Daughter," a Christian boy who throws his ball over the garden wall of a Jewish neighbor and seeks to retrieve it is abducted and ritually murdered.

So this was the tale related as a recent event. Its current revival can be explained by its embodiment of two of the most anxiety-laden issues of modern times: racial fears and the decline of downtown businesses. In reflecting these two phobias, the legend of the mutilated boy exemplifies contemporary urban folklore.

A related legend that has caught the attention of journalists changes the crime from mutilation of a boy to attempted abduction of a girl. Here is the version printed in the Des Moines (Iowa) *Register,* November 4, 1979.

### The Attempted Abduction

+ A mother and her 15-year-old daughter were shopping at the Midlands Mall in downtown Council Bluffs. The daughter told her mother she was going to the restroom. The mother waited, but when the daughter didn't return she went to investigate.

.She found two women dragging her semi-conscious daughter out of the restroom. One of the women said to the mother, "Look out, my daughter is sick and we have to get her to the hospital."

To which the mother replied, "That's not your daughter. That's MY daughter!"

At that point the women dropped the girl, who had, it turned out, been drugged with chloroform, and fled.

It was suspected that the women were planning to abduct her and take her to Chicago where she was to be sold on the white slave market.

The journalist reporting the "shocking story" noted that it had been told repeatedly and had alarmed many residents of southwestern Iowa. Yet no hard evidence for the allegations could be found. The Pottawattamie County attorney declared that the incident never happened; no one had complained to the police or to his office, although he had received calls from individuals, newspapers, and radio and television stations throughout the country. On the other hand, Donna Timson, a mother of five, in Henderson in Page County, Iowa, believed the story to be true. "I think it happened," she was quoted. "I was raised in a city so I know these things go on. I've warned all my children never to go into a restroom alone."

In this variation of the restroom legend the crime was not carried out, and in terms of our typology it would belong with lucky escapes. This family of variants adds to urban folklore and reflects the fears and anxieties of city dwellers.

Just as "true" stories of mill thefts have replaced trickster fictions of yore, and immigrant escape sagas substitute for fairy-tale dangers of olden times, so crime-tales fill the gap left by the decline of scary ghost and horror legends. Earlier generations thrilled to narratives of haunted homes and eerie revenants; urban society today does not need recourse to supernatural demons and ogres when natural ones walk the streets and enter domiciles. As one once learned protective behavior from ghost and devil stories—for instance, the invocation of the Lord's name as a magical incantation driving off the spirits—so now the listener absorbs survival techniques from the crimelore narratives. Muggers that stalk prove even more terrifying than ghosts that walk.

# EPILOGUE

This report of my sojourn in the Region could continue, and many more sojourns could yield many more returns. But enough has been said, I hope, to make a case for the reality of urban folklore. All three great folk traditions in the United States—the regional, the ethnic, and the occupational—can be observed and recorded in cities. But, unlike earlier fieldworkers, urban folklorists will not collect tales and songs from a homogeneous society. They will encounter the most diverse cultural traditions.

One day in particular, July 6, 1976, stays in my mind as epitomizing the vagaries of fieldwork and the complexities of the Region. That morning I set out for East Chicago to revisit a Serbian steelworker who supported the mother church in Yugoslavia. Bosko was jubilant for, although he had recently suffered a severe injury in the mill (the account is given in Chapter 2), he had just received news of a Supreme Court decision that resolved a long legal battle over church properties in favor of his side, the Federalists, against the Raskolniks. His friend Jovan, president of their church and an East Chicago police detective, was there rejoicing with him. The two explained that the schism had sundered the Serbian communities in East Chicago and Gary and across the land, and had led to physical confrontation over possession of church buildings, as well as continuous litigation since 1963.*

The schism I had known about, but Jovan surprised me by identifying a third group of recent Serb immigrants, called the Vuk Karadjič society in honor of the famed Serbian philologist and folklorist, which opposed both factions. These Tito agents spread Communist propaganda through radio and TV, by means of tapes and films obtained from the Yugoslav consul, and infiltrated the older Serbian communities in the Region. Through his police connections Jovan kept track of their actions and intimidated them with threats to put their jobs in jeopardy. I left bewildered by the factionalism that rent a seemingly monolithic ethnic stock and puzzled by the conflict of ideals. Bosko argued for separation of church and state, saying that the sins of Tito's Communism should not be visited on the historic church, and the opposition argued for freedom of religious choice.

On impulse I called on Bill Garza, an active young member of the Mexican community in East Chicago with whom I had been trying to set up an appointment for months, to no avail. (Bill and his wife, Milly, had befriended me earlier, but an odd incident had led to an estrangement. They had also assisted a student of mine collecting from Mexican *curanderas,* or healers, but after the student's husband was jailed on charges of embezzlement, Milly avoided me.) I was fortunate in finding the Garzas at home. Ordinarily Bill took an early morning train to Chicago to his office as coordinator of a six-state federal program for Hispanics, but they had returned from a holiday in Las Vegas late the night before, so Bill had taken an extra day's vacation. A former millworker who, after graduating from Indiana University Northwest, had entered government service, Bill's mission was to persuade other Hispanics—the term he preferred to Latinos—to follow his own career. Though in his early thirties, Bill displayed the serious and troubled countenance of an elder statesman as he explained the difficulty in attracting Spanish-speaking Americans into civil-service positions. Work in the mills paid well, and laborers felt uncomfortable wearing suits. The strategy he adopted with Mexican-Americans was to instill pride in their heritage, bolster their self-esteem, and urge them to aspire to white-collar managerial posts. In talks and writings and local political activities Bill cultivated the Mexican national legend and could cite a string of contributions by Mexicans to American life,

---

* The Supreme Court on June 21, 1976, decided in favor of the unity faction. See *Harvard Encyclopedia of American Ethnic Groups* (Cambridge, Mass.: Harvard University Press, 1980), p. 922. For the Raskolnik point of view, see Chapter 3, the remarks of Jelena Branimirović.

from cowboys to chocolate to color TV, and a list of Mexican military heroes in American uniforms, some of them natives of the Region.

Garza's version of Hispanic folklore thus differed from Nick Kanellos with his Latino theater of protest and Juan Gomez with his covert folk beliefs. In our typology of ethnic folklore, Bill speaks for the historical-civic, Nick for the promotional-public, and Juan for the esoteric-private modes.

In East Chicago resided another long-standing but lapsed acquaintance, Dr. Edward C. L. Broomes, a Guyana-born physician whom I had recorded in 1968 and run into, with his wife, Anna, in Monrovia, Liberia, in 1970. I found Anna entertaining a young nurse from Guyana, in their elegant mansion. Jennifer Abdullah, friendly and merry, proved to be a fount of familiar folklore, such as I had encountered in my field trips to rural black settlements in Michigan and Arkansas, but not among the Region's residents. For two hours she unreeled into my tape recorder personal accounts of ghosts, spirits, obeah, snakes, dreams, spells, and visions, in a seemingly endless flow of occult adventures. Jennifer chuckled while she talked, but obviously believed in the supernatural. At the end of the afternoon she departed for Chicago, en route back to Guyana. So by the merest chance I stumbled upon a most unexpected source of unanticipated folklore, which did not at all fit in with my collecting plans. The folklorist never knows what surprises the field may hold.

An even stranger encounter awaited me that day. I had an appointment with Adrienne Seward and Gil Cooley of the Gary Gang field team to meet in downtown Gary in the evening to videotape a black teenagers outdoor dance. To our dismay, the youths chose not to dance; they turned the event into a rock concert. We were about to leave, when a soft-spoken, short black man in his mid-thirties began chatting with us about our equipment. Frank Jenkins was a steelworker, who had produced, directed, and starred in a home movie he shot on a super 8 mm camera. We all went to Frank's tiny apartment and he showed us *The Takeover*, a film running nearly two hours, set entirely in the Gary area. Frank's relatives, friends, and co-workers took on the roles; Frank himself played the leading character, Big Al, who returns from prison to take over the Gary rackets—numbers, gambling, brothels, drugs. One lurid scene after another showed Big Al's hit men rubbing out the rival gang, beating up store owners, taking a racketeer who didn't make his quota "for a ride" to the city dump. In a softer mood, Big Al turns lover and squeezes the bulbous breasts of a voluptuous girl friend. (Frank confided that he had his clothes on under the bedsheets during the filming, and that the girl's boy friend was watching.) In spite of the crudities of acting and camera work, or perhaps because of them, the film fascinated us right up to the unresolved end, when Big Al's girl friend betrays him to the cops (as did Dillinger's). The finale was to include a great chase, but

## Epilogue

Frank could not decide whether to let Big Al be killed off or escape to star again in a sequel.

A cog in the mills where, like most of his peers, he despises his work, Frank feeds his ambitions and fantasies through his movie career. In real life he creates the film; in the movie myth he enacts the gangster-overlord who conquers tough men with force and beautiful women with sex appeal. From stereotypes in Hollywood gangster films, climaxed in *The Godfather,* from local legends in the Region about Al Capone and John Dillinger, and from the immediacies of Gary lowlife, Frank fashioned his film, much as the märchen-teller of old wove magical fictions from the story elements at his disposal. And, as is often the way with storytellers, Frank has made himself the hero of his tale.

Thus went the sequence of chance meetings on one eventful day in the Region. Taken by itself, this day illustrates major themes of ethnic and black folkways in the urban scene. With the Serbs, it is the church schism that consumes their passions and energies and breeds a folklore of suspicion and distrust. With the Mexicans, it is the struggle for acceptance in the mainstream culture that induces a legendry of collective and personal achievements. With the black steelworker turned moviemaker, we find the patterns of the success story and "the other life" syndrome perfectly exemplified, if in a novel medium.

Having seen some of the bricks upon which this edifice was constructed, let us return to the five questions I posed in my Introduction.

Has the Region generated a distinctive folklore, in itself and about itself? Yes to the second part, no to the first part. No physical area in the United States corresponds to "de Region," with its four core cities, each with a separate personality, bounded by the expanding white-flight suburbs, overshadowed by high-culture Chicago to the west, set apart from farmlands in southern Lake County and in Porter County on the east, terminated on the north by the shoreline of Lake Michigan. We may assert that the Region has indeed produced its own myth, that of a cultural desert peopled by blue-collar workers living in the midst of polluted skies, garbage dumps, and violent ghettos. Some reality lies behind the myth, but we have seen that enormous cultural vitality enlivens the Region and passes unnoticed by the world at large.

It is the production of steel that bonds the people of Gary and East Chicago and links them with factory workers in Hammond and refinery workers in Whiting, under a blue-collar mantle. The ethnic and racial diversity of the Region results from wage-labor opportunities in this heavily industrial corner. East Europeans, Latins, blacks, and southern whites possess their own subcultures, but they share the work culture of mill and factory, which provides them with a common tongue and gives the Region its distinct character.

If the myth of the Region is special, the urban folklore within it can

# Land of the Millrats

stand in microcosm for metropolitan centers throughout the nation. Cities such as Buffalo and Pittsburgh and Youngstown would surely reveal comparable caches of steel, ethnic, black, and crime traditions. The themes that dominate the conversations of Region residents—the withering of the inner city, black-white tensions, fluctuation in housing values, the race to the suburbs, the tedium of work coupled with the threat of unemployment, factory horseplay and trickery, safety at home and in the streets, corruption in politics—are all-American concerns. In these respects cities have become mirror images of each other, with one row of gutted tenements, sleazy bars, seedy cafes, and littered alleys replicating another. Frantic efforts to revivify the downtown area and to improve the quality of life on the assembly line characterize the policies of city officials and factory management everywhere. No social class is exempt from city folkways, and every urban dweller, old or young, rich or poor, black or white, possesses a mental map of the city that is collectable by the folklorist.

Do steelworkers possess a body of folklore as do cowboys, lumberjacks, miners, and oil drillers? My answer here, based on the sizable store of tales presented in Chapter 2, is an unequivocal yes. In several ways, however, steelworkers' folklore departs from the traditions of the outdoor and underground industries. Those traditions, with the exception of the oil drillers, most technological of the group, heavily emphasized the singing of folksongs—on the open range, in the lumbercamp bunkhouse, in the railroad roundhouse, and in the mine patch. Millworkers could not possibly sing on the job, nor did they, like the miners, live in isolated company towns that fostered communal entertainment. Millrat folklore runs to the oral narrative, delivered in anecdotal swap-sessions at the lunch break, in the canteen, in the union hall, in bars and cafes, in the parking lot before work, or in homes where several family members work in the mills. The heroes that emerge from this accumulated saga do not follow the pattern found in the older occupations—of physically powerful workmen, dedicated to the job and loyal to the company, upholders of the American work ethic. Millworkers tell of no figures like Casey Jones who died with his hand on the throttle, or Gib Morgan who drilled into buttermilk and champagne sand, or Young Monroe who lost his life poling logs on Sunday, or the valiant miners who perished in the cave-in at Avondale. Those who die in the mills are nameless, careless, and unlucky. The mill heroes are pranksters and tricksters who sleep on the job, sneak metals and tools past the gate guards, smash the canteen, and foul up the production line. They are proud not of work done but of work avoided. Theirs is an adversary relation, pitting the union against the company.

In the codes of the outdoor occupations the workers displayed gallant manners toward women outside their work sites. In the mills, women

236

have become co-workers and are portrayed in demeaning roles in the stories told by male laborers. Cranemen seduce "chicks" aloft in their cranes; a big buck laborer ejaculates at the sight of a Rosie the Riveter in tight-fitting slacks; jealous wives divorce husbands who work too closely with women; female apprentice workers fail the training program because of menstrual periods and physical weaknesses that prevent their doing a man's job.

An exciting issue of *Western Folklore* (July 1978) devoted to *Working Americans: Contemporary Approaches to Occupational Folklife* confirms my findings on many points. Robert Byington, special editor for the issue, declares that folklorists must alter their expectations of finding the conventional genres in urban/industrial occupational folklife and concentrate on narrative lore. Jack Santino adds that narrative arises along each of the relationships a worker is involved in, from underlings to peers to bosses to management to the public. Archie Green boldly asserts that "factory behavior is itself folklife" and that folklorists should view the expressions of assembly line and service workers as folklore and "see machine tenders as creative performers in an interactive ballet." Roger Abrahams perceives a flow of workers' rebellious energies into repeated pranks, which elevate a new kind of folk hero, the trickster-prankster, who replaces the strongman hero of preindustrial times. Robert McCarl believes that the industrial–factory–assembly-line system has led to shamming, faking, and intentional degrading of skill by the workers.

The anti-work ethic finds forceful expression in the folklore of pranks and thefts and sabotage. Companies operate on the premise that workers hate their jobs and must be supervised and regulated continually; and the workers respond in kind. But it was not always so. The work ethic existed as late as the Depression, according to one of Terkel's interviewees, when people wanted to work and could not find jobs. In the steel folklore the older generation, who antedate the unions, express pride in fulfillment of the task, loyalty to the company, and sacrifices for their children. Yet those of their children who work in the mills for the good pay scoff at the job. They possess more means and more education than did their parents at the same age. They learn quickly enough to applaud the cool fellow who steals a wheelbarrow every day.

Yes, there is a folklore of steel, and it reveals a changed America from the nineteenth-century toilers who sang the virtues of loyalty, chivalry, and an honest day's work.

How did ethnic folkways and cultural traditions fit into the life of the Region? To deal with this complex question I outlined a fourfold scale of involvement on the part of ethnic groups and individuals in the Region. At one end of the scale lies the public face of ethnic behavior, in the form of presentations—festivals, parades, celebrations—intended for the entire multiethnic and nonethnic community. At the other end is the private face, turned inward and away from any eyes and ears outside the ethnic stock, contemplating esoteric beliefs and practices that avert evil and cure disease and ensure fortune's favors. One step removed from the private beliefs are the communal and socializing activities that unite the ethnic group, the rites de passage and saints' days and calendar customs its members celebrate among themselves. The remaining gap between the public and semi-private is filled by what I have called the civic face, which brings to the attention of the schools, the courts, and other agencies the needs, desires, and even demands of the ethnic group for recognition of its historical traditions. Such traditions, rooted in the language, religion, and fabric that give substance to the ethnic heritage, are endangered in the new land.

In this four-tiered scheme, the ethnics use folklore to entertain and win over the public, at the upper level; to protect their inheritance from the dominant culture, at the second level; to enjoy and sustain their group identity, at the third level; and to do battle with the forces of darkness, at the most secret level. In recounting in Chapter 3 various meetings, conversations, and performances of an ethnic nature experienced in the Region, I applied this scheme; it seemed to fit all circumstances, from a broad-gauged ethnic festival to an intimate revelation of the evil eye. I suggest that this analytic model may be extended to expressions of ethnic folklore and folklife throughout the United States, to chart ways in which such expressions permeate the American consciousness.

What is urban about long-held ethnic beliefs and attitudes that come to light in the Region? We can distinguish between traditions that move into and those that grow within cities. The ethnic festival emerges in the city, made possible by the juxtaposition of many ethnic groups; belief in the evil eye moves into the American city from Old-Country villages. But the dichotomy rests on false oppositions of rural versus urban, European versus American. Children suffer from the effects of the evil eye on the island of Chios or in the heart of Gary. The persistence of traditional animosities—Greeks against Turks, Romanians against Hungarians—results from the crush of urban population. But the old enmities must make room for new ones—ethnics against blacks, Latinos against Anglos. And new friendships emerge, as of the Mexicans and Puerto Ricans. The imported and the indigenous blend in urban ethnic folklore.

What is the folklore, if any, of middle-class blacks in a northern city where, for the first time in American history, they have become the dominant culture? No strand of American folklore has been more amply documented than the Afro-American, but the collections on our shelves derive from rural southerners, ghetto dwellers, and prison inmates. From these folk emanate animal tales, Old Marster tales, stories of hants and hoodoo, jokes about preachers and Irishmen, spirituals and blues, cries and hollers, toasts and dozens—a feast of oral genres. None of these appear in my chapter on "Black Outlooks." I do not say they cannot be unearthed in Gary—of course they can—but the most prominent genre I encountered was new to the folklore collector. This is the personal success story, an autobiographical narrative told on the plane of reality, but shaped by the American cultural myth of the upward climb: the rags-to-riches saga of an Andrew Carnegie, the log cabin to White House ascent of an Abe Lincoln, the rise from slavery to eminence of a Booker T. Washington. These preachers and teachers, well-paid millworkers, and aspiring businessmen are as fluent as the storytellers of the old plantation, but they spin a different tale.

To these black Americans, the city of Gary is not the armpit of America but the promised land. They tell not of Brer Rabbit outwitting Brer Fox, or John the favorite slave outsmarting Old Marster, but of Richard Gordon Hatcher being elected mayor over the candidates of the white political machine, and similar triumphs of blacks in the white man's world. I am sure these middle-class success stories are duplicated in other cities, in some of which—Detroit, Los Angeles, and Atlanta, for example—black mayor-heroes have already risen.

Can recitals of muggings and rapes be classed as modern folktales? Again the answer is a resounding yes. These are, alas, the stories of our times. Even since writing the chapter on crimelore, at a meeting of the New York City chapter of the New York State Folklore Society, I heard a cycle of personal mugging tales develop spontaneously and travel like an electric circuit throughout the room. It was odd to hear folklorists becoming informants to recount their own misfortunes, but any urban group nowadays can react similarly. Newspaper stories daily swell the crimelore repertoire with gruesome reports.

In an earlier day folks frightened themselves with stories of ghosts and specters, ghouls and hants from the invisible world, finding a perverse excitement in the dread aroused by such accounts. The supernatural has receded from our minds, but we still shudder at tales of stalkers in the night, the rapists and muggers who strike in dark streets or pounce from cars, lurk in subways and spring from doorways, or the purse-snatchers and molesters who in broad daylight descend on the unwary.

In this swirling spate of crime tales we can recognize stereotyped characters and repetitive patterns. Each situation may be unique, but the basic cast of characters remains the same: narrator-victims call themselves dupes for walking into ambush, or trickster-heroes for outsmarting the stupid ogre.

The foray into the Region ends thus: an urban folklore does exist and can predictably be entrapped in every city in the United States, and in other nations as well. Much of this folklore is rooted in episodic experiences that people relate about themselves or retell from the narrations of friends and acquaintances. We need not venture onto distant trails to find folklore: it is all about us, in places of work and worship, in our homes and neighborhoods, projecting our tensions and anxieties, devilishness and saintliness, struggles and ideals.

# A BIBLIOGRAPHICAL NOTE

This book depends for its primary data on taped interviews conducted in the field situation and supplemented by my field diaries. The original 117 tapes are on deposit in the Archives of Traditional Music of Indiana University, Bloomington, under "North America—U.S.—Indiana—Calumet Region—76–136–F, and the tape transcripts are on file in the Calumet Region collection in the Folklore Institute of Indiana University. Some relevant publications follow.

## CHAPTER 1. *MYSTIQUE OF THE REGION*

Awareness of the special character of "de Region" was recognized in *A Standard History of Lake County, Indiana, and the Calumet Region,* ed. W. F. Howat, 2 vols. (Chicago and New York: Lewis Publishing Co., 1915). It was followed by *The Calumet Region Historical Guide,* compiled by the Workers of the Writers' Program of the Works Projects Administration in the State of Indiana (Gary: Garman Printing Co., 1939). The subtitle reads "Containing the early history of the region as well as the contemporary scene within the cities of Gary, Hammond, East Chicago (including Indiana Harbor), and Whiting." A reprint edition was issued in 1975 by the AMS Press, New York. Powell A. Moore wrote the standard history, *The Calumet Region: Indiana's Last Frontier* (Indianapolis: Indiana Historical Bureau, 1959), concentrating on the same four core cities. The Bureau published a new edition in 1977 with an Afterword by Lance Trusty, who singles out minority relations, housing problems, the economic growth of Porter County, the Save-the-Dunes movement, and the emergence of the Indiana University Northwest and Purdue University Calumet campuses as major developments in the recent period. Some of Moore's information turns up in oral tradition; cf. his references to Henry Schrage and Oklahoma, pp. 184–185, 195, mentioned in Chapter 1. James B. Lane has written *"City of the Century": A History of Gary, Indiana* (Bloomington: Indiana University Press, 1978), an intimate history based on personal interviews and newspaper files. Lance Trusty has issued *The Calumet Region: An Historical Resource Guide* (Hammond: Purdue University Calumet, The Regional Studies Institute, 1980). The citations from Howard W. Odum and Harry Estill Moore are from Chapter 1, "The Implications and Meanings of Regionalism," in their *American Regionalism* (New York: Henry Holt, 1938).

The folklore of the Calumet Region was first investigated by my colleague Linda Degh, who made contact with the Hungarian community there. She has published from her fieldwork the following: "Two Old World Narrators in Urban Setting," in *Kontakte und Grenzen: Festschrift für Gerhard Heilfurth* (Göttingen: Otto Schwartz, 1969), pp. 71–86; "Two Hungarian-American Stereotypes," *New York Folklore Quarterly* 28 (1972): 3–14; "Symbiosis of Joke and Legend: A Case of Conversational Folklore," in *Folklore Today: A Festschrift for Richard M. Dorson* (Bloomington: Indiana University, 1976), pp. 101–122.

My own preliminary trip to the Region in 1968 resulted in "The Ethnic Survey of Northwest Indiana," *Kontakte und Grenzen,* pp. 65–69, and "Is There a Folk in the City?" *Journal of American Folklore* 83 (1970): 185–216, reprinted in Dorson, *Folklore: Selected Essays* (Bloomington: Indiana University Press, 1972), pp. 33–79. The field trips of 1975–1976 have produced two special journal issues, both edited by Inta Gale Carpenter, to which each member of the Gary Gang and I contributed articles: *Indiana Folklore* 10:2 (1977), entitled *Land of the Millrats: Folklore in the Calumet Region* and containing photographs and tape transcripts as well as field reports (reprinted in hardcover by Arno Press, New York, 1980); and *Folklore Forum* 11:3 (1978): *Folklorists in the City: The Urban Field Experience.* My article there, "Team Fieldwork," also appeared in *Fabula* 20:1–3 (1979): 69–78, as "Team Fieldwork in Northwest Indiana" in a Festschrift for Max Lüthi. Philip B. George has separately published "The Ghost of Cline Avenue: 'La Llorona' in the Calumet Region," *Indiana Folklore* 6:1 (1972): 56–91.

On ways of looking at cities, empirically and symbolically, Anselm L. Strauss has written one stimulating volume, *Images of the American City* (New York: Free Press of Glencoe, 1961; repr. Transaction Books, New Brunswick, N.J., 1976), and edited another, *The American City: A Source Book of Urban Imagery* (Chicago: Aldine, 1968). Kevin Lynch, *The Image of the City* (Cambridge, Mass.: MIT Press, 1960), approaches the subject from the perspective of an architectural historian. A group of geographers move beyond urban to regional imagery in D. W. Meinig, ed., *The Interpretation of Ordinary Landscapes: Geographical Essays* (New York: Oxford University Press, 1979); Meinig's essay on "Symbolic Landscapes, Models of American Community" is especially suggestive. Gerald E. Warshaver, "Psycho-Geographic Traditions of City Folk in the 1890s as Revealed in Writings by Mariana Van Rensselaer, H. C. Bunner, and Stephen Crane" (Ph.D. dissertation, Indiana University, 1979), considers urban authors who formulated cognitive maps of New York City as frames for their work.

# A Bibliographical Note

## CHAPTER 2. *THE FOLKLORE OF STEEL*

An older study that sets forth with abundant data the factors favoring steel manufacturing in northwest Indiana is John B. Appleton, *The Iron and Steel Industry of the Calumet District: A Study in Economic Geography* (Urbana: University of Illinois Studies in the *Social Sciences* 13:2 [June 1925; copyright 1927]). The human side of the creation of Gary as a steel town may be read in Ida M. Tarbell, *The Life of Elbert H. Gary: The Story of Steel* (New York: Appleton, 1925).

Occupational folklore and folklife of the blue-collar and white-collar worlds is beginning to command attention. An excellent set of essays outlining concepts and strategies is available in a special issue of *Western Folklore* 37 (1978), reprinted as Smithsonian Folklife Studies Number 3 (Washington, D.C., 1978), and titled *Working Americans: Contemporary Approaches to Occupational Folklife*. The patterns of factory folklore are outlined, on the basis of his own participant-observation, by Bruce E. Nickerson in "Is There a Folk in the Factory?," *Journal of American Folklore* 87 (1974): 133–139, and in "Industrial Lore: A Study of an Urban Factory" (Ph.D. dissertation, Indiana University, 1976).

Two volumes based on interviews with Americans about their work point the way to folkloric investigations of men and women on the job. The mammoth tome of Studs Terkel, *Working* (New York: Pantheon, 1974), covers a wide range of occupations and includes statements by two steelworkers. In the more personal account of Barbara Garson, *All the Livelong Day*, with its revealing subtitle, *The Meaning and Demeaning of Routine Work* (Garden City, N.Y.: Doubleday, 1975; repr. Penguin Books, Harmondsworth, England, 1977), the author takes one of the demeaning jobs she has interrogated others about.

A variant to the theft of wheelbarrows occurs in the science fiction novel *The Dark Designs* by Philip José Farmer (New York: Berkley Medallion Books, 1977), pp. 269–270:

"Nasruddin crossed the border from Persia to India on his donkey many times. Each time, the donkey carried large bundles of straw on his back. But when Nasruddin returned, the donkey carried nothing. Each time, the customs guard searched Nasruddin, but he could not find any contraband.

"The guard would always ask Nasruddin what he was carrying. The Mullah would always reply, 'I am smuggling,' and he would smile.

"After many years, Nasruddin retired to Egypt. The customs man went to him and said, 'Very well, Nasruddin. Tell me, now it's safe for you. What were you smuggling?'

" 'Donkeys.' "

"They laughed again. Frigate said, 'I heard the same story in Arizona. Only this time the smuggler was Pancho, and he was crossing the border from Mexico to the United States.' "

(Thanks to Breon and Lynda Mitchell)

Alan Dundes informs me of Lithuanian, Czech, and Russian versions and cites Greg Benton and Graham Loomes, *Big Red Joke Book* (London: Pluto, 1976), pp. 103–104.

A variant to "A Piece of the Heat" is found in the novel of H. L. Davis, *Honey in the Horn* (New York: Harper, 1935), pp. 205–206:

"Most of Baker's stories about the iron foundry tended to get mixed up with reminiscences of his wife before she quit him, but he did tell one about a man who was detailed to watch a three-ton vat of molten iron alone, and when they went to call him at the end of his shift he was nowhere to be found. Failing to locate him around town, the company called in an assayer to analyze the vat of iron. The analysis showed a trace of gold that could have been his watch and his teeth-fillings, and a trace of brass that was probably his belt buckle and his pants buttons. So it was decided that he had been overcome by the fumes of iron and had fallen into it and burned up; and the company, by way of showing its sense of bereavement, had the whole three-ton ingot carted out to the cemetery and interred with appropriate ceremonies, several large floral pieces from officials and fellow workmen, and a full set of honorary pall-bearers assisted by two donkey-engines."

(Thanks to Michael S. Licht)

## CHAPTER 3.  *A SPECTRUM OF ETHNICS*

Overviews with references to key published writings and to doctoral dissertations are Stephen Stern, "Ethnic Folklore and the Folklore of Ethnicity," *Western Folklore* 36 (1977): 7–32; and Roger D. Abrahams, "Folklore," in *Harvard Encyclopedia of American Ethnic Groups* (hereafter cited as HEAEG) (Cambridge, Mass.: Harvard University Press, 1980), pp. 370–379. The dissertation I cited by Robert B. Klymasz is "Ukrainian Folklore in Canada: An Immigrant Complex in Transition" (Indiana University, 1970; published by Arno Press, New York, 1980). American immigrant/ethnic folklore remains an underdeveloped field. Some writings pertinent to this chapter include:

Serbian: Stella Alexander, "The Schism in North America, 1962–3," in *Church and State in Yugoslavia since 1945* (Cambridge: Cambridge University Press, 1979), pp. 276–280; Richard March, "The Tamburitza Tradition in the Calumet Region," *Indiana Folklore* 10 (1977): 127–138; Djuro Jovan Vrga and Frank J. Fahney, *Changes and Socio-Religious Conflict in an Ethnic Minority Group: The Serbian Orthodox Church in America* (Palo Alto, Cal.: Ragusan Press, 1975). Michael B. Petrovich and Joel Halpern in their article on "Serbs" in HEAEG discuss the tamburica, *krsna slava*, and *kum* (pp. 924–925).

Greek: Robert A. Georges, "Matiasma: Living Folk Belief," *Midwest Folklore* 12 (1962): 69–74; George Gizelis, "The Use of Amulets among Greek Philadelphians," *Pennsylvania Folklife* 20 (1971): 30–37; Robert T. Teske, "On the Making of *Bobonieres* and *Marturia* in Greek-Philadelphia: Commercialism in Folk Religion," *Journal of the Folklore Institute* 14 (1977): 151–158.

Mexican: Catherine J. Hinckle, "The Devil in New Mexican Spanish Folklore," *Western Folklore* 8 (1949): 123–125; Soledad Pérez, "Mexican Folklore from Austin, Texas," in W. M. Hudson, ed., *The Healer of Los Olmos, and Other Mexican Lore* (Dallas and Austin: Texas Folklore Society, Publication 24, 1951), pp. 71–127; "Mal de Ojo and Susto," pp. 108–112, reprinted in R. M. Dorson, *Buying the Wind* (Chicago: University of Chicago Press, 1964), pp. 455–459.

Puerto Rican: Philip B. George, "Reaffirmation of Identity: A Latino Case in East Chicago," and "Tales of a Puerto Rican Storyteller," *Indiana Folklore* 10 (1977): 139–158.

Latino: Nicolás Kanellos, "Folklore in Chicano Theater and Chicano Theater as Folklore," *Journal of the Folklore Institute* 15 (1978): 57–82.

## CHAPTER 4.  *BLACK OUTLOOKS*

Background information and valuable photographs can be found in Dolly Millender, *Yesterday in Gary: A Brief History of the Negro in Gary, 1906–1967*

# A Bibliographical Note

(Gary: Dolly Millender, 1967); and Alex Poinsett, *Black Power Gary Style: The Making of Mayor Richard Gordon Hatcher* (Chicago: Johnson Publishing Co., 1970); both books advance the theme of black struggle to success. Also pertinent is the chapter on "The Middle-Class Way of Life" in St. Clair Drake and Horace R. Clayton, *Black Metropolis* (New York: Harcourt, Brace, 1945), pp. 658–715, especially the section on "Middle-Class Religion," pp. 670–688, with its discussions of "mixed-type" or "mass" churches and the preacher as a race leader in Chicago.

Three members of our team have made notable contributions to appreciation of black folklife in Gary in *Indiana Folklore* 10:2 1977: John Hasse, "The Gary Black Religious Experience: A Photo Essay" (pp. 165–181), and " 'The whites runnin' because the blacks are movin' in': An interview with Rev. Roosevelt Robinson" (pp. 183–190); Gilbert E. Cooley, "Root Doctors and Psychics in the Region" (pp. 191–200), and "Conversations about Hoodoo" (pp. 201–215); Adrienne L. Seward, "Gary's Black Self-Image" (pp. 217–221), and "An Urban Black Philosopher" (pp. 223–228).

## CHAPTER 5. *CRIMELORE*

Eleanor F. Wachs, "The Code of Survival: The Crime-Victim Narrative within an Urban Context" (Ph.D. dissertation, Indiana University, 1979) treats personal and second-hand narratives of criminal attacks related by New Yorkers as a folklore genre.

The contemporary legend of the child mutilated in a restroom by racial assailants is traced by Florence H. Ridley, "A Tale Told Too Often," *Western Folklore* 26 (1967): 153–156, to the fifth century A.D., through Chaucer's The Prioress's Tale and the Child ballad of "Sir Hugh, or the Jew's Daughter," up to current accounts in urban shopping centers. Donald A. Bird, "Rumor as Folklore: An Interpretation and Inventory" (Ph.D. dissertation, Indiana University, 1979), cites references to reports of "Mutilation of a Child" from newspapers in Detroit, Denver, Washington, D.C., and Philadelphia between 1956 and 1975 and discusses "Blood Ritual Murder of a Child," citing David J. Jacobson, *The Affairs of Dame Rumor* (New York: Rinehart, 1948), and Cecil Roth, ed., *The Ritual Murder Libel and the Jew* (London: Woburn Press, 1934).

# INDEX

# Index

# Index

George, Philip B. (Gary Gang), 4, 20
Georgia State College, 181–182
Germans, 7, 14, 27, 34, 37–40, 111, 162, 191–192, 214
Glen Park, Ind., 14, 16, 30, 122, 131, 196–197, 212
Gomez, Juan (informant), 147–158, 226–229, 234
Grambling College, La., 202
Greater Calumet River, 7, 13
Greeks, 3, 33–34, 110, 112, 114–117, 121, 128, 130, 132, 133–138, 164, 216, 238
Griffith, Ind., 13
Guadalupe, Shrine of the Virgin of, 152

Hammond, George H., 8, 26–27
Hammond, Ind., 7–13, 15–18, 20, 24, 26–33, 35, 41, 113, 119, 121, 124, 127–128, 148, 218, 221–222, 235
Harlan, Wilbert (informant), 185–196, 212
Hartford, Conn., 181
Hasse, John (Gary Gang), 4, 175
Hatcher, Mayor Richard Gordon, 3, 28, 121, 143, 165, 184, 193–196, 201, 218–219, 229, 239
Hoskins, William (*The Making of the English Landscape*), 6
Highland, Ind., 13, 28, 34
Hillbillies, 34–35, 39, 41, 93, 101, 105, 189, 192
Hobart, Ind., 13, 20, 121
Hoodoo, 1, 119, 178, 185, 202, 207, 238
Housing: stories of, 12, 15, 19; depreciation of, 16, 20–21, 23, 25
Howat, W. F. (*A Standard History of Lake County, Indiana, and the Calumet Region*), 7
Hungarians, 39–40, 112–113, 214, 238
Hyatt, Rev. Harry M., 1
Hyles Anderson College, 127
Hyles, Rev. Jack, 124–127

Indiana Harbor (the Harbor), 11, 13, 20–21, 37, 45, 118–119, 221, 225
Indiana Northwest University, Gary, 4, 13, 16, 115, 138, 146, 233
Indiana University, Bloomington, 9, 11, 120, 138, 165, 219
Indianapolis, Ind., 14, 178

Indianapolis *Star,* 215, 229
Inland Steel, 8, 12, 21, 34, 37, 42–43, 45–46, 51–59, 66–67, 72, 76–77, 81, 94, 96–97, 100, 102
Irish, 34, 238
Italians, 93, 115, 119

Jackson, Mrs. F. Brannan (informant), 171–173
Jackson, Rev. F. Brannan (informant), 167–174, 185
Jackson, Rev. Hobson (informant), 222–223
Jackson, Rev. L. K. (informant), 179–184
Jackson, Robert (informant), 197–202
Jeffries, Kirby (informant), 202–207, 212
Jenkins, Frank (informant), 234–235
Jones, Casey, 236

Kanellos, Nicolás (informant), 138–147, 234
Kissinger, Henry, 135–136
Ku Klux Klan, 24, 29, 33

Lake County, Ind., 7–8, 13, 17, 26, 183, 210, 219, 235
Lake Station, Ind., 13
Lane, James B. (*"City of the Century"*), 13, 184
Lansing, Ill., 12, 28
Latinos, 4, 8, 11, 41, 45, 47, 110, 118, 120, 138, 140, 143, 145–148, 214, 233, 235, 238
Lever Brothers, 34–35
Lithuanians, 4, 105, 112
Little Calumet River, 7
Lomax, Alan, 166
Lomax, John, 1
Louisville, Ky., 186

Macedonians, 115, 117–118, 120–121
Maddox, Lester, 20, 24–25
Malamud, Bernard, 229
March, Richard (Gary Gang), 4, 117, 119, 161, 177
Marquette Park, 18, 40, 112
Meinig, Donald W., 6–7
Merrillville, Ind., 14, 16, 18–20, 114, 121, 132, 204, 228
Mexicans, 3, 13, 21, 23, 31, 41, 65, 98–99, 106–107, 110–111, 113, 116, 119–120, 139–140, 143, 147,

# Index

# Index

Vidutis, Richard, 4, 117, 120
Voodoo. *See* Hoodoo

Wallace, George, 20, 24
Washington, Booker T., 186, 239
White, Rev. Catherine, 204
Whiting, Ind., 7–8, 12–13, 15, 33–41, 148, 235
Williams, Prophet E. N. (informant), 177–179, 184–185

Wisconsin Steel, 13, 42, 46, 67, 76, 82
Woodman, Ind., 34

Youngstown, Ohio, 45, 236
Youngstown Sheet and Tube, 37, 42, 45, 80
Yugoslavia, 132, 161, 232–233

Zivich, Ed (informant), 33–41